FROM
VIOLINS
TO
VIOLENCE

MARSHALL FRANK

MARSHALL FRANK

FROM VIOLINS TO VIOLENCE

Marshall Frank

EVERLY BOOKS
PUBLISHING CO.

New York   Boston   London   Paris   Vancouver

From Violins To Violence

Printed In Canada

54 24 66 74 12 98 15 01 14

by

EVERLY BOOKS
PUBLISHING CO.

Everly Books Publishing Co., 1918 BOUL.SAINT-REGIS
DORVAL, QC, H9P 1H6
CANADA
www. EverlyBooks.com

Third Edition © 2021 by Marshall Frank

LIBRARY OF CONGRESS CATALOGING-IN-PUBLICATION DATA

ISBN: ISBN: 1777278120
ISBN-13: 978-1-7772781-2-0

PUBLISHER'S NOTE

This is a nonfiction book. Names marked with an asterisk * indicate the author is not using the true name of the person in question.

Editor-In-Chief: Christopher S. Douglas
Cover design by Everly Books Publishing Co.,

To Brookley Hazen Rene Beamer
and all her children

A Memoir

CONTENTS

Marshall Frank

PREFACE

It's been said that anyone who sits down to write a book of personal memoirs and then has them published must be a flaming egomaniac, particularly non-celebrities who nobody knows or cares about other than the author's inner circle of family and friends. Well, that's what I thought.

Not too long ago I received, unsolicited, a self-published book in the mail from a casual friend named Scotty, a retired police officer who had served a long and distinguished career fighting crime in the steamy neighborhoods of Miami-Dade County. I didn't know him well, but I read the book with interest. Knowing it was not destined for the shelves of Barnes & Noble, or the review page of the *New York Times,* he wrote it for no other reason but to leave his story to posterity. He cared about legacy to grandchildren, and their children, and so on.

I thought about my ancestors from both sides of the parental aisle, including my father whom I never met. I wondered if I would have been interested in learning more about his life in vaudeville, what motivated him, what made him happy, what didn't. Was he really engaged to

Ginger Rogers at one time? Was his friendship with show biz stars like Milton Berle, Rudy Vallee and the Dorsey Brothers for real, or did he tolerate them for professional gain? Were my mother and father truly in love, or were they talented performers who enhanced each other's career?

What drove him to the insane asylum where he died, just across the street from Sing Sing prison in Ossining, New York? Did my mother have an affair with a Mafia gangster while he was still alive? What struggles lingered in his heart as he wallowed in loneliness the last two years of his life, staring out dusty windows of a mental institution?

These are questions that will never be answered, for me, and for my children's children. And what of his parents, my grandparents who died in separate pedestrian accidents in New York City long before I was born? Would I have not longed to read their memoirs about life in Eastern Europe in the 19th century, when anti-Semitism stewed and Jewish people longed for freedom across the ocean in America's paradise? Why did they make the decision? How difficult was the journey, from idea to arrival? How did they support seven children, one of whom was my father? And is it true that so many of their offspring's offspring changed their surnames in order to hide their Jewishness? Frank became Franklin.

Weinberger became Wayne. And so on. Then, there is the mystery of the Norwegian side of my heritage. Mom rarely spoke of her feelings about family and early struggles. I would love to have known about my grandfather's view of the world at the turn of the 20th century in Minnesota and South Dakota. Neither of my Norwegian grandparents could carry a tune nor play an instrument, yet they sacrificed and spent their last nickels and dimes to make sure their two daughters became accomplished dancers and classical pianists. What was the vision? What were their struggles growing up in the rural mid-west? Who were their parents, why did they immigrate, and what were their dreams?

The questions are endless, to those who care. I would have read any of their memoirs with passion and zeal, if they only existed. Instead, their lives are gone with the wind. While we know little or nothing about our ancestors from two hundred or two thousand years ago, there will soon be a day when my life, and those around me, will be gone to that same wind. Most of my great-great grandchildren will not care that I ever existed. But, there might be one. Just one.

And so, on behalf of that great-great granddaughter in the year 2103, I present these professional and personal memoirs for the same posterity as Scotty, my police friend who sent me his self-published book. His was a good idea, and so is this.

One never knows. Some young man with a Frank surname in the next century might wonder why he's afflicted with an attention deficit disorder, or schizophrenia, or why he's able to pick out tunes on a piano by ear, why he's easily subject to addiction, or what drives his libido out of control. I'm not sure to what extent genetics and lineage can affect the personality. I've been told by many how much

I walk, talk, act, laugh and even think like my natural father, though I never shared a single moment with him.

I have lived a full life, replete with all the trimmings, including show business, dance, classical music, living with the Mafia, zero self-esteem, foiled marriages, children scattered, misery, friends and enemies, violence, killers, rapists, corruption, politics, good cops/bad cops, the face of suicide and the wonder of happiness as I approach the finale. Many ask how a violin student, high school drop-out and stepson of a Miami Beach bookie ever ended up wearing a badge and a gun. It is time to share all this, before it's too late.

People tend to pigeonhole others, seeing them as one dimensional, attaching a quick label for easy recognition, like sound bites from CNN News. Sally the slut. Max is a millionaire. Sam the homeless man. Tiger the golf pro. Jack the police officer. Many see me as just a cop, a homicide detective, a captain, and nothing else. Kids see me as an authority figure. Ex-wives see me as a man who let them down, and therefore, I owed them something.

Friends see me as loyal. Others see me as a person who once hurt them. Just like Richard Nixon, Bill Clinton, Monica Lewinsky and Mark Foley, whatever good they accomplished in life will be overshadowed by a single deed. That can happen to anyone.

It all doesn't matter when the hole is dug. What really matters is what we leave behind. For some, it's money, property, memories and a few pictures. For me, as always, it has to be words.

Writing is the ultimate catharsis. It brings it all together. We have no idea what impact we may have had on another individual. I've received letters—out of the blue—from long since retired cops who wanted to thank me for whatever it was I did for them twenty-five years earlier. One man recently showed up at a library book talk in Clearwater, Florida, for no other reason but to thank me for setting his life straight when he was a wayward teenager thirty years before. I had no recollection, but he hugged me anyway.

Scotty has no idea that he inspired me to pen a book of memoirs. He does now.

While these pages were mostly intended to describe the world of policedom, it was impossible to exclude personal milestones that formed the mosaic of my life, why and how they impacted my behavior, my performance, my struggles as a human being, and how it all impacted those who I worked with and who I loved. Rest assured, at least fifty percent of the personal side has been edited out, or else this book would have looked like a Michener opus.

For that great-great grandkid somewhere down the calendar, I want him or her to know this: More important than any solved murder, failed or successful marriage, violin recital, mystery novel or newspaper accolade, I wish to be remembered most as one who loved from deep inside the heart. No matter how it ever may have appeared on the outside, no matter my imperfections, my love has always been genuine.

And so it goes...

CHAPTER ONE
A Cop's Toughest Job

November, 1966. Miami, Florida

Sergeant Ray Beck and I stood at the bank of the manmade rock pit, wiped our brows with already sweat-soaked handkerchiefs and waited for the divers to bring the body to shore. At noon, the overhead sun baked the southern suburbs of Dade County into a megalopolis of steamed roadways and sweltering humanity. A small gathering of children and neighbors stood behind yellow barrier tape to look on while the squawk of police radios broke the silence.

Ray was familiar with Miller Lake, an old rock pit nestled in the upper side of a new development named Kendall. It was his fourth case here since being assigned to Homicide four years earlier. With all the interviews, sketches and photos taken, it was time to examine the body. With plenty of witnesses, there was little doubt about what happened. No foul play. Miller Lake had claimed another drowning victim.

The pathetic, limp body of a shaggy-haired eight year-old boy was laid onto the shore as his playmates stood by staring. His name: Rolando. He had stood up in an aluminum canoe when it suddenly tipped over. He couldn't hold on. Two of his friends could swim. He could not.

The examination would not take very long. All the common signs were there; Foaming from the mouth, fingernail imprints in the palms of his hands, goose flesh and the idyllic gaze from lifeless eyes.

After twelve years on the job and four of probing unnatural death cases, Ray was calloused all right, but he admitted feeling a lump in his throat each time he was compelled to touch a dead child. Shootings, bodies, blood—he took it all in stride. But kids were something else.

Haunting images suddenly flashed from an early memory bank.

Bennett! Behhnnett! Behhhhnnehhhtt!

The field investigation was complete and the boy was on the way to the morgue, but the worst was yet to come. We walked back to the car where we soaked up the air conditioning and Ray had me begin the initial report. The radio dispatcher asked if we were ready to take on another case. Ray picked up the mike. "That's negative," he replied. "We're not yet clear for calls."

Quizzically, I looked to my mentor. "I thought we were finished here. What's up?"

"Finished? Afraid not." Ray shifted into drive. "Time to visit Mama."

Now I felt light-headed. As my heart began to race, my mouth turned dry as I anticipated the dreadful moment, me designated to inform an unsuspecting mother that her child was no longer alive. Oh God, do I have to do this? I was concerned how other detectives perceived me, knowing that the bureau captain and lieutenant hadn't wanted want me in Homicide. All they needed was a good excuse. If Ray told them I didn't have the stomach for this job, I'd be back in uniform somewhere. It was important to appear stoic, though the anxiety burned inside of me.

Bennett! Behhnnett! Behhhhnnehhhtt!

As I thought about Rolando's wet little body, visions of my own brother flashed into my mind, from that fateful day in April of 1943. Who was it that informed my mother? What did they say? I could only imagine the horror of her reaction.

"Is this your first notification with a kid?" asked Ray.

"Yeah."

"Get ready for a rough time."

"Why don't we just use the phone and call?" I asked.

"Never, Marshall. You never call. Imagine, if you were home

alone, and you just received a cold phone message."
Twenty minutes passed before we arrived. Gravel rock crunched under the wheels as we pulled in front of the coral pink, one-story apartment building in the Little Havana district of Miami. It wasn't far from the salsa beats and sounds of Calle Ocho, known six years before as, simply, Eighth Street.

Olive-skinned kids with dirty faces frolicked about in bare feet while they glanced curiously at the two conspicuous men wearing polyester suits. Slowly we walked to the row of mail boxes in the courtyard where I spotted the name "Arguello" scribbled in pencil under the number "8." Beads of perspiration formed on Ray's temples. The trek to the last apartment was like walking the final corridor on death row. Sounds of lively Spanish music blared from inside the Arguello apartment as the aroma of baked chicken and yellow rice permeated the air.

"Hope she speaks English," Ray said, under his breath. "You okay, Marshall?"

I had to play it tough. "Yeah. I'm fine. Let's just get this over with."

Ray took a deep breath, hesitated, then knocked. I could feel the pulse on my temple. No answer. He knocked harder this time, with the gold ring on his finger. Almost immediately, the volume subsided and footsteps approached the door. Sweat trickled down my sideburns. Ray patted me on the shoulder. The jalousies cranked open and she asked, "Yes, may I help you?" I was struck by her eyes and her flawless skin. Petite, no more than thirty, the woman wearing wide-rimmed glasses had full, red lips that formed an infectious smile. So trusting. So unsuspecting. I felt a nudge from Ray.

I displayed my silver shield. Ray's was gold. "My name is Detective Frank. This is Sergeant Ray Beck. May we please come in?" I could barely look her in the eyes. I knew this would be a moment that would impact her until the end of her life.

Smiling wide, Mrs. Carmen Arguello hurriedly opened her

door, then said she had to attend to her oven.

"I'll be right with you. Please sit."

Seconds seemed like hours as we sat nervously fiddling with pens, wiping brows, scanning the room, not saying a word. It was difficult to breathe inside the sweltering apartment as an oscillating fan gave movement to the drawn window curtains. A partial ray of sunlight beamed through the glass jalousie door. A portrait of Jesus hung on the wall and an arrangement of framed photographs were set in layered rows upon end tables, mostly of a smiling, laughing, shaggy-haired, eight year-old boy. I swallowed hard at the thought of what lay ahead.

The lady emerged clutching a dish towel. "Please excuse the mess, I am making supper for the little one and myself."

Little one?

"Yes, how can I help you?" Her smiling eyes opened wide. There was no turning back. A million thoughts raced through my head in a micro second as she stood there with her curious, innocent smile. Ray stood behind me as I took the lead.

"Is there anyone here with you, ma'am?"

Her brow furrowed. "No, I am a widow. What is it please?"

"You have a little boy named Rolando?"

"Yes," she replied nodding. "Oh dear. What has he gotten in to now?" The broad smile disappeared. Her expression changed to exasperation, impatience. "Has he been throwing rocks again?"

There was only one way to do this. I stood, wetted my lips and made hard eye contact. "I'm afraid there's been an accident, ma'am." My voice quivered. I couldn't help it.

She looked confused. She paused, peering deeper.
Then the transparency in my face told it all. I felt the weight of a bowling ball in my chest, and the urge to cry out.

I'm sorry Mommy.

After three words, she knew. "We're very sorry," I said.

As though a blunt instrument struck her from behind, her face transformed into a compression of crevices and wrinkles and distortions. First, it was disbelief. No tears. Not yet. Then her lower jaw protruded outward baring teeth while she choked, grabbed her chest and staggered away. Then came the wailing and the sobbing, the oh so pathetic sobbing.

Images of my mother's contorted face appeared into my brain, as she shouted, *"Oh God! Why God? Oh no, please God!"*

Alone with this woman we had just met, Ray Beck and I spent the next hour allowing her beat on our chests screaming in a language we did not understand, holding her, comforting her and trying to explain something that was unexplainable. Ray's eyes welled up. That was good, because it validated my own emotions.

Before the end of that torturous hour, three human beings of disparate cultures and tongues shared a moment that would be etched in their hearts for a lifetime. I steeled myself as best I could, braving the depth of emotions while in her presence. But no matter how hard I tried to remain unaffected, old childhood images whittled me down to a member of humanity. I broke into a sob the moment we sat alone back in his car. I simply couldn't control myself. Ray looked away, allowing me my tears.

Carmen Arguello remained with neighbors and relatives who would see her through the emotional abyss and to help palliate the shock.

Ray waited and looked at his watch while I gathered myself and thought about the perils inherent in this job, the crime, the riots, drugs, weaponry, the incessant tidal wave of violence that secures the very need for the existence of police. It is all dangerous. But I would gladly have faced a thousand thieves or plunge into the bowels of any street riot than have to face one more Carmen Arguello.

Ray picked up the mike to check back in. The dispatcher said they were backed up with calls and there was no one else available to handle a report of child abuse.

The victim was at the morgue.

"QSL. We're on the way."

CHAPTER TWO
Through the Eyes of Squidgie

Queens Borough, New York April, 1943

"Bennett!... Behhnnett!... Behhhhhnnehhhtt!"

We lived in a small apartment on the first floor of a tall brick building, amid rows of many tall brick buildings.

It is my earliest memory, Mom screaming through a sash window overlooking a busy street in Flushing, Long Island. Cars, all black, were parked along the curb while kids ran back and forth on the sidewalk below, each stopping to look up, curious at the shrill in my mother's voice.

"Behhhnnehhht!... Behhhnnehhht!"

I was not yet four years old, but I knew something was terribly wrong. I stood on my toes, poked my blond curls out the window and hollered with her,

"Bennett!... Bennett!"

I'll never forget the expression on her face, because it was a departure from the bright smiling beauty I'd always known. She seemed in pain, gulping, crying, holding her chest, pacing the floor, cursing, screaming, pleading to God that nothing had happened to him.

My brother never came home that day. He was only seven.

Bennett had been at play on a floating log with two other boys in Flushing Bay. He slipped off and could not swim. One of the boys was named Bruce. My mother thought that Bennett might have been pushed. Ever since, I've held a secret prejudice against anyone named Bruce.

The next morning, police dragged the bottom of the bay and recovered Bennett's limp and lifeless body. I can only imagine the reaction my mother had the instant she was told.

It was my first encounter with grief, seeing my mother's contorted face wailing in sorrow, shouting, "Oh God! Why God?

Oh no, please God!" I cried hard, until my stomach hurt, because she cried hard. She loved my brother so very much.

"I'm sorry, Mommy."

For the next few days, I stayed with my grandparents and aunt, my home away from home. I had visited there often. Later on, I was brought to a ritual where all the people— hundreds, it seemed— wore black clothing and somber faces. Bennett lay asleep in an ornate coffin as the chamber echoed from my mother's wailing again and again, constantly throughout the services, unable to control herself until she passed out from exhaustion. My father sat nearby trying to calm her. She collapsed into his arms.

I often reflect on her screaming out that window, a spring day I would never forget.

"*Behhhhnnehhht!*"

From that day on, my mother's hair was no longer natural auburn. At thirty-three, her roots turned pure white, though she continued to color her hair until the end of her life.

* * *

Born in Chicago on September 13, 1910, Vivien Marie Peterson was the elder of two daughters whose parents, Carl and Anna, were first generation Norwegians. Twenty-nine years later, in a Manhattan hospital on the 28th of April, 1939, she would become my mother.

Hers was a life of glamour and good times. And hard times. Raised in a strict musical environment, she had mastered classical piano, winning every competition she entered, performing such difficult pieces as Rachmaninoff's Prelude in C Sharp Minor, and other great works by Liszt, Beethoven and Schubert. But dancing was her passion: ballet, tap, jazz, where she could dazzle audiences, not only with her grace and finesse, but her ebullient personality and a smile that lit up an entire theater.

Vivien Peterson was born to entertain.

She lived through the flapper era of the roaring '20s, performed on vaudeville in the '30s, and then sang torch songs and danced in New York City nightclubs into the early '40s. People likened her to Rita Hayworth, famed actress of breathtaking beauty with long wavy red hair, just like my Mom's. It was in those nightclubs that she met the boys. The wise guys. Hot shots. Gamblers. Hustlers—The mob.

She soaked up the adulation. Furs, diamonds, booze, cigarettes, laughs, all-night entertainment, country club vacations while consorting with show biz stars like young Jackie Gleason, Larry Storch and Sophie Tucker. It was the good life, fun on top of fun, all of them Jews and Italians. The "boys" loved her and she loved them.

Especially one, a Jewish gangster named Willie Strauss. He was the man I called—Dad.

In later years, I would wonder what it was that a glamorous woman like Vivien Peterson saw in Willie Strauss, when she could have had her pick of anyone. Paunchy, not handsome, inarticulate, and prone to wild drinking sprees, he never saw a day of hard labor in his life. I remember his hands, soft as a baby's ass.

Willie and his brothers, Ruby and Joey, were notorious bent-nosed gamblers, operating back room casinos and paying off the cops in Queens for protection. Their disfigured faces were remnants of having grown up in the rugged streets of New York where fist fights were as common as clouds and sunshine.

From the time I was born, until I was four years old, I often stayed with my Norwegian grandparents and their other daughter, Frances, my Aunt Tootie. She also played piano, sang opera and danced as one of the Rockettes at Radio City Music Hall. Tall and blonde, and two years younger than my mother, Frances was more reserved. She lived at home her entire life and never married.

I think my mother was too busy working and having fun to care for her two sons very much, until Bennett died. After the tragedy, everything changed. For the next couple of years, she rarely let me out of her sight.

Then came the big war. Though he was 37 years old, the army drafted my father, a trauma which ultimately gave him a case of stomach ulcers. He never went overseas. Illegal gambling in New York City was in big trouble during war time. A hot-shot prosecutor named Thomas E. Dewey had cracked down hard on organized crime, which helped him to get elected as governor of the state. Florida, however, was still wide open to pay-offs, a perfect lure to gangsters. In January of 1945, the three of us climbed into the family sedan—a black Cadillac LaSalle—and moved to Miami Beach, Florida, with Chico, my tiny white Chihuahua.

I remember the excitement of the trip, having heard all about the ocean beaches, palm trees, hotels, and wide open spaces. It had been snowing in Queens on the day we departed. By the time we crossed the Florida line, the sun shone brightly over a warm land laced with a myriad of tropical trees that captured my curiosity, particularly the coconuts. We stayed overnight in roadside bungalows along the way, whacking mosquitoes against the wall during in the night. By morning, the walls looked like burst of blood spots. Mom drove the entire journey down U.S. Highway #1, a two-lane, pot-holed road often blocked by crossing cows. We stopped to visit St. Augustine where we visited the fabled Fountain of Youth and then an alligator farm where I freaked out at the sight of the huge reptiles inside a wire enclosure. I screamed hysterically like a little idiot until they got me out of there.

We finally arrived at Miami Beach and checked into the Silver Palm, a small hotel on 37th Street and Collins Avenue, where we all embarked on our new lives. Down the street, new beachside hotels were under construction, so tall they seemed to reach the clouds. I was amazed that so many sun-tanned people walked around in shorts in the middle of January.

* * *

As the story goes, I was about three and a half years old when my older brother was given piano lessons. I watched from a corner of the room while the teacher sat with Bennett, instructing him on finger exercises and a simple Indian song, which he practiced every day. When the lesson was over and I thought no one was watching, I would climb up on the bench and work through the Indian song by ear until I could play it as well as Bennett, without music lessons.

A year after we moved to Florida, at the age of seven, I was told that I was going to take lessons in some instrument. Mom gave me a choice: Piano, violin, or trumpet. I have no idea what prompted me to ask, "Which one is the hardest?"

"The violin," she responded.

When given choices, tackling the hardest of tasks would become part of my life's pattern. Perhaps something in my early years induced such insecurity or feelings of inferiority which compelled me to prove my worth by demonstrating what feats I could accomplish. I learned much later, from relatives, that Bennett had been the favored child, well behaved, gorgeous, affectionate and fun, while I was the accident, less good looking, hopelessly hyperactive, the one who got into the most mischief, who challenged authority, who wanted answers to questions that could not always be answered. In modern terms, I probably had an Attention Deficit Disorder. To be sure, I was a challenge. After watching Bennett receive all his adulation, I sought approval by what I could accomplish.

That's my stab at personal psychoanalysis. But the "choice" launched a life of not only playing violin, (and piano) but a love and appreciation of all great music, popular and classical, for which I'll always be grateful. While other kids received toy guns as birthday gifts, I received 78 rpm albums of Jascha Heifetz playing Beethoven's, Mozart's and Brahms's concertos, then other records by The Andrews Sisters singing *The House of Blue Lights*, or Bing Crosby's Blue Skies. My mother took me to violin concerts and shows like South Pacific and Guys And Dolls. I studied movies and actors like no other kid my age. Not just the big stars, but relative unknowns today, like Diana Lynn, Randolph Scott, Wallace Beery, and Paul Muni. When the family was home together during evenings, rare as it was, we listened to radio programs like *Inner Sanctum, The Great Gildersleeve* and Toscanini concerts by the NBC Symphony. I was destined, I thought, to be in show business someday or, at the least, a professional musician.

My mother arranged private violin lessons for me from an Italian maestro named Attilio Canonico who, I was told, would not accept students unless they showed promise. He had been the concertmaster of the Miami Symphony Orchestra and was a strong musical disciplinarian. Short, stocky and balding, he smoked incessantly, often holding a burning cigarette between his fingers while he bowed the violin. He would remain the only teacher I ever had. More important than anything, more important than playing well or playing hard, he insisted, was, "Practice! Practice! Practice!"

And practice I did, at least one hour a day, often two and sometimes four and five. Those were my requirements if I wanted any free time outside with friends. I never thought of it as a task, but compliance with my mother's wishes. The better I became, the more I enjoyed playing.

* * *

As a child, I thought Miami and Miami Beach was sheer paradise. Warm weather year around. No snow, no ice. Beaches, hotel swimming pools, pony rides on Biscayne Boulevard near where The Miami Herald building now stands, sparkling waterways with boats cruising back and forth, and deep sea fishing. Dressed in colorful garb, Seminole Indians shopped in downtown Miami. They were seen more often than Hispanics who, as of today, have converted the city into Little Havana. Tourist sights abounded, like the Parrot Jungle, Monkey Jungle, Serpentarium, air boat rides in the Everglades and the world famous Crandon Park Zoo. I felt the envy of an entire nation, living in a place where other Americans spent fortunes just to visit for a week or two.

The Silver Palm Hotel was a small six-story hotel on Collins Avenue, one of many in a row near beachfront hotels. Later, we moved into a two bedroom apartment on Indian Creek Drive and 63rd Street, across from the Kingston Hotel, which no longer exists. I watched many high rise hotels go up in those years, and then, years later, watched the same ones fall under the wrecking ball, like the Martinique, Lombardy and McFadden Deauville which featured the largest oval swimming pool I had ever seen.

Under the protection of paid-off cops, (gambling was technically illegal in Florida) my father opened a clandestine casino room in the St. Moritz Hotel on 16th Street and Collins Avenue, in what is now called the Art Deco District. It was his way of life. Booze, broads, playing cards, shooting craps, running the casino, being a big shot, showing off with my mother on his arm.

To no one's surprise, Mom gave me private swimming lessons. On weekends, I spent time at the hotel swimming pool, soaking up the smells of suntan oil, salt water and cigarette smoke which pervaded my parents' cabana. They each smoked four packs a day, Parliaments and English Ovals. I dreaded their friends, especially the women who had a penchant for running their fingers through my frizzy blond hair and comparing me to Harpo Marx. They'd pinch my cheeks until it hurt and call me names like "Bubbala" and "Mishugana," whatever that meant. It was bad enough being called "Squidgie" from birth, a nickname that stuck with me until I reached my teens. Virtually everyone knew me as "Squidgie." Few knew my true name.

It wasn't all fun and glamour.

If I wanted a quarter to play pinball machines, I'd have find my dad. That entailed a short walk down one of the corridors where I knocked on a specific door and waited for a gravel voice holler from inside, "Yeah?"

"Hi. It's Squidgie. Can I see my dad?"

"Yeah, sure."

When the door opened, the room was abuzz with dozens of people sitting at tables playing cards and shooting dice, drinking booze and smoking so much, the air seemed like a London fog. A pretty woman walked around in a short skirt carrying a little table with a strap around her neck, smiling, calling..."Cigars, cigarettes?"

In the Silver Palm Hotel, I spent much time alone in my room which was nothing more than a converted closet. I had a girl friend, a limp rag doll almost my size with listen to my records and radio programs. When I practiced my lessons and played the exercises well, my mother was happy with me.

But the fights were horrifying.

Night after night, it seemed, my father screamed at my mother until he was hoarse, squealing, angry, loud, throwing things, breaking lamps, wheezing, like he had just sprinted for two miles. I would peek through the crack in the door then hide under my cot with my doll, protecting her and my violin until the screaming ended. But the fights did not always end. One night, the sounds came so close to my door, I thought he was coming in to yell at me. He was a heavy man, and when he fell, everything in his way came crashing down with him, lamps, tables, pictures. Then my mother went down.

Frantic now, I closed my door, heart racing. I heard my mother scream back. "No, no, Willie, don't. Stop, please." I cracked open the door again and spotted my father dragging her across the floor by her flaming red hair while she grasped his hands and held her head. Grimacing, crying, her face transformed again, like I had seen when my brother died. "Please, Willie, no!" she shouted. "You're hurting me!"

I started to shake. Fear swarmed over me, I closed the door again, afraid that he might have seen me. I slammed the doll against the bed and began punching her over and over again until she was nothing more than puffs of cotton and ragged material. I cursed her, pulled at her hair, then collapsed and wept in my pillow.

After all fell silent, Mom came into the room and saw that I was out of breath, curled in a fetal position, trembling. I thought she might be angry at me for peeking, but she tucked me in calmly and stroked my hair. Her eyes were swollen black and blue, her hair a mess, but with effort and difficulty, she offered her angel's smile and I felt whole again. "It's okay, Squidgie," she whispered. "I love you Don't worry. Everything is okay."

She remained a long time, stroking my hair until I fell asleep.

* * *

The year I was nine, 1948, New York Governor, Thomas E. Dewey, was running for president against Harry Truman, Gandhi had just been assassinated, Babe Ruth died at the age of 53, and the State of Israel was born. Of course, I knew none of that at the time, but I did know that Jascha Heifetz was the greatest living violinist. That same year, Mr. Canonico had me attend a Heifetz concert from the wings of the stage. In those days, the concerts took place at the auditorium of Edison High School. That's where I met the great virtuoso in person after the performance and obtained his much treasured autograph which I own to this day.

Shortly after eight o'clock one evening, I was in my room practicing from my book of etudes (melodic exercises) when, suddenly, I heard crashing and grunting sounds from outside my bedroom window. I crouched from my bed and peeked through wooden blinds at the edge of the window. Through the darkness outside, I could make out figures in the moonlight. In the alley, next to the garbage cans, my father was being held from behind by one man while another punched him in the stomach, over and over and over, until the grunting sounded more like a painful wheeze. Frightened and confused, I wondered why they were hurting my father and hoped they would not kill him.

From outside my door, my mother called out in a harrowed voice, "Keep practicing, Squidgie. Keep practicing!" With my heart racing in high speed, I nervously lifted my violin and started playing scales rapidly, up and down three octaves like a musical roller coaster, high... low... high... low... all the while thinking that those angry men might come and beat me up too. Then the front door to the apartment slammed.

I stopped playing and cracked open my bedroom door enough to see my mother tending to the bloodied face of my father who had collapsed, holding his stomach, on the couch. When she spotted me, I quickly retreated back to the violin and started practicing again.

This wasn't the first time I saw my father beaten. It would not be the last. Spurts of violence, it seemed, erupted all around me without warning.

Friends often came for dinner and Mom would create lavish dishes and culinary displays that high class restaurants could not duplicate. Lobster *fra diavolo*, veal parmesan, braccioli, meat balls, pastas and the greatest meat sauce in the history of cooking. I savored the smells of garlic, basil, oregano, sweet sausage and... chocolate cake. A perfect Virgo, Mom was meticulous and orderly. She set a table adorned with silver cigarette boxes, chrome lighters, her finest china and bottles of scotch, bourbon, Sambuca, red wine and, of course, chocolate milk for me, poured into a wine glass.

The living area became the dining room, accommodating up to ten people by adding leaf extensions to the table. Everyone was Italian or Jewish, yet no one called themselves that. "Guinea, wop, dago, heeb, kyke, yid, nigger, spic, broad, faggot, and queer were common sobriquets used to describe everyone, even friends. Without exception, Bronx and Brooklynese prevailed: "Da bum woiked at toity-toid street," and they smoked one cigarette after another. All of them. No exceptions. I smoked, by breathing the air.

"Bubbala!" the women would say, pinching my cheeks, patting me on the head. Ugh! Then, those comments about my hair looking like Harpo Marx. So predictable. So annoying. I wanted to hide under my bed.

Mom made me part of the show. "Squidgie, get your violin. We'll play a piece for everyone." Time for a performance.

The group of smoking, boozing mobsters patronized my mother and me as she accompanied me on a baby grand piano while I played a flawed rendition of Brahms's Hungarian Dance No. 5, or an easier piece like The Swan. From the corner of my eye, I could see the exasperated expression on the mobster's faces, eyes rolling, sucking on cigars, bored out of their brains. Finally, I'd acknowledge the obligatory applause, tolerate a few more pinches on the cheek and feel a great sense of relief when Mom said,

"Okay, Squidgie. Go on in your room now."

Whew!

Those evenings were not always laughs and pinches and songs. Sitting at the table with gangland company was a hazardous position, because no one knew when laughter would suddenly erupt into violent pandemonium.

I rarely paid attention to table conversation while I ate. One night, with my mind in a far away place and six other people sitting around, my father suddenly leaped to his feet and screamed so loud his voice started squealing in that familiar hoarse sound. "Get outa here you dirty son of a bitch!" I jumped from the table. Everyone jumped with me. With his fist raised in the air, another man rose from his chair, causing bottles to tip and plates to smash on the floor. Women ran. When the two men started grappling and hitting each other's faces, my mother grabbed me by the neck and led me directly into my room without saying a word.

I think the women also got involved. I could hear them screaming at the men, more glass shattering, loud voices, sounds of pain, then, "I'll kill you, you guinea bastard! Get out!"

The front door slammed. Cars drove away.

Everyone had gone. I peeked into the living room and saw my mother tending to my father's bloodied face—a familiar sight. When she spotted me, I knew just what to do.

I took out my book of etudes.

* * *

In the summer of 1949, we spent two months at the Arcady Country Club in upper New York State. Situated at the north shore of Lake George, it was a Mecca for gangsters, gamblers, hookers and top night club entertainment. Every morning, card tables were set up around the patio and men of all ages engaged in gaming while their women basked in the sun's rays around the pool. It was a wonderful vacation; I played croquet, swam in the lake and learned to water ski behind a wooden speed boat.

It was also where I fell in love with Sonia.

The duo of Ramon and Sonia was one of the nightly acts at the outdoor club, a lively team who wore lavish costumes and danced to Latin rhythms, invariably sparking the audience into uproarious cheers and applause. My personal favorite was The Peanut Song, where she and Ramon would separate around the dance floor and hand out little ornate bags of peanuts to the audience as they passed by. She always gave me extras.

Sonia had bright red lips, a broad smile and golden hair pulled tightly over her ears and back into a bun. Her accent fascinated me. It mattered not that she was a head taller and fifteen years older, I loved that woman. And she loved me.

During the daytime, while everyone else gambled and lounged around the pool, she taught me to cha cha cha, tango, and rhumba. No "bubbalas." No pinches on the cheek. No Harpo Marx comparisons. She seemed to enjoy her ten-year-old admirer. My heart melted each time she lay her hand upon my shoulder and then placed mine around her waist.

Ay carrumba. Oye, Squidgie, come and dance with me, yes?   Larry Storch was a funny man who performed at the outdoor nightclub, keeping the audience in stitches. Somehow, Mom arranged for him to use me in one of his gags. I was impressed, indeed, performing on stage with the star of the show. My parents sat at a table drinking with raucous people who hooted and hollered when I delivered the punch line. Then, I had to play the violin, a gypsy song. I always had to play violin for people. My mother enjoyed showing me off. I made mistakes, but the audience was either drunk or had no ear for music, and I kept on without missing a beat.

The audience applauded loudly. In truth, they wanted my mother to step up and perform a dance number, then take the microphone and bellow out a few songs.

"This town is full of guys...who think they're mighty wise... because they happen to know a thing or twoo-o. But you can find them any day... strolling up and down Broadway... telling of the wonders they can do-o-o."

Except at the nightclub, I rarely saw my father. He was too busy gambling.

One afternoon, after he'd been gone all night, my mother told me to hurry and pack because we were leaving. She now drove a Studebaker Land Cruiser, green, stick shift. We traveled many miles, it seemed, until we reached a bus station in Saratoga Springs. That's where my father was, waiting for her to pick him up. Wearing dress pants and a sweat-soaked shirt and tie, he looked stressed and worried.

Earlier that day, the body of a man was found in a watery ditch just south of Lake George. He'd been shot in the head. Adults don't think kids pay attention, but I overheard my mother telling him about the news that had just come out. She asked a question. He told her to shut up.

I never saw Lake George, or Sonia, again.

CHAPTER THREE
Death and Deception

October 1949

Party time screeched to a halt when my father took sick. Bleeding ulcers. Mom stayed up around the clock, night and day, for two long weeks caring for him, feeding him baby food from little glass jars, cleaning his bed, helping him sleep while he moaned and groaned. He lost a lot of weight. I noticed little else, going to school by day, practicing violin, and occasionally making time to play with friends outside. Mr. Canonico still came to the house for my weekly violin lessons. Previously, he would stay and discuss my progress with my mother, but now the atmosphere was grim.

I remember the dire expression on my mother's face, the worry and the rushing to and from the doctor's office while she found someone to stay with me. She seemed so dedicated, so intense, so loyal and loving. In a strange way it was comforting, for it gave me a strong sense of knowing she would be there for me if I ever became sick.

"When you love someone," she said, "you must always be there, no matter what, especially in the hard times. That's when it counts. Never turn your back on someone you love."

I'll never forget her face, so beautiful yet so distorted at the twist of emotion.

* * *

Whack!

It was the only time my mother ever hit me. Across the face, the one swift slap caught me completely off guard. I had been resisting, disobeying. Just two blocks from our apartment, the lobby of Saint Francis Hospital was crowded with people gawking at us.

"Your father is dying," she said, fire blazing from her eyes. "Don't give me any more trouble. You are coming with me upstairs.

He wants to see you." She grabbed my arm firmly and shook it, leaving me no doubt who was in charge. As a father, Willie Strauss had been but a passing fart in the wind. No memories of fishing or playing ball; no long talks or great advice, nor deeds that would make a young boy brag about his father. He was just there— sometimes. My most vivid memories were watching people beat the shit out of him, or seeing him beat the shit out of my mother. That, or eating at the table, talking loud, cursing, or finding him at a card table with his cronies, smoking and drinking.

I had never seen anyone who was about to die and it frightened me. At ten years old, how was I to act? What could I say?

From the lobby to the halls and into the patient's rooms, the Saint Francis Hospital reeked of antiseptic smells. When we arrived at his door, I hesitated. Mom pulled. Slowly, she led me inside his room. Soft airy noises emanated from strange machines while wires and tubes hung over the bed. When I saw that his eyes were closed, I thought he might already be dead. I hadn't seen him in over two weeks when he went in for an operation for his ulcers. The operation was a success, but he contracted a major case of uremia.

The bed seemed very high, for my eyes were barely higher than his. His skin was pallid, and his face so thin I barely recognized him. A green oxygen tube dangled out of his nose, hissing. I felt my mother's eyes, intensely watching, approving. He opened one eye, turned his head painfully, then slowly raised his left arm from the side, gesturing for me to hold his hand. Again, there was that soft, "baby's ass" flesh that had never worked a day of physical labor in his life. He held my hand weakly and whispered, "Take care of your mother."

The mood was ominous and grave. What else could
I say? "I will."

I wanted to run out, but Mom told me to give him a kiss. I stood on the edge of the rail and leaned over to kiss his forehead, but I don't think he felt a thing. I think he died right there.

"Go outside, wait for me," she said.

Minutes later, she stepped awkwardly from the room, her face in tears, grimacing.

It occurred to me; My eyes were the last he ever saw, my hand the last touch he ever felt.

Two days later, funeral services were held in a local synagogue. It all seemed like another flashback to when I was four. Crowds of people wore black, Mom sobbed out of control, her face contorted, and the rail-thin body of Willie Strauss lay in a fancy coffin wearing a dark suit and tie, his face powdered white, lips sewn together, almost unrecognizable. She told me to wear a yarmulke (skull cap,) to show respect. Though in the presence of Jews all my life, I'd never been to a Jewish service in my life.

My mother must have loved him very much. When the funeral was over, she said to me, "Don't you ever forget that man."

I didn't. Neither would I ever forget the revelation that followed.

The morning after the funeral, Mom removed three large photo albums from a closet and sat me down with an announcement. "I have something to tell you. Willie Strauss was not your real father."

"What? What do you mean?"

"Come sit next to me." She patted the sofa. "He didn't want you to know, so I never told you. But now that he's dead, it's only right that I tell you."

"Who is my father?" I asked.

"Willie adopted you when you were three. Your real father was Art Frank. He was also Jewish, and a famous vaudeville star. He died of pneumonia in a mental institution when you were two. Here are all his pictures and clippings."

In my thirst for truth, I took the books, and the pictures, and the old movies and tore through them until I memorized everything about my real father, including all the shows and theaters he performed in on the Orpheus Circuit. He had been a headliner, often sharing the same stage and on the same show biz level with greats like Burns and Allen, Rudy Vallee, Milton Berle and Jack Benny. A sense of pride washed over me. I thought, what a wonderful man he must have been and how deprived I was of knowing him, of being his son. Instead, I was led to believe my father was a mobster, a boozing, gambling, ranting and raving wife beater.

I'll never forget the sense of betrayal, of being deceived those ten years. "It was for your own good," Mom said. But I didn't believe her. I believed it was for their own convenience. In the meanwhile, I had been stripped of my true identity.

CHAPTER FOUR
Fairyland

For the next five years, my only competition for Mom's attention was a bottle of Dewar's White Label.

Despite all the good times and rolls of cash, Willie Strauss left his wife with nothing other than her good looks, a couple of furs, diamond rings, furniture, piano, a 1949 Studebaker and me. Beyond that, she was broke except for a small pension ($68 a month) from the U.S. Army, the government's apology for Willie's ulcers. A few hoods came around to settle up debts, but there was nothing to settle with. Willie and his money were gone. The hospital got what he owed the shylocks.

One day, a young twenty-year-old bespectacled redhead named Yvonne emerged from obscurity (along with her lush mother) claiming to be a long lost illegitimate daughter of Willie Strauss. They knocked on the apartment door, demanding some of the inheritance. "Fine," my mother said. "You can have his shirts, pants, ties and shoes. Oh yes, there's a few decks of cards."

They threatened to sue, but never did.

Nearing forty years old, weathered by years of booze and cigarettes, Mom was no longer nightclub material or a Broadway starlet. She had a son to raise. He needed violin lessons. She had to work. All she knew was music and dance.

She landed a part-time job at the Fithian Dance Studio, off 48th Street and Pine Tree Drive on Miami Beach, where she played a dilapidated upright piano for ballet and tap classes, and served as an assistant teacher when needed. The $15 a week income, with the monthly pension, enabled her to retain Artie Canonico as my violin teacher. I think she would have starved so that I could continue those lessons.

The Fithian Studio experience offered another bonus, if you could call it that. As I look back, it was more a nightmare. Because my mother worked there, I was entitled to free dance instruction, complete with leotard, tights, ballet and tap shoes. I became adept for a ten- year old boy with Harpo Marx hair, leaping around like

Peter Pan, doing splits and acrobatics like an Olympic gymnast, tap dancing like Gene Kelly and Ray Bolger, and spinning pirouettes like a New York ballerina. I was the only boy in the dance school, but I didn't give it any notice. It didn't mean anything. When the end-of-year recital came, I was one of the stars of the show, not only dancing, but you guessed it, playing that violin. Ta daaa.

I didn't see much of Mom then, except at the studio. In evenings, I was either with baby sitters or confined to my room after dinner to practice violin, read, write, or listen to my records. She cooked dinners for me and fresh hamburger for my dog, Chico. Atop the table sat the omnipresent bottle of Dewar's, the oversized shot glass, and a tumbler of ice water. By early evening, she was usually bombed, blurry eyed, and reeking of booze. Each night, I had to help her stagger into bed. "Come, Mom, stand up, hold on to my shoulder, you gotta get into bed."

On occasions, she would pass out at the kitchen table while I was eating dinner. One time she fell sideways off the chair to the floor like a sack of potatoes. I didn't know what to do. I couldn't lift her, so I summoned a neighbor who helped get her into bed. The old man told me she had not been eating. I knew she had eaten because I watched. Crackers. Tea. Scotch. I realized, then, she had been cooking for me and the dog, but not for herself.

Sometimes, Mr. Canonico brought sandwiches when he came for a lesson, often staying longer than one hour, making sure I understood how to practice, and how to perfect those scales, double-stops and trills. He and Mom would talk after, while I remained in my room, practicing,. listening, opening my door a crack, curious. Mr. Canonico drank scotch as well, and often stayed with Mom long into the night until I was asleep. I thought about Mr. Canonico and my mother in a romantic way, hoping she would find someone to make her happy again. But there were two problems. He was four inches shorter than she was, and he had a wife and two kids.

At eleven years of age, I was already in seventh grade at Nautilus Junior High, near Alton Road and 42nd Street. Academic progress had vaulted me from 3rd to 5th grade in elementary school, skipping the fourth grade. On a routine day, my mother dropped me off at school, equipped with violin and briefcase. I attended classes and played in the orchestra. When school was over, I'd walk the ten to twelve residential blocks to The Fithian Studio where I'd take my dance lessons and be with my mother.

Until...

* * *

On a warm November afternoon in 1950, my world was altered forever.

During that year, a school bully named Stanley Press had been harassing me, cornering me against the wall during classroom breaks, cursing, calling me names and threatening to beat me up. Press was much bigger than me, which isn't saying much. I was a skinny lightweight of a kid. And though he was unnerving, I basically dismissed it all, thinking he was just a jerk. I figured he'd go away if I ignored him.

One Thursday afternoon, the school bell rang and, as always, I sped out the side door for my one-mile trek to The Fithian Studio, holding my brief case in one hand and violin case in the other.

Led by Stanley Press, they were lined up outside, waiting for me, sinister grins on their faces, seven or eight kids, boys and girls, laughing, pointing, calling names. Taken by surprise, my heart started to race. I tried to run through them, but it was impossible. They formed a circle around me, taunting, cackling, pushing me from one to another like a dodge ball, chanting to the tune of Ring Around The Rosey, changing the lyrics to, "Marshall is a fairy, Marshall is a fairy," over and over, and over again. "Marshall is a fairieee, Marshall is a fairieee." I felt their fists and hands hitting my shoulders, stomach, and face, then they shoved me to the ground, kicking, spitting. I lost control of my brief case and violin as I crawled into a fetal position and wrapped my hands over my face for protection from the onslaught. Then came belly dives directly on my back. It was like a shark frenzy. I thought they were going to kill me. "Marshall is a fairieee." I looked up and saw my violin go airborne, landing into the bushes. They pulled the black leotard and tights from my briefcase and draped them over a tree limb, a memento for all to see. "Marshall is a fairieee." The grit of Florida sand coated my tongue and lips as they finally ran off in different directions, leaving me there like a beaten slab of meat.

The body heals, but the mind remains scarred forever. The incident changed my world and the way I saw it. It also changed the way I intended for others to see me.

Marshall's fairy days were over.

* * *

"How did it go today in school, Squidgie?"

"Don't ever call me Squidgie again, Mom!"

"Look at you. You look a mess. What happened to you?"

I explained the incident. She tended to my minor injuries and said she wanted to complain to the school authorities the next day. I pleaded that she not.

"I'm not taking dancing lessons any more. No more violin lessons either."

We argued. It was the first time I ever stood up to her. It must have been very confusing. "Okay," she said.

"You don't have to take dance lessons, but you must continue with violin. You are not throwing it all away. You have no choice."

No matter, my days as a burgeoning virtuoso came to a halt as I resisted practicing any more than I absolutely had to. Two to three hours a day dropped to a half hour. I closed the windows on my room so no one could hear outside. My student progress slowed to a near stop. I frustrated Mr. Canonico who had visions of my becoming first-chair symphony violinist, if not a soloist. I began to dread school and saw the kids around me as my judges, my enemies. For the first time ever, my grades went below straight A's, plunging so low that I failed the seventh grade.

I began to study boxing, baseball, football and anything else that was considered masculine. Alone in my room, I practiced curse words in the mirror. I wanted shorter hair, no more Harpo Marx. I started lifting barbells, trying to emulate Charles Atlas in his famous advertisement where he emerged from a ninety-eight pound weakling into a muscle man.

No one would ever call me a fairy again, even if it meant being a football player, a prize fighter, a Marine or a gun-toting cop, and not a concert violinist.

CHAPTER FIVE
Death, Booze, and Baseball

June 1952

While the Korean War was in high gear, Dwight Eisenhower and Adlai Stevenson were the front runners for the next presidential election. A new television show called *The Hit Parade* featured Snooky Lanson and Dorothy Collins singing songs like *How Much Is That Doggie In The Window* and *Kiss of Fire*. That same year, Rocky Marciano knocked out Jersey Joe Walcott for the heavyweight championship.

This was also a time when Jews were persona non grata at selected motels and hotels along Miami Beach. In the off season, when parking lots were empty, desk clerks at beachfront resorts like the Golden Strand Motel would announce "no vacancy" if your name was Greenberg. Worse, black people were not only segregated on buses and public facilities, they were not allowed on Miami Beach after dark, unless they could produce a work permit.

Two years earlier, during a summer break with the Fithian Studio clan, I had experienced my first kiss in the back room of a clapboard summer home in Belgrade Lakes, Maine. Her name: Idola Miller. I was ten, she, seven. We were teamed to dance together during shows, mostly tap. I thought her beauty was unmatched by any girl I ever knew, perfect features, dark eyes, wavy hair. I remember my heart fluttering, knees shaking and being rejected when I tried a second time. Ah, the tribulations of young love. Maine is an enchantingly beautiful state in the summer, with the smell of pine and flower blossoms permeating the air, blue jays, cardinals, and sparrows fluttering in the countryside, glistening lakes and rustic harbors lining the oceanfront. My grandparents and Aunt Frances drove there during summer vacations to get away from the heat and hustle-bustle of the big city; New York. Carl Peterson, my grandfather, had just purchased the latest model 1952 Ford, four door. This was to be its maiden voyage, so to speak, the first long drive into the country. He had worked long hours at the

Philadelphia press room, traveling one hour by train each way every day, while Anna sewed custom-made dresses for the ladies of New York.

A giant of a man standing at least 6'4", he had pure white hair, false teeth, and a quiet lumbering personality who rarely spoke unless spoken to. My fondest memory of him was playing catch together with a tennis ball across the street from the Forest Hills tennis courts in Queens, New York.

As always, Aunt Frances did the driving. Anna, my grandmother, was sitting in the front seat, passenger side. Carl relaxed in the back seat. As I learned later, they had been talking about music, art, the beautiful scenery and national politics when they reached a construction site and a temporary wooden bridge crossing a river. Frances stopped, then carefully eased the car across wooden planks.

* * *

Cesar Lamonica was a prominent Miami figure for many years among music enthusiasts. Besides other gigs, the gangly old maestro conducted the Youth Symphony at the outdoor band shell on Bayfront Park in downtown Miami, a landmark which has long since succumbed to the wrecking ball. He was a tall man who always wore a white dinner jacket, had wild graying hair and a thick Italian accent. He looked and acted every bit the role of Arturo Toscanini moved south.

The Youth Symphony was comprised of child musicians in junior or senior high school, an invaluable experience for youngsters aspiring to the profession. For me, it was not voluntary.

We convened in the evening hours, playing and performing some pretty tough music, including Beethoven's Fifth Symphony, songs from Student Prince, Strauss waltzes and other opera overtures. Occasionally, opera singers performed solos with the orchestra.

A family friend—a woman named Bunny—drove me to the band shell one night because Mom had just received an important phone call and had to remain at home. Halfway through the rehearsal, during a rest period, Bunny hurriedly approached my chair from the wings, tapped me on the shoulder and said we had to go. Mr. Lamonica did not seem very happy.

When I arrived home thirty minutes later, Mom was at the kitchen table, scotch in hand. I saw that expression again. Something terrible must have happened. She was sobbing, her features contorted, hysterical. While sitting on the couch, she held me close and gently cupped my face in her hands. "Your Grampa died today, Squidgie."

I flinched at the nickname, but it was not the time to say anything. "How?" I asked.

"In a car accident. We have to go to New York."

Three days later, once again, people were all dressed in black, my mother wept and my grandfather lay in a fancy casket, face powdered, lips sealed.

The tires of the new Ford had slipped from the wooden planks and plunged, trunk first, into the river. Fortunately, the front windows were open, enabling Frances and Anna to exit and reach the surface. Carl Peterson was trapped in the rear seat. It was the fourth family death in nine years, two by drowning.

Once a dancer with the famed Rockettes of Radio City Music Hall, Aunt Frances lived another fifty-two years, until she died at the age of 91. She never touched the wheel of a car again.

* * *

I don't know how she managed on the measly income, but with the help of her VA benefits, Mom bought a small, three-bedroom house in the newly developing region of North Miami Beach and then opened her own dance studio on West Dixie Highway, calling it The Vivien Melby Dance Studio. "Melby" was her mother's maiden name.

Her resilience and stamina were nothing less than amazing, though I did not recognize it then. She drank herself into oblivion every night and smoked four packs of cigarettes a day (Kent, with the micronite filter for better health), yet she danced on her feet six or seven hours daily with students ranging from ages of four to teens to adult women in their twenties. She ran the business, took care of me and the house. Gone were the days of huge dinner parties and male friends, other than weekly visits by Mr. Canonico.

The main street in North Miami Beach, 163rd, was then a remote two-lane road that extended east all the way to the beaches. Except for a gas station, a few small stores and a couple bars, it was like moving to the boondocks.

Within three years, the forest areas on 163rd street gave way to huge shopping centers and other commercial enterprises and the road was widened into a major thoroughfare. In 1952, the population of North Miami Beach was approximately 2,000. In three years that number grew to 10,000.

North Miami High School must have been the prototype for Rydell High in the Broadway Show, Grease. Kids, clothing, ducktail hair styles, cars with loud mufflers and spinner hubcaps, lingo and the advent of Rock 'n Roll music was nothing less than identical, including the innocence of teachers. I didn't realize what a great place it was then.

Life for me was a matter of going to school, making friends, practicing violin at least forty-five minutes a day (mandated, no exceptions), trying out for sports and, most importantly, remaking my image.

Everyone knows that a varsity football player is the ultimate jock, guaranteed a spot in any list of most popular and admired kids. I was thin for my five-foot ten inches, but big enough, I thought. I wanted to try out, but Mom refused to sign the permission papers. "No football," she said. "You'll break a finger."

I forged her name.

First day of practice, I suited up with shoulder pads, cleats, helmet, jersey with a number, doing jumping jacks in line with all the other jocks. Then came the first scrimmage. Assigned to play offensive center, I joined the huddle, heard the play, bent over the football, wrapped my hands about it, then felt the quarterback's hand in my crotch while listening to the call of numbers. So cool!

When I glanced upward, another helmeted fellow growled directly into my face, a bulldog kinda guy named John Lewis who had lined up as defensive center. When he assumed the position, he looked at me with such hate in his eyes, spewing steam from ears and nostrils. I almost shit right there.

The quarterback hollered, "Hike!"

The next thing I remember was lying face up on the ground with the world spinning, my upper lip the size of a jellyfish.

Face guards didn't exist in 1954.

Okay. No football. But I had studied a lot about boxing and knew all the terminology, the history, the champions, the moves, and so on. So, I tried out for the boxing team, and entered my first sparring round against a student named Monte Steel. The round lasted less than twenty seconds.

Okay. No boxing.

I did have a good throwing arm and no one beats you up in baseball. While I settled for the less violent sport, I actually excelled as a pitcher and outfielder on local Pony League and Babe Ruth league teams. Being accepted on a sports team validated my masculinity. My image and being "accepted" meant more than anything—more than girls, more than music, more than love itself. Mom was no longer calling me Squidgie, my Harpo hair had transformed into a more conservative cut, and the days of "Bubbala" were

over.

I had made good friends with two distinctly different groups, one predominantly Jewish and the other, gentiles. No particular reason. It just turned out that way. They didn't hang out with each other. I would go with one group on a Saturday, for example. And then the other group on Sunday. It was great. Among them, I still remain best of friends with Harvey Glaser and George Reincke, and stay in close touch with several others as well.

Having been raised in a secular environment, religion didn't matter to me. I was never brought to a church or synagogue other than for weddings and funerals, and there were plenty of them. Mom was born into a Lutheran family, but religion didn't guide her life in any manner. At Art Frank's request (my natural father), she had converted to Judaism so they could marry. But she never really practiced it. Then she married Willie.

Once, I asked my mother what religion I was supposed to be. After all, other kids had a religion, why not me? She said, "Study them all, then choose."

As I matured, I came to realize that was the best advice a parent could give, suggesting that I educate myself, rather than being indoctrinated with subjective beliefs or having me follow the masses into blind faith.

So, I did.

As my early teens sped by, Mom seemed to be more tired. She worked long and hard during the day and drank at night. Sometimes we fought. Seeing her with her eyes crossed, spittle at the corners of her mouth, staggering and stammering night after night angered me more as time passed. On one occasion, I poured her scotch down the kitchen drain, pleading with her to stop. She screamed, reminding me the price of a bottle of Dewar's. More than anything,

I wished she'd find a man and get married. Then, maybe, she would not be so depressed.

It wasn't long. My wish came true.

CHAPTER SIX
Bernie The Bookie

In the fall of 1954, Willie Mays won his first batting title with the New York Giants; a little known singer named Elvis Presley debuted on a country music show in Shreveport, Louisiana; and a nutty senator from Wisconsin named Joe McCarthy saw communists around every corner. Miami was still a medium-sized resort town made up of 85 percent white—mostly transplants from northern states—percent black, four percent Hispanic and one percent Native American.

I November of that year, my mother was on a long distance call with an old friend and sister "moll" named Chickie Stein. They talked about the good old days, when Willie Strauss, and Chickie's husband, Bernie, ran bookmaking operations in Manhattan, along with a card room or two, and about all the cops and politicians they paid off in the process. The four of them had always been good friends. Mom enjoyed the surprise and rare phone call. Moments after they hung up, Chickie died of a brain hemorrhage.

Apparently, my mother and Bernard Stein had a thing for each other I hadn't known about. Two months later, Bernie drove from California to Miami with his two kids, Jerry, eight, and Phyllis, six, and moved into the house with my mother and me. In an instant, I had three new steps: brother, sister, and father. Mom had a new common-law husband, a man four years older, whom she had known in New York during the early '40s and, a bonafide gangster besides. Life was good again.

Bernie took over bookmaking and shylock operations for the upper beach area called Sunny Isles where four miles of motels lined the Atlantic, tourists flocked by the millions, and all the lures for organized crime were in good standing: prostitution, gambling, loan sharking, murder, mayhem and political pay-offs. Drug trafficking was taboo, however. Not part of his repertoire. An imposing figure with a large head and barrel chest, Bernie would have stood over six feet if he straightened up, but he stooped slightly and walked with a labored shuffle. With a perennial Tiparillo cigar between his teeth and receding grey hair swooped back with no part, Bernie fit the mobster stereotype because he talked the talk and walked the walk. From childhood, he had been groomed with the best of them.

For Mom, it was like riding a bike, back in the saddle. After five years of depression and financial woes, money was rolling in again. She curbed her drinking habit. Her dance studio was thriving. Once again, the household hosted huge dinner parties for mobsters with "New Yawk" accents and names like Maxie, Philly, Guido, Carmine, Sally and Frankie. Then, the familiar around-the-table repartee: "Guinea, wop, dago, heeb, kyke, yid, nigger, spic, broad, faggot and queer." Equal opportunity. No one was left out.

For me, it was *déjà vu*, with the omnipresent aroma of Jewish and Italian food, booze flowing, cigar and cigarette smoke permeating the air, howling laughter, and my mother playing piano and singing torch songs. "Frankie and Johnnie were sweethearts...oh yeah!
Oh lordy how they could love."
"Am I bluuuuue... Oh, am I bluuuuue..."
"This town is full of guys, who think they're mighty wise."

My role was to eat, perform and disappear, and hope no one got pissed off at one another. I played the usual Gypsy pieces on the violin, accepted polite applause and slipped into my room where I basked in solitude.

All in all, Bernie's presence was a welcome relief. I no longer worried about my mother's welfare, no longer grappled with putting her to bed at night, no longer poured her scotch down the drain. Our arguments came to a halt. I relished my new found freedom and the ability to be with my friends, provided, of course, that I practiced violin that minimum forty-five minutes a day. Mr. Canonico still came once a week, but I think his visions of me becoming a concert soloist had long dissipated. Besides all that, I was accepted as a starting baseball player on two local teams. I had friends. I had a new image. Life was getting better all the time.

* * *

Bernie's "office" was the small master bedroom of the house. His work attire: skivvy undershorts and a white tee-shirt. Tools of the trade were his bed and pillow to lean back on, a telephone atop the nightstand, a pencil and a pack of flash paper which were narrow betting slips coated with a special chemical. Bernie chuckled each time he demonstrated how the paper would catch fire and disappear without a trace when torched with a match or lit cigarette. No ashes. No residue. Next to the bed, a mere two feet from his burning Tiparillo, stood an oxygen tank, just in case of a heart attack.

His ducks were all in a row because of his dire fear of the FBI. His regulars spoke coded lingo on the telephone because he thought the wires might be tapped. Special conversations required that the "customer" come to the house in person. A full supply of flash paper ensured that his betting slips would disappear in the event of a raid. And, he had the loyal services of Dr. Phil Basso at his beck and call, a mob physician on retainer in case he needed a timely heart attack.

It worked.

Two FBI agents came to the house one day to talk to Bernie. He thought they might have a search warrant. After Mom let them in, they walked down the hall to the bedroom and asked, "Are you Bernie Stein?"

Bernie grabbed his chest. "Yeah, yeah, What's the matter. I ain't feelin' too good here."

"We want to talk to you about..."

"My chest, it hurts. Call my wife in here."

Perplexed, the agents summoned my mother and waited off to the side. "What's the matter, hon?" she asked.

"Call Doc Basso. I think I'm having a heart attack."

As I learned later, Doctor Basso, a gynecologist, was in the middle of an examination when he took the call. He dropped everything and rushed to the house, arriving in fifteen minutes. He hurried inside, rushed by the agents who were standing confused in the living room, ran down the hall and put a stethoscope to Bernie's chest. By now, Bernie was breathing so heavy, the windows fogged up.

Doc Basso yelled, "Call an ambulance. This is an emergency. My patient is having a heart attack."

The FBI agents departed, never to be seen again. Bernie remained in North Miami General Hospital for the next four days recovering from heart failure. And Doc Basso went back to work, satisfied that he had fulfilled his obligation to mob money. The ploy worked.

* * *

Though Bernie had a son and daughter, there was a certain chemistry between me and him that wasn't there with his own kids. Jerry was ill-mannered, lazy, and often in trouble in school. He sauntered around like a big shot because his old man was a big shot. As the years passed, I never heard Bernie say a kind word to him. Even as Jerry grew into manhood, he was ever the loser, eventually a convict and a drug abuser, finding a miserable existence somewhere in the universe. During his teen years, fights often erupted in the house with Bernie in a rage, degrading Jerry, calling him a "piece of shit" followed by a few well placed smacks across the head. The sounds were a throwback to my early years— squealing voices, wheezing, fire and anger.

Phyllis was a sweet and gentle girl who sought approval from everyone, including my mother, her father and me. But Bernie treated her around the house like a pet that had to be fed and nothing more. The parenting of Phyllis was relegated to my mother, which she took on willingly.

I eventually became very close to Bernie. He had that slick, New Yawk gangster charisma, like a character out of a movie. He cared for me and I cared for him, despite his foibles. He probably held dark secrets that no one should ever know, and I never pried. I often sat on the edge of his bed listening to him talk about his good old days while he intermittently answered the phone to take a bet. I was flattered, indeed.

He had met Al Capone once or twice. "A crazy bastard," he called him. "Totally nuts. And a fucking slob besides. He didn't have much to do with me 'cause I was a Jew, and he didn't trust the Jews."

He ran around with Bennie (Bugsy) Siegel when they were kids together on Manhattan's lower east side.

"Another crazy bastard," he called Bugsy. "A fuckin' whacko. I stayed away from him after he got me into a lot of trouble.

"He was a protection racketeer. He'd walk up to a poor pushcart vendor selling fruit and demand money. When the guy wouldn't give it to him, Bugsy set the cart on fire. From then on, they gave him what he wanted." Bernie chomped on his Tiparillo, his mind swimming in the past.

"We done a few things together, but when he started that shit, I broke it off."

"Ever know Meyer Lansky?" I asked.

"Know him? He's still living over on the beach.

Wanna have him over for dinner?" Bernie formed an impish laugh. "Well, we ain't exactly talkin' these days, but we were friends once. Let's just leave it at that."

CHAPTER SEVEN
Troublemaker

Mom didn't like many of my friends. She felt they weren't good enough for me, preferring that I hung around with musicians, artists and dancers. But that was out of the question. *Sophisticated* kids weren't fun. My friends were.

Harvey Glaser, she thought, was a little Napoleon, a wise guy, a smart ass.

She liked Larry Epstein because he played violin. We also shared the same violin teacher.

The first time she met George Reincke, she thought he walked like a giraffe. He drove a 1948 Mercury with glass back mufflers that could be heard ten blocks away. And when he pulled off from Mom's driveway, he spun gravel all over the neighbors' yard. She was not happy.

She thought Jim Murphy was a nice kid, but a loser, not going anywhere. Besides, he liked to tinker with mechanics. His future would be a grease monkey, she figured. Not what she had in mind for her son.

Murphy and I hung out together for no other reason than to find things to laugh about, make fun of strange people, drag race, sneak into drive-in movies, make up dumb lyrics to popular songs and sample various forms of alcohol.

One night after dark, while cruising around in my black, 1947 Ford coupe, we were passing through a darkened residential neighborhood on the way to the main highway. Jim suddenly hollered, "Marsh, wait! Back it up."

We looked to our right and saw that a light was on in the center window of a house. In it, clear as daylight, was a young woman getting dressed. So, we sat there for a couple seconds until the front door of the house tore open and two guys like big gorillas started running to the car.

"Oh shit," Jim said. " Let's get outa here. Gun it! Quick!"

I could see two large men running to their driveway, enter a sedan and back up quickly. Sudden panic set in. I squealed tires and drove like a maniac, around turns and through yards trying to elude them for, it seemed, an eternity, our hearts racing, scared to death. But they chased after us in a bigger and better car, and when we reached a stop sign, they pulled up directly in front of my jalopy and stormed out.

When the driver's door came open, I think I pooped in my pants. In an instant, two powerful hands grabbed my neck and shirt collar and dragged me to the street while these guys screamed, cursed and threatened to kill us. I didn't see what happened to Jim, I was so worried about myself. We begged for mercy and promised that we were not Peeping Toms, just passing by in a car. "I'm sorry! I'm sorry!" we both screamed.

Fortunately, the two angry men eased off and left the matter to the local North Miami Beach Police, who brought us to the station where we shivered and shook until our mothers came to get us. The police filed a report, but somehow, it got lost. As it turned out, Bernie knew the chief, Red Lieper.

Jim and I were even more relieved after we learned that one of those men was Willie Pastrano, who would later become the Light-Heavyweight champion of the world. Thank goodness for Bernie.

* * *

A year later, I went to jail.

After a few jobs washing dishes, cleaning swimming pools and bagging groceries, I bought my second car, a 1951 Chevrolet fastback, stick shift, green. Harvey and Larry suggested we take it for a long drive to see how it ran on the highway.

I don't know why we traveled so far up Highway 27, but the car's engine started knocking just as we entered the town of Lake Placid, Florida, about one hundred miles north of home. The car threw a rod. We were stranded.

"Mom? Help!"

It was late in the afternoon and none of our mothers were prepared to rescue us on the spot. We had barely enough money between us to stay in a dumpy motel room for the night and eat a cheap hamburger. They would come and get us the next day.

A year younger, bigger and burlier than Harvey or me, Larry was more the conservative, tagging along, trying to keep calm. The room had one double bed. I slept in the middle. Well, I tried to. Harvey was a hopeless prankster. He would not let up, tickling, rubbing his feet on me, laughing and jabbing until it was impossible to stay in the bed with all the jumping and hollering. We spent about four hours howling with laughter, poking fun and raising hell. Harvey sneaked into the bathroom while I showered, stood atop the toilet seat, reached over the curtain and grabbed my head, causing me to scream like a maniac. The ruckus went on for hours.

Neighbors complained. A knock came at the door. Minutes later, we were handcuffed and riding in a Sheriff's car, on the way to the jail in Sebring. Charge: Disturbing. The Peace.

The instant conversion from innocent teenager to jail inmate was a sobering experience. The old gray two story jail building seemed to lean much like the Old Jail tourist attraction in Saint Augustine. We arrived in the darkened cell at 4 A.M., and immediately realized we were in a drunk tank that held twenty-one prisoners but had only twelve bunks. It reeked of urine, sweat and alcohol breath. Because he was still a legal minor, Larry was required to sleep outside the cell. One toilet and one sink against the back wall was supposed to accommodate everyone. After tiptoeing in the dark around sleeping prisoners, Harvey and I set a blanket on the floor inside the cell and lay awake listening to the cacophony of farts, grunts and snoring. It wasn't funny any more.

The next morning at 11 A.M. , tired and frightened, we were escorted into a courtroom before a crippled judge who chewed us new assholes, inside and out. I thought for sure we were going to the state penitentiary. He let us go. The arresting deputy gave us a few dollars to buy a bus ticket and in a few hours we were safe at home. Mom sent him the money back the next week. Never booked. No record of being arrested.

I sensed Bernie was behind it all.

* * *

Gary (Bob) Minium was the biggest, baddest son-of-a bitch in the entire high school. Kids got out of his way when he strode down the halls, his nose high in the air, sneering, angry, and tough. Besides being a hard-hitting football player, he had a reputation as bully, known for picking on kids, beating them up and engaging in gang fights after school. He was one mean-ass guy. No one messed with Minium.

Despite playing on a baseball team and having my own coterie of friends, I was still paranoid of my image and did my best to sneak into school the back way every morning to drop off my violin in the orchestra room. I managed passing grades because I showed up most of the time, but studied little and did even less homework. I was one of those kids who blended into the wall, unnoticed.

Until...

One day, I was sent to the Dean's office. I don't recall why. When I arrived, the secretary told me to wait in the meeting room. There, at the same table sitting with some other big kid was Gary Minium... the bully. Fear instantly swept over me. I thought my heart would explode from my chest. For me, any bully was a menace. I broke out in a cold sweat. Minium sneered and seemed really mad. I just knew this guy was going to beat the shit out of me. There he was, Stanley Press all over again as visions of kids dancing in a circle around me swarmed into my head. *Marshall is a fairieee. Marshall is a fairieee.* I probably looked like a human vibrator.

But it all ended with no commotion, no bullying. The perceptions were all in my head. And as the years passed, it was not the last I would see of Gary Minium.

I used to sneak into the school orchestra room early in the mornings to drop off my violin, so no one would see me. Orchestra was sixth period, so I'd leave the violin there after school, and come back later when the coast was clear, to pick it up. It was an old and valuable instrument. Mom wouldn't allow me to leave it overnight.

I was concertmaster and the school's alternate conductor, beside the teacher, Mrs. Dinino. Sometimes, other musical kids would ask me to play solos on the violin. I was viewed as the school's best musician, until another kid arrived, a dark-haired Italian boy who played an incredible piano, just as good as any professional. Kids crowded around after school when he played one dazzling piece after another. Name: Bill Conti. He would go on to become one of Hollywood's premier composer/conductors, writing such famous music as the theme from Rocky.

CHAPTER EIGHT
Employed by the Mob

1955 was the year of wrap-around windshields, glass pack mufflers and spinner hubcaps. Young Marlon Brando starred in a new movie, "On The Waterfront," and the newly constructed Fountainbleu Hotel was in its first year of operation on Miami Beach. With Mom's help, I had purchased my stick shift, 1947 Ford Coupe for $295. On one of its first evening runs, I drove a car full of friends to Miami Beach where I boldly drove the jalopy up the gilded driveway to the sparkling new Fountainbleu Hotel and parked it between a new Chrysler Imperial and a Rolls Royce. The bellhops were not impressed.

At sixteen, my first on-the-payroll job was a coffee shop dishwasher at the beachfront Caravan Motel on the north end of Sunny Isles' Motel Row. Bernie knew the owner, a "customer" who owed him. Seven days a week, no days off, eight hour days, for twenty bucks a week. I figured that amounted to 37 cents an hour. But, it included all I could eat for one meal a day. The manager insisted that nothing be thrown away. Leftovers, like lettuce and tomato, pickles, toast, and cuts of meat, could always be recycled to another customer in one way or another. I lasted about three weeks until I got a job at a grocery store that gave me Sundays off.

Between the ages of sixteen and eighteen, I held at least thirty menial labor jobs: bag boy, stock boy, pool boy, dishwasher, and valet runner at the parking lot of the landmark Lighthouse Restaurant, south of Haulover Beach. (Since burned down) I also taught private violin lessons to a few beginners for $2 a lesson. My first sexual encounter was with a fifteen year-old violin student named Zaidee whose mother worked as a night nurse at a hospital. She would pay me the $2, then go to work, leaving me to her daughter who gave me free lessons of her own.

Sometimes I played violin in small local productions, like *Carousel* and *South Pacific*, but that was never steady, nor did it pay well. I was not in a musician's union, so getting regular jobs in music was impossible.

I fell madly in love with a brown-haired Louisiana girl named Nita Taylor who moved into the house next door with her mom and dad. She was a year younger than me. It started with passing glances and waves of the hand. Then, she invited me over for punch. Punch led to holding hands, and then making out. When she said she loved me, I melted. She had the softest skin on earth. Nita fully acquainted me with the love experience. I went totally nuts. We made out in my car and in her house when her parents were not home, and for hours we danced to love songs like *The Great Pretender* and *Only You* until we dropped. I must have blathered over her like a wimpy little kid, which is why she dumped me after a couple months.

Worried she would find another love, I kept constant track of her, peeking through the blinds, calling incessantly, being a nuisance. One night, I saw a car pull into her driveway. I ducked under the window and turned out my lights, then watched. The driver was a guy I knew from school named Henry Papale. She got in, and they drove away. I paced the floor for four hours, until the car returned to the driveway at midnight. I turned out the lights once more, then peered out the window. She stayed in the car for eons. I wondered if they were making out, but I couldn't tell. It was too dark. So, I went outside and climbed on the roof of the house and crawled across the tiles like a wartime G.I. She finally kissed the guy, got out and walked to her door. It ate my insides.

My insides developed another problem. I was stuck. The garbage can that I used to vault myself up, had tipped over. No way down. I could not stay on the roof all night. Time to suffer embarrassment.

"MOM?"

A week later, I was sent to stay with relatives in New York where I had three visits with a psychiatrist.

Diagnosis: Immaturity.

Despite my image remake and acceptance by many friends, I still floundered. Emotionally wrecked over the loss of my first love, I paid no attention to responsibilities. School bored me; my grades were deplorable. I set no goals, had no accomplishments, saw no real future. I existed for the day and saw nothing beyond.

Bernie was in some kind of partnership with a Mafioso figure named Frank Dioguardi, better known as Frankie Dio. Frankie was more famous for being the brother of Johnny Dio, a tough wise guy whose claim to notoriety came when he threw acid in the face of a news photographer in 1948, blinding him for life.

Short and heavy set with smooth olive skin and a lazy eye that drifted from center, Frankie had his fingers in a little of everything, and probably more than I ever knew about. But he did own three restaurants, one of which was an Italian bistro and nightclub on Biscayne Boulevard, just across and down the street from Rocky Marciano's Restaurant, which later became the Playboy Club. I don't remember its name, but grape vines hung from the ceiling lattice, the servers were all men, and there were always lots of people. And, of course, the "cigarettes, cigars" lady pranced about along with a photographer cruising tables hoping for a sell. One far corner of the main dining room was regularly reserved for "the boys" whose quiet meetings often extended past closing hour.

Thanks to Bernie, Frankie hired me on as a strolling violinist on Friday and Saturday nights for five bucks a night plus tips. I thought that was pretty good pay. It reminded me of the nightclubs my mother and Willie Strauss used to take me to, with the prevailing sounds of laughter, booze, cigarette girls, and New York accents. All I had to do was walk around tables when the singer or the band took a break and play songs like *The Story Of Sorrento* and *Fascination*, or take special requests, not all of which I knew. Lights were low, food was good and the tips equaled the pay, and sometimes more. I did this for about six weeks.

One night, during my rendition of *Autumn Leaves*, (or was it *Sorrento?*) sharp staccato sounds suddenly burst into the air... Pop!... Pop!... Pop! They came from the kitchen area. People in every direction jumped from their tables, knocking over glasses and bottles of wine, and headed for the front door in a speechless stampede. The head waiter named Tony, a slick, bent-nosed Italian in a dark suit, rushed from the kitchen trying to stop everyone, shouting, "Firecrackers. Just firecrackers! Hey, don't go. There's no problem here. Just firecrackers."

Yeah. Sure.

I stood riveted to the back wall, violin at my side, waiting to see if they were going to carry out a body, or if there was some way I could sneak out without being noticed. No chance. I was on the opposite side of the room. Moments later, a perspiring Frankie Dio emerged from the kitchen and spotted me. "Hey, Kid. Come 'ere." When I walked over, he handed me a ten dollar bill, patted the side of my cheek, and said in a very soft voice, "You didn't hear nothin' but firecrackers, Right?"

"Right."

"Okay. Go on home."

To this day, I have no idea what had transpired. No bodies ever turned up, no cops were called in and the incident vanished like it never happened. Who knows? Maybe it was firecrackers? But would that have been worth an extra ten bucks and Frankie saying, *"You didn't hear nothin' but firecrackers. Right?"*

The restaurant closed. Frankie Dio continued to operate Dore's and Angelo's restaurants further north in Sunny Isles, plus other business ventures. It would not be the last I'd see of Frankie Dio.

* * *

By the time I was eighteen, I met another girl who would be the second love of my life, Sheila Epstein. Small, dark-haired, petite, and very well-endowed, Sheila Epstein was a lot of fun, for we danced and danced in her living room until we collapsed from exhaustion, then made out in my car... all with our clothes on. But Sheila was not to become a permanent part of my life either. She had been raised in a devout religious family who didn't see me as passing Jewish muster, never having been through a Bar Mitzvah, or attended any Jewish services, other than at funerals and weddings. As the relationship fizzled, my heart cried wishing for a miracle that was not to be.

Despite offers for music scholarships to LSU and FSU, I quit high school three months prior to graduation. Poor grades, too many skipped classes, boredom and the desire to work two jobs made classrooms less inviting each day. Mom was devastated. First, I had stopped the dancing lessons, then violin. And now, she would not have the pleasure of seeing her son graduate.

Dumb decisions were a big part of my life. Such was the case when I joined the Marines. It was time to prove to the world I was a man. I could be as tough as the toughest. Grrrr.

In 1958, creative military reserve programs were in effect like the one I joined: six months of active duty, then six years of attending reserve meetings. For me, it was draft evasion because I certainly didn't want to be drafted into the Army for two years.

Parris Island boot camp was thirteen weeks of pure hell. I knew it was going to be rough, but I didn't know that Drill Instructors would unmercifully beat the shit out of recruits. I was one of the lucky ones who managed to stay less noticed because I performed well. But I felt sorry for the poor slobs who struggled, because they got the swagger sticks, the rifle butts, and quite often, hard fists slamming into their stomachs. Other than Drill Instructors, sand fleas were the most difficult to deal with. Not because they were everywhere all the time, or because they went up your nose, into your eyes, and buzzed in your ears, but because we were prohibited from swatting them. "They gotta eat, too!" the D.I.'s yelled.

Then, I learned the meaning of prejudice. The first Sunday morning there, the head D.I. entered the barracks, seemingly all pissed off. We all spun to attention. He strolled up and down the floor, telling us what the rules were about the outdoor church services. Then, in midstream, he looked left, then right. "I want all the Protestants to line up outside on the right. I want all the Catholics to line up outside on the left." Then he lowered the brim of his Smoky Bear hat, peered and sneered, "Thar ain't no Jews, in here, are there?"

I became an instant Methodist. Every Parris Island platoon had to pull a week of mess duty. For those who don't understand military jargon, a mess hall is the place to eat. While most recruits were assigned to the serving line or to peeling potatoes, I was one of the lucky ones—D. I. Waiter. My job was to stand at attention, take orders from any D.I. entering the mess hall, run to the back and then serve his meal.

The first day was a disaster. An overweight redneck D.I. sat at the table, and sneered up at me with his order. "I want some pork chops, some spuds, gravy on my spuds, iced tea and dessert. Heah?"

"Aye Aye, Sir!"

I must have lived my life under a rock. I had never heard the term "spuds" before. I thought to myself, *what in the hell are spuds?* As I rushed to the serving line, I asked the recruit serving Jello, "Hey, quick, tell me. What are spuds?"

"Celery," he said.

"Thanks."

At that, I ran back to the locker room and placed four stalks of celery on the plate next to his pork chops. Ah, yes, he said he wanted gravy on his spuds. I ladled a healthy portion of gravy over his celery, ran back to the D.I. and set the plate in front of him. I stood at attention for at least five minutes wondering about the sudden silence. He kept looking at his plate, then at me, and back at his plate.

His voice echoed throughout the room, "What in the fuck is this, you turd?" I thought I'd shit in my pants right there. He tossed the plate across the room, food flying everywhere. "Get me some Goddam spuds, now!"

By the time my knees stopped shaking, I learned that spuds was a slang term for potatoes. For certain, I have never forgotten that.

When the boot camp was over, I had proved to the world, and my mother, and my friends, that I was a tough guy after all. I had made it through Parris Island, with honors as well.

But when the six months of active duty was over, I reverted to the same old floundering. Besides cleaning pool decks, bagging groceries and parking cars, I sold ladies shoes at a store called A.S. Beck's. They let me go after two months. "Cutting back on staff", said the manager. I knew better. I was a lousy salesman.

I took up a job with an Arthur Murray-style studio teaching ballroom dancing. That turned out to be more a sales job than teaching, arm-twisting customers into believing it was their moral and civic duty to know the cha-cha-cha. Teachers were rated on how many contracts they sold, not the quality of dance instruction. Mom later fixed me up with a dance partner named Connie Schare, who joined me as a cruise boat teacher aboard the *SS Evangaline*. It was a fun experience, hopping the Caribbean Islands, though most of the get-away housewives who took lessons were more interested in the horizontal mambo. For a short while, I performed some night club shows with the Palumbo sisters, Betty and Patty, two of my mother's star pupils. We danced a fabulous jazz number to the music from the Frank Sinatra movie, *Man With A Golden Arm*. I had this uncanny ability to leap to the ceiling from a standing position. (Why didn't I ever try out for the track team?)

A year later, Bernie had me working for Frankie Dio once again, this time delivering cigarettes to his vending machine route along Miami Beach. This was a great job. And it paid well in more ways than one.

Frankie's nephew, Vito, (honest, that was his name) was moving back to New York. Cocky, thin and wiry, Vito had worked the route for a couple of years and spent a week showing me the system. We drove the van up and down the length of Miami Beach, stopping at the fifty or sixty bars and hotels each day where Frankie owned the cigarette machines, removing the money and refilling the cigarettes according to the sales. Excess leftover change which did not break even with the number of cartons, was left in the change receptacle until next time.

Frankie paid me a penny for every pack sold in the machines. That averaged $50 a week. But Vito showed me his system for doubling that by removing all the money from every machine, leaving no change in the cup.

"Frankie never does inventory," he said. "Piece of cake." For another six months, I would come to work at Angelo's Restaurant in Sunny Isles and see Frankie surrounded by beautiful women lounging around his table, lipstick smears on his face, a glass of scotch in his hand and a cigarette between his fingers, barking orders to waiters. His wife never came to the restaurant but I'm sure she knew. He was just too flagrant. The route took me to all the famous bars along the beach, including the Dream Lounge in the Johnina Hotel, a notorious hangout for mobsters. I also delivered cigarettes to Jake LaMotta's bar, but never met the Raging Bull in person.

At the end of the work day, I'd bring Frankie a cloth bag full of quarters and nickels with a smile on my face, amused that I'd just robbed the Mafia. In retrospect, that was pretty stupid.

* * *

One might think that my stepfather, being a bookie and a local mobster, would have groomed me in his mold—tough, crooked, a thief, gambler, gangster, living on the edge, dealing with organized crime elements day after day. Not so. Matter of fact, I attribute my future life away from organized crime directly to Bernie.

I had become an expert in sports trivia, especially boxing and baseball. I knew all the teams by heart, the individual statistics, the history of the game, and the fighters in all weight divisions. Listening to Bernie take bets whetted my appetite to gamble, because I knew which teams would most likely win based on pitchers, hitters, home team advantages, and so forth. I finally garnered the courage to ask. "Hey, Bernie. How about letting me make a couple bets on the games. I know my shit. I'll win, I know. Mantle's on a streak, Whitey Ford is pitching and..."

Bernie abruptly pointed his Tiparillo at me and squinted. "Shut-up, kid. Enough. You listen to me. I do what I do, because I don't know nothin' else. You see. It's all I know. It's all I will ever know. You? You're goin' places. You got a long life ahead of you. You gotta keep your nose clean, don't fuck around with this shit. You understand? Keep your nose clean. I don't wanna ever hear you ask me that again."

Amen.

* * *

Attending Marine Corps Reserve meetings was a pain, one weekend a month in fatigue uniform, playing soldier, listening to gung-ho kids barely older than me with chevrons on their collars, barking orders and acting like gods. I was obligated for six years, until 1964.

Weekend drill meetings were at the Naval Air Station in Jacksonville, which entailed flying on a military transport from Miami's industrial airport on a Friday night, then flying back on Sunday night. Had I caught that plane in September of 1959, much of my life, and the lives of others, would have taken a different course. But because I'd arrived late, my only option was to hitchhike.

The first ride dropped me at Biscayne Boulevard and 135th Street, in front of Weigel's, a small roadside motel where the swimming pool area faced the street. As I began thumbing again, I noticed a girl on a chaise lounge with her parents sitting nearby. Boldly, I hopped the rail and introduced myself. I was astonished by her soft beauty and impeccable features, like a cover girl model. I remained talking to her for three hours. I never made it to Jacksonville that weekend.

A petite sixteen-year-old blonde with perfect features and a southern accent, Betty Jo Ricker had just moved to Florida with her parents from Anderson, South Carolina. When she accepted a date, I was ecstatic. This girl could have been a homecoming queen, or a model, the girl other guys would gush over, yet she was going out with me. She was still in high school, but we dated every weekend and every night. Love abounded. She said she loved me too. Betty Jo had become my trophy. Two months later, I knocked her up in the back seat of a Chevy Bel Air in front of her parents' house.

That changed everything.

CHAPTER NINE
Me? A Cop?

Tangle-Toes did it.

Frankie Dio had sold his cigarette route, leaving me on the hunt for another job. That was bad, because I had just married Betty Jo in a rushed ceremony at a North Miami Beach Methodist church, and had a new wife to support, two months pregnant. Mom was beside herself, not only because I had become a loser, she thought Betty was white trash, a southern belle with no other redeeming attributes, not good enough for me. All those violin lessons had gone to waste.

When I first had announced that Betty was pregnant, Mom exclaimed, "Oh my God."

Bernie raised his eyebrows, shrugged and smirked,

"Well, you gotta admit. She's a good lookin' dame."

Regardless, playtime had caught up to me and I was suddenly facing the responsibility of a family.

Selling ladies shoes certainly wasn't what I wanted for a career path, but a job is a job, and it was better than construction or digging holes for swimming pools. Physical labor and I didn't get along very well.

The 163rd Street Shopping Center had several shoe stores, including the upscale boutique, Chandlers. Working in an air-conditioned environment, wearing a white shirt and tie, I figured, would be easy enough while meeting women and earning seven percent of every sale. Actually, the job was a colossal pain in the ass. Salesmen milled around inside the store like sharks circling prey waiting turns to pounce on customers, hoping to land the big one. I remember how envious I'd get, watching other salesmen ring up four or five boxes of shoes, while I'd sell a pair of slippers now and then. It never ended, my carrying out stacks of boxes for whimsical women who were mostly interested in seeing their feet in a mirror. No sale. I felt so insignificant, hustling a few dollars a day in hopes of paying the rent and feeding my pregnant wife.

Then I met Tangle-Toes. It was not my turn on the floor. No matter. Other salesmen saw her coming in and walked the other way. "You can have her," one said.

The heavy-set old woman waddled with difficulty into the store, collapsed into a chair and spoke to me with a thick East European accent. She removed her wedgies and asked, "Vell, young man, if you vant to try and fit my size, I have zis problem here."

The poor lady had crusted feet and deformed toes wrapped around each other like spaghetti. I determined the make of her old shoes and headed back to the stock room, checking stacks, styles and sizes. That's when I stopped and took a long breath. An awakening came over me, like an epiphany. This was bullshit. It wasn't me. I really didn't want to be doing this. Where was my life going? What had I done to myself? I felt trapped.

To my right, I could see the old lady through the doorway, sitting in the chair, listing to one side, waiting for me. To my left, another open doorway, the delivery entrance leading out to the back of the shopping center. I looked at her again, then looked at the back entrance. I could talk to the boss, but...what for? I made up my mind. Out the back entrance I went, to my car and off into the vast wilderness of no future, leaving the poor woman sitting there. As far as I know, she may still be sitting there, in rigor mortis, perhaps mummified, waiting for a pair of shoes that fit her tangled toes.

* * *

The scene was familiar. Bernie leaning back against a pillow in his underwear, smoking a Tiparillo, oxygen tank to the side, telephone ringing every five or ten minutes, flash paper, and me on the edge of the bed shooting the breeze, dumping all my problems. Bernie always had the best answers, or at least a temporary solution to my woes.

After a lull in the conversation, with a burning cigar between his teeth, he asked a stunning question. "How would you like to be a cop?"

Huh? I thought I'd bust out laughing. "Me? A cop?

You gotta be shitting me."

"I'm dead serious."

To me, policemen were big, tough guys who kicked ass. I still felt like a scrawny teenager. Visions of all my past troubles with police flashed through my mind, including a host of speeding tickets, the last one only a couple weeks before. "Bernie, how can I be a cop? Look at all the trouble I've been in."

"Ah, big fucking deal. You were never booked, there ain't no record. And a few speeding tickets don't mean nothin'."

I pondered a few moments longer and imagined myself in a uniform carrying a gun, barking orders to adults, arresting people, writing tickets. I simply could not see myself in that role. I felt too much like a boy, not yet a man. "I can't."

Bernie waffled his head and looked at me as if I was a first class asshole. "Listen to me, you got your GED, you're twenty-one, you got the brains and you're in shape.

It's a good job, kid, with benefits, decent pay, vacations, sick leave, even retirement down the road."

It sounded pretty good. "Don't they check backgrounds?" I asked. "I mean, what about my jobs working for Frankie Dio, and you being.... I mean, they'll never hire me."

"Yeah they will."

"How do you know?"

He bit down on his cigar and squinted his eyes. "I got connections."

* * *

Bernie had connections all right. Three days later, a plain clothes bulldog detective named Maxie Berman* arrived at Mom's house to take me downtown for the written test. Built like a cinder block, Maxie spoke in a hoarse, New York voice and looked like a tough guy from a George Raft movie. We talked very little, other than his telling me what to say and not to say down at headquarters.

"Don't put down that you worked for Frankie Dio," he said. "Or anything about your jail thing. You were never arrested for nothin'. Understand?"

"Understand."

I aced the test. Two weeks later, the formal interview before a panel headed by a skinny lieutenant named Bill McKee was a cakewalk.

I listed my past employers as The Marine Corps, Chandler Shoes and The Vivien Melby Dance Studio where I had taught a few ballroom dancing lessons, off and on. When I visited Mom at her studio one afternoon, a detective named Bob Minervini from Internal Affairs was sitting there conducting the so-called background interview. The instant we shook hands, he looked directly into my eyes and winked. The fix was in the bag. I was going to be a cop.

   * *Fictitious name*

CHAPTER TEN
Eyes and Ears Open, Mouth Shut

In July of 1960, Senator John F. Kennedy had received the democratic nomination for president while the first Negro ever (from Ohio) was allowed to compete in the Miss Universe pageant being held on Miami Beach. I had just come back from a Marine reserve weekend where they flew us by helicopter to a base in Cuba called Guantanamo. Tensions were high there, because a revolutionary rebel named Fidel Castro was reveling in victory, having assumed power one year before. Little did any of us realize what an impact that event would have on the future of South Florida.

Meanwhile, Brenda Lee's song, *I'm Sorry,* was atop the charts, which is what I listened to just before I parked my car in downtown Miami at 11 P.M., the night of July 26th. It was my first day on the job, hired on as a pre-academy recruit to learn jail procedures, help out with errands and be a general gofer. The academy would start in two weeks.

A classic granite and marble building with stately columns and a pyramid roof, the Miami Courthouse stood twenty-five stories, the tallest in the state of Florida at the time. The County Jail occupied the top six floors. The streets were quiet and barren, yet when I looked up, I could see lights were on from the 19th floor up, reminding me of the well-lit upper tower of the Empire State Building. They had given me a blue bus driver's uniform to start, because I wasn't a cop yet. Having just turned twenty-one, replete with peach fuzz and pimples, I felt more like a kid playing a game. My heart raced in anticipation of meeting police officers as a peer, not some punk traffic violator. A pudgy old deputy named Gus Campbell, with puffs of thick hair protruding from his nose, operated the manual elevator. He looked like a punch-drunk old fighter. As I stepped off onto the administrative floor, an odor of sweat, smoke and urine invaded my nostrils. I could only imagine what the cells smelled like.

Those first images will remain imbedded in my memory forever. I stopped and gathered my senses. Low slung ceilings, dim lighting, steel walls in need of paint, narrow halls, the thick stench of smoke and body odors, and the sounds of metal doors slamming and keys rattling jarred my consciousness. This was the real thing. Two large deputies hustled a shirtless, filth-covered black man into the elevator lifting him by his arms while his hands were cuffed behind. I covered my face from his rancid smell. I had never interacted with a real criminal or a black person in my life, and I felt suddenly apprehensive. I wondered if I really wanted to be there. But I thought about my pregnant Betty Jo at home, old Tangle-toes and all the other failed jobs. This was it. Suck it in.

Tall, gray and slightly bald, Captain Noah Scott called me into his office like a doting old southern grandfather, spoke in cop jargon during a pep talk, then assigned me to a burly young deputy named, *Wesley

Harmon. "Follow Wes here. Do what he says."

"Yes sir."

Wes was an ex-Marine and immediately took a liking to me because I'd also been to Parris Island. Stocky, about five years older than me, crew cut and a classic redneck, Wes walked with a lumbering gait and liked to brag about being from Texas. I caught him smirking at me, eager to show this runny-nosed kid all the ropes.

"I'm gonna show you how to fingerprint a prisoner."

A youngster, about nineteen, the inmate was tall and gangly with blond hair way too long for pre-Beatle times. His charges: Disorderly Conduct and Public Drunk. And drunk he was. My first encounter with a prisoner would be one to remember.

"First thing, Frank, is you strip search him, then check his asshole. Tell him to bend over and spread his cheeks." Wes smiled with a lecherous glint. I felt nauseous. Here I was, with only thirty minutes tenure on the job, and my assignment was to inspect an asshole—literally. I really did not want to do this. Wes ordered the teetering boy to take off all his clothes. It was routine. All inmates must be checked for weapons and contraband.

The prisoner was slow to act, head bobbing, speech slurred. Suddenly, without warning, Wes reached back like he was about to throw a fast ball and whacked the kid across the head with an open hand. Then a backhand, and another forehand. Then two more. My eyeballs must have boinged from my head. I gasped. The kid staggered left and right, grunting and groaning and wheezing, slipping on bare feet, dazed, holding on to the wall. Wes punched him once in the stomach, then grabbed his hair and smashed his head against the wall, screaming and cursing, ordering him to speed it up and to bend over. The cop's face had turned blood red with anger as the kid slumped to the floor. Wes then cooled off and looked at me with a wry grin, proud to have shown off his best stuff. I wondered if I was expected to join in and start whacking this kid around for the sheer joy of it, to show I was one of the boys who could be trusted.

I crouched from my bed. It was dark outside but I could still make out the figures in the moonlight. My father was being held from behind while another punched him, over and over, the grunting sounded more like a painful wheeze.

Wes' behavior, I figured, must have come from a sense of omnipotence that is automatically endowed by wearing a badge. After all, cops are the good guys, they are the bad guys. Right?

For me, it was foreign. The idea of being a cop was not so palatable any more. I could never hit someone, just to hit. I think Wes caught on to that, and I wondered if he trusted me from that time on.

The commotion had echoed throughout the floor so loudly that supervisors at the front certainly heard it all, the sergeants, the lieutenants, and even Captain Scott. That's when I realized, it's routine. Just an everyday occurrence. They assumed it was justified. The inmate must have resisted.

Within one hour of my first night on the job, I learned the meaning of arbitrary brutality , those same kinds of acts I had always dismissed when reading about them in a newspaper or seeing reports on television, because I thought the cops had to be right and the media wrong.

I also learned that color didn't matter. Wes Harmon imposed no racial prejudice when it came to knocking a prisoner around. He felt just as much pleasure by felling a white boy as he did a black.

For a kid once perceived as a "fairy," a violin student and dance instructor, the training session with Wes Harmon was a rude awakening, indeed. So many new questions. Would this happen every day? How far would this man go with beatings? Would he kill? Could I turn a blind eye? Could I turn him in? Would I survive this?

Should I look for another job?

* * *

Underwear. Tiparillo. Flash paper. Phone ringing.

"How was your first night, kid?" Bernie asked.

"Okay, I guess. I mean, look, I'm not sure I'm cut out for this."

"Yeah? How come?"

I told him about Wesley Harmon and the beating of an inmate. "What do I do?" I asked. "I can't do that kinda stuff."

"You didn't hand him up, I hope?"

"No. I wouldn't do that. But I might not fit in, you know what I mean?"

Bernie puffed his cigar, then pointed it directly at me. "Look, kid. You're gonna see a lot of shit on both sides of the fence. There's only one way to survive. You keep your eyes and ears open, and your mouth shut. Don't ever forget that. Say it to yourself anytime you have doubts. Eyes and ears open, mouth shut."

Amen.

CHAPTER ELEVEN
Academy

I didn't work with Wes Harmon again during my two-week gofer assignment in the County Jail. I figure he pegged me as a wimp when he caught the look on my face, then told the bosses he'd rather work with a different recruit. It was fine with me.

Captain Scott assigned me the now-obsolete task of operating a manual elevator, hoisting personnel and prisoners between the 19th and 25th floors all night long. A boring job, indeed, though I became an expert at lining up the floor of the cab perfectly even with the landing. But, the assignment provided a central location where I met many police officers, prisoners and all the brass, including the Sheriff, Thomas J. Kelly. Kelly was a crusty old Army general into his second career, though he had no background as a cop. There were also rumors he was a closet homosexual, but who dared to ask? Not me.

It was all easy enough, but it didn't teach me anything. The jail atmosphere was dour, the air stale, the food bad, the prisoners depressing, and the police attitudes cynical and aloof. I was glad to get out and prayed I would not be assigned there.

Eight weeks of a grueling police academy went by in a flash. Recruit Class 16 was a great bunch of guys, some of whom remain my friends to this day. The group was comprised of white males, between 5' 9" and 6' 4", the required criteria of that era. Women had their own classification, "Policewoman," hired only in small numbers for special assignments like searching female prisoners and handling children. Blacks were not officially exempt from the job, but they might as well have been. With over six hundred deputies on the payroll, the Dade County Sheriff's Office employed three or four black officers, used only for special assignments in the black community.

As the youngest among twenty-two new rookies, I blended into the walls, excelling in nothing, graduating with scores somewhere in the middle, a mediocre shot with a revolver, physically average and anxious to start policing.

As a break away from classroom studies and physical training, we looked forward to riding on weekends as an observer with regular police officers. It was time to learn first hand, how police officers track criminals, chase violators, handle crime scenes and investigate murders and assaults. I would see why these men become icons for justice, centurions for the people, protectors of law and order, true heroes.

It didn't happen. I spent most of my time waiting in a patrol car while officers wrote reports, and reports, and then more reports, mostly on domestic arguments, fender benders and bicycle thefts. This was it? This was police work?

Besides the ride-alongs, the academy weeks were dotted with few memorable experiences.

At first, I was disappointed to learn our long anticipated visit to the Medical Examiner's Office had been canceled. But my ghoulish curiosity prevailed, and I managed a special invitation which I accepted on my own time. I had seen dead bodies in caskets, never in the raw. I could smell the blood and chemicals the moment I entered the bright tile-covered autopsy room. Men in white bloodied smocks busily moved around, attending to supine nude bodies on steel trays in different corners of the room, like slabs of meat. I instantly felt light-headed and hoped I would not embarrass myself.

"Over here," announced one of the doctors. "Stand around." A group of men and women in white smocks, probably students, stood around, pads in hand.

Wearing nothing but a toe-tag, the dead man looked no older than forty, his mouth agape, eyes gazing into nowhere, the underside of his skin a deep purple. This was not a casket. No powdered face, no sealed lips. The distinguished looking pathologist seemed to enjoy the teaching experience. He had to know there were queasy stomachs standing there. Some would not be there much longer.

I steeled myself, trying to appear stoic, like the others. The pathologist narrated as he went along. "This case is an apparent natural death. But because he was not being treated by a physician for any illness, we must determine the exact cause of death and make sure there was no foul play." Interesting. "And remember, if he died by accident, it could make a big difference in the life insurance benefits." Interesting. "We'll also do a number of laboratory tests to see what foreign agents may be in his blood. That's how we've solved clever homicides before, like poisonings." Interesting. "First we use a scalpel to make a vertical incision in the torso." Not so interesting.

"Here we go."

Everything went black.

For a second or two anyway. One of the students, a tall fellow the size of a linebacker, stepped away, hand over face. I regained my composure, took a breath, and waited until all the incisions were done then took another look. The carcass had been dissected completely, with folds of fat and skin lying open, exposing the rib case and organs. For me, it was a struggle between surviving the distasteful moment, looking unaffected and then utter fascination with it all. After all, this was an unveiling, a first-time eye witness account to what we all are on the inside.

Step by step, the doctor told us what he was doing and why, removing the liver, heart, kidneys, weighing them all, dissecting to see if tumors or other growths were present. Then, he said, "Very often, it is important for us to know what the deceased ate before he died, and how long it had been." Interesting. "Some foods digest faster than others. And it takes about four hours, under normal circumstances, for food to pass through into the intestines." Interesting. "Naturally, we'll test the stomach contents for foreign substances." Interesting. "Now let's cut open the stomach and see. Not so interesting. "Here we go."

Tempted to look away, I remained attentive though my stomach was not doing well. The doctor said, "Freshly digested food in here. Let's see what it is." He smiled, leaned over the gaping cadaver to the open stomach, inserted his finger, then the lay the finger to his own tongue. "Ahh, chili, peas and carrots."

Everything went black.

For a few seconds, anyway. But I didn't faint.

Another student, a woman, walked off. As it turned out, the pathologist was having fun with us. He had actually inserted his middle finger into the stomach, then switched to his index for the taste test. Funny guy.

* * *

The low barometric pressure of tropical storms has a tendency to bring late term pregnancies to an abrupt delivery, which is the reason

I checked Betty Jo into a hospital ward with numbers of other pregnant women on the night of September 9, 1960. She was at the end of her ninth month when Hurricane Donna started approaching the southeast Florida peninsula. We'd been living in a small apartment in North Miami Beach where my mother often looked in on her when I was attending academy classes. We recruits were told an emergency was pending and to prepare for twelve-hour shifts. If the disaster hit Miami, we would be the front line troops, working in the field with an experienced officer for reconnaissance and rescue duties. They needed all the manpower possible, and recruits were cheap labor.

Meanwhile, Betty Jo would be safe at the hospital ward, and if she delivered, I'd weather the storm, so to speak, as a new father.

I had been through hurricanes before; I knew the force, and the aftermath. At the Silver Palm Hotel in 1947, the ocean and bay came together, submerging the entire island of Miami Beach. During the '50s, Mom and I hunkered down in the house, awning shutters closed, listening to the powerful wind and rain, crashes of rock and metal flying and smacking into objects outside. This time I would be a real hero, rescuing people, fighting the storm, saving lives, working along side of an experienced and heroic cop. I looked forward to the challenge. Another bubble burst.

We weathered the hurricane all right. *My experienced and heroic cop* was an old-timer named Garland Fox, short and balding, sixty year-old Missing Person detective who needed a swig from his flask every time he turned a corner. We rode in a broken-down, 1957 Studebaker Lark, stick shift, which Fox could barely get out of second gear because his short legs couldn't push the clutch to the floor. I had imagined having a partner like Superman or Joe Friday, but got Elmer Fudd instead.

But we did work the storm as it raged on, ravaging Miami with a direct hit, felling trees, power lines, rooftops, overturning cars, bending street signs, and flooding Dade County from the Atlantic to the Everglades. Our job was to check out Key Biscayne and areas along Coconut Grove, just south of Miami, to report downed lines, stranded motorists and other hazards. It was quite exciting, patrolling as a potential hero and not hunkering inside a candle-lit kitchen with my mother. Fox held the radio mike as if it were a vibrator, shaking in his hand, his voice quivering with anxiety. Poor guy. Wind and rain became so fierce that we eventually had to return to headquarters and wait the storm out in the building.

* * *

The morning after Hurricane Donna, September 11, 1960, my son, Bennett, was born at Biscayne Osteopathic Hospital. My best friend, Harvey, helped me pace the floor in the waiting room, taking pictures and sharing my joy at becoming a father. In my mind, I now became the person I never knew—Dad.

* * *

As the appointed head of 650 officers, with scrambled egg patterns adorning his uniformed hat brim, Sheriff Thomas J. Kelly gave a non-inspiring speech during the graduation ceremony in October of 1960. Twenty-two of us lined up in brown uniforms. Betty Jo pinned the badge on my shirt with baby Bennett asleep in a stroller. We all raised our hands and took an oath to uphold the constitution, protect the citizens and enforce laws fairly. At twenty-one years and six months, I joined my comrades in becoming the most powerful person in the community: a full fledged police officer with the government sanctioned authority and discretion to strip anyone of their freedom as I saw fit.

It felt like make believe.

CHAPTER TWELVE
Halloween

The academy class that graduated before us had been disbursed to assignments throughout Dade County's five police districts covering 2200 square miles of patrol and serving a population base of one million people. When Class 16 graduated, I thought I'd be assigned to a patrol car in a district somewhere with seasoned cops, riding around using the radio, turning on the red beacons, chasing speeders, handling calls, arresting criminals and showing off how tough I was with a gun and badge.

Not so. With the exception of three lucky guys, my entire class was shipped off to the Miami International Airport. Translated, that meant walking a beat on the road ramps, writing parking tickets, whistling down speeders and answering questions from citizens.

I'll never forget that awesome feeling, the first day on the job, walking a beat on upper ramp. It was all surreal, like acting in a play. The uniform felt like a Halloween costume.

People suddenly called *me* "Sir." Adults, professionals, military, elderly, pilots, all called *me* "Sir."

So cool. When I blew my whistle, cars screeched to a halt, automatically.

Tweet! Screech!

Young people my age were in awe of my very presence. Perhaps it was fear. I issued commands like I knew what I was doing:

"Only five minutes for loading or unloading, sir."

"Move that car!"

"No, I will not watch your bag, ma'am."

"Show me your driver's license."

Men and women begged me to stop when I wrote a parking ticket. A crowd looked on the first time I arrested a drunk who caused a disturbance inside the terminal.

Minutes later, he was in the back seat of a patrol car being taken to the jail. I, Marshall Frank, took his freedom away.

All minor stuff, but the sense of power was incredible.

I knew I did the correct thing, but I still thought about who and what he was, and how this might affect his life and the lives of others around him. After all, I, too, was once arrested for disturbing the peace. Now I was the arrester, not the arrestee.

I still had pimples. The hat fell down to my ears. My chest puffed three times its normal size. In truth, I had no business being a cop. To this day, I don't believe any kid at twenty-one should be empowered with the discretion and authority of a law enforcement officer.

The best part of the job was its unpredictability. Contrary to working in factories, grocery stores and motel swimming pools, no day was boring. No assembly lines, no pressures to sell, nothing to clean besides my revolver.

Of all the duties, I mostly dreaded the incessant writing of reports any time we did anything official. Television and movies never showed cops writing reports, but I learned quickly that was fifty percent of a cop's day. Pen to paper. Getting it right, before the sergeant's review. Then, there was the feeling of shaking in my boots every time a gold badge walked by. Facing a sergeant was like facing a god.

Short, gray-haired, Earl Craver was surely born pissed-off and remained that way for life. The first day in the squad room, he gave me a look as if to say, *"What am I supposed to do with this snot-nosed kid?"* Craver had false teeth which he never wore, leaving him with a gummy-speech impediment. He didn't talk. He barked.

On days off, his relief was a former Marine named Ray Beck. Statuesque, articulate and persnickety about written reports, he would reject any document that wasn't absolutely perfect, and the cops all knew it. Beck was a sergeant's sergeant, not interested in being liked, only in making sure the job was done and done right. Some cops called Craver, and others, by their first names. Not this man. To everyone, he was "Sergeant Beck."

In my first encounter with Sergeant Beck, I was in the squad room, standing in line three or four back waiting my turn to present two written reports for the day. A short, older cop got into line behind me and saw that Beck was reviewing the reports. "Beck's here? Oh shit," he said. "I better go rewrite these things. They'll never get through him."

Shaking like an idiot, I stood there as this god-like man with gold chevrons slowly read over my reports. I was stunned when he glanced upward and said, "Very good,

Frank. Next officer?"

While I managed to get on the good side of Sergeant Beck, it mattered not to Earl Craver. He still didn't like me. And Gabe Spina didn't help. A cocky young officer with two years on the job, Spina was a cut-out from *West Side Story*, slick skinny New York Italian with an attitude and always the jokester. He reminded me of Vito, the thief who taught me how to steal on Frankie Dio's cigarette route.

It must have been payday in mid-December when Spina asked me, "Hey, Marshall. You got your Christmas bonus, didn't you?"

"No. What Christmas bonus?"

"Geez. They must have screwed you. We all got ours."

"I didn't know we got a bonus for Christmas," I said.

Spina wiped off his customary smile, now deadly serious. "Well, you better ask Sergeant Craver. He'll make sure you get it."

At the end of the shift, while waiting for the sergeant to review my reports, and with a line of other cops behind me, I bumbled, "Sergeant, Uh. I didn't get my Christmas bonus today."

Craver dropped his pen without looking up, then slowly raised his head. The minute I heard laughter in the room, I knew I'd been had. I leaped from my pants when Craver bellowed, "WHAT?"

"Uh, never mind, sir."

* * *

The pay wasn't much, but the checks were reliable. No such thing as overtime. No extra bonuses. Just the $312 a month, less taxes and FICA. Not bad.

An airport rookie generally rode one day a week in a patrol car with a veteran cop. Two days if he was lucky. The district had only two patrol zones which encompassed the perimeter regions of the airport. Each day or night at roll call, I hoped for a riding assignment, for that's where I could act as a bonafide police officer, pulling people over, handling calls, making arrests, traffic accidents, and, of course, writing reports and reports and reports.

Roy Humston was on the job three years, assigned to the South District where he established a reputation for being an aggressive officer who racked up impressive statistics. His only problem had been a proclivity for wrecking police cars. When the department grounded him, he was transferred to the airport.

Not to worry. Craver and the other sergeants knew they had a statistics machine in Roy Humston, so they had him ride the zone every day with a rookie driver. Stats meant everything. The more tickets, the more arrests and the more warrant apprehensions a month, the better your evaluation would be. With good evaluations came choice assignments, praise and future preferences for promotion, once you passed the test. After all, sergeants had their own bosses as well, lieutenants and captains who had nothing to gauge performance from other than a monthly rating system. If a sergeant's squad performed well, the sergeant performed well. If a shift lieutenant had sergeants who produced monthly reports with high stats, the district captain would be pleased. And so on, up the line.

I rode with Humston one or two days a week and learned everything there was to know about searching for traffic violators, stolen cars, thieves and wanted persons. Unfortunately, that often entailed racial profiling, though the term had not yet been invented.

Gabe Spina and others taught me similar tricks, but Humston had that eagle eye for catching people, the best at it. Unassuming, average height, portly, always amicable, Humston looked more like a friendly bus driver than a cop.

"Look for coloreds in a broken down car. Pull 'em over for anything, tail-light out, bald tires, whatever.

Chances are 50-50, he'll be wanted on a bench warrant for failure to appear in court or not paying a ticket."

He was right. It was easy. At the time, I never gave thought to honest but indigent black folks caught in a Catch 22, unable to pay their mounting fines while struggling to make a living doing lawn maintenance and other labor. All

I thought about was the sergeant's praises at the end of the shift when we produced four or five arrest reports, and three "criminals" apprehended for bench warrants, plus ten to fifteen traffic tickets, making sure the revenues were coming in.

I never saw Humston falsify a report or do anything illegal. For him, and others, looking for blacks to write tickets and make arrests was like fishing in a trout pond. Each situation was a matter of an officer's discretion, unless the dispatcher came back with the record's check with notice that the man was wanted. Then, the cop had no choice but to haul him in.

Years later, I looked back and realized how terrible it all was. I have no regrets about legitimate arrests and enforcing bonafide violations of the law, regardless of race, but targeting people like prey, simply because they were poor and black, unable to pay for legal problems, knowing they were likely wanted for warrants, has given me a great sense of retro-guilt.

But we came by it honestly, a cycle or sorts. After the academy, police training came from old hand-me-down methods that had worked over time. Cops who taught me were only teaching what they had been taught years before. Humston and the others were just good soldiers following the prevailing process and procedures. I quickly learned the means for acceptance and survival: Please the sergeant.

* * *

Other than routine arrests, traffic control, parking tickets and assisting citizens, not one noteworthy event occurred in my first year on the job until waves of Cuban refugees started to come into the United States. The advent of Fidel Castro into Cuba forever changed the ethnic and cultural make-up of South Florida. Professionals and hard working Cubans, stripped of their property and worldly goods, formed a mass exodus. Thousands arrived at the airport in droves with nothing but the clothes on their backs, elderly and children included, to start a new life in the strange promised land they knew as The United States. It was an impressive sight, indeed, because I knew history was in the making. And my heart went out to them.

Until the spring of 1961, I don't think I ever heard Spanish spoken other than in a school classroom or from my heart-throb, Sonia, at the Arcady Country Club in 1949.

Ay carrumba. Oye, Squidgie, come and dance with me, yes?

My job was to maintain order, assist, regulate parking and hold back crowds. Cuban immigrants were demonstrative folks who made their thoughts and feelings known. Little did we realize then, that Miami, the small tourist town on the southeast coast of Florida, would eventually become a city transplanted from across the seas:

Little Havana.

Marshall Frank

CHAPTER THIRTEEN
Turning To The Mob

For my first annual performance evaluation, Sergeant Craver wrote a scathing report, suggesting that I find another line of work. He thought my head was up my ass, that I walked around in a daze, I wasn't aggressive, I was immature. He was right on all counts. But he passed my probation anyway, despite the fact that I couldn't shoot my way out of a paper sack.

Once a year, department officers were required to demonstrate proficiency at the pistol range. A passing score was 240 out of 300.

I shot a 216. Another rookie, Dick Ward, also flunked.

Most cops enjoyed range days and the shooting experience, like it was a day at the park. Not me. I had no fascination with guns. I dreaded shooting. Carrying a weapon was part of the necessary paraphernalia, like handcuffs, whistle, and ball-point pen. But it was important to know how to shoot. I knew how, all right, but the bullets went everywhere but where I aimed.

Ward and I were ordered to work with empty holsters until we rescheduled another shoot date and fired a passing score. I thought that was pretty stupid. After all, here we are before the public in full uniform exposed to harm's way. What would happen if either of us were in a situation that required defending our lives, or the lives of other citizens? No one ever said that the police lords had to have brains.

Fortunately, nothing serious happened. I don't know how Ward finally qualified, but I managed to become friends with the range master who shook his head when he saw my spray pattern of shots on the target. "It's for my probation," I pleaded, as he checked my target.

The old crusty range sergeant had worn chevrons since they were invented. He started scanning the target, circling the holes. "Okay, this one time, Frank." He looked around, furtively. "We'll just use this thirty-eight caliber pencil."

And so, my score was turned in as a 248.and I was given back my revolver.

* * *

After one year at the airport, boredom and frustration started to set in. I was envious of other cops working in outlying districts where real police work was taking place. Walking ramps and chasing after indigent Negroes for bench warrant arrests was not real police work. A police friend named Bob Eiland suggested I submit a written transfer request to Station One, the North District, near where I was living. It took a while, but I finally garnered the courage and turned a memo in to Sergeant Craver at the end of one shift. Not surprising, he formed a broad, toothless smile and told me, "Forget it, Frank. You ain't going nowhere. You'll be here at least five years."

Oh yeah?

Bernie was a well-kept secret. No one knew that I had ties to the mob. Neither did I ever ask Bernie for any favors. Favors, in that environment, meant owing. I didn't want to owe Bernie any more than I already did. I had been a good soldier, enduring my probationary year at an undesirable assignment, but I was having thoughts of resigning and returning to my music. With a full year behind me, it was the longest I'd ever held a job. But Bernie had been right. It had benefits, and the pay was steady. With a wife and new baby, quitting would be disastrous.

Sergeant Craver's remarks gnawed at me. *"Forget it, Frank. You ain't going nowhere."* After all, he was really just a little guy in the overall scheme of things.

Time for a Sunday visit for dinner at Mom's house. Other friends were coming over, like Guido, Angie, Carmine, Louie and Philly. *"Guinea, wop, dago, heeb, kyke, yid, nigger, spic, broad, faggot, queer"* Later, they would ask me how I liked being a cop. Here I was, arresting criminals by day, and breaking bread with them by night. Some of the faces were familiar, like I'd seen them on roll-call bulletins. Mom cooked all day then set an extended table to host a full course Italian dinner second to none, cigarettes, wine and booze included. Then, of course, a tune on the violin, just like old days.

This particular day, Betty Jo and I arrived early. I wanted time alone with Bernie.

The scene was familiar. Underwear, Tiparillo, oxygen tank, phone and flash paper. "How's it going, kid?" he asked.

I lit a Pall Mall, took a deep drag, paced the floor and exhaled. How would I go about pandering for another favor, without really asking? "Ah. My sergeant says I'll be at the Airport District for five years. It's a bummer. Other guys are out in the zones riding every day and every night. Me? I blow whistles on the ramp. I'm thinking about quitting"

Bernie furrowed his brow. "Don't even think like that. You ain't quitting nothin'. Let me see what I can do." Two days later, Sergeant Craver called me into his office. With a scornful expression and from a toothless mouth, he said, "Frank, you're transferred to the North District next week, on the road. Damned if I know how."

I smiled. "Thanks, Sarge."

Thanks, Bernie.

* * *

It all came into focus later that month when I happened to stop over at Mom's house to help her with yard work. Bernie was in the back bedroom. I was sitting on the living room couch, drinking a soda, looking at the television. Mom was in the kitchen.

A white car pulled up on the gravel drive. Then came a knock at the door. Mom answered. Two tall men wearing dark suits, one bald, the other with thick black hair, nonchalantly strolled through the living room with somber expressions, nodding at me as they passed by on the way to the back bedroom. They looked familiar, but I couldn't place the faces.

Less than five minutes passed, and the two men strolled back out of the house, nodding at me once more. I shrugged. They drove off.

Minutes later, barefoot, wearing a tee shirt and skivvies, a burning Tiparillo fixed in his teeth, Bernie shuffled down the hall with an impish smirk on his face.

"Heh, heh. Monday. It's pay day. Gotta pay the bills, right?"

I thought the faces were familiar. That night, at the squad room, I checked the boards for pictures of the department hierarchy. There was that dark-haired fellow: Manson Hill, Chief of Detectives. The bald man: a detective lieutenant, one of Hill's cronies.

Connections.

CHAPTER FOURTEEN
Lost Love

After more than a year on the job, I finally rode with experienced zone cops, no more walking beat, no more parking tickets, no more whistle. Each night brought new events and, often, a different trainer. Now I was handling domestics, burglaries, robberies, sex assaults, traffic accidents, missing persons, making arrests, chasing speeders and recovering stolen property. This was police work. I became enthralled, fascinated, obsessed. My every thought, night and day, focused on the excitement of law enforcement, acceptance from my peers, keeping up with department politics, rules, training, uniforms, court appearances, the shooting range, and making those reports picture perfect.

I never saw it coming.

Every day during the first two weeks of my new assignment, I spent hours telling Betty Jo about the night before, the arrests, accidents, reports, the guys, the sergeants.

My son, Bennett, now one year old, was a beautiful blond boy, the pride of my life, the child who gave me the opportunity to be the father I didn't have. I cherished every moment I spent with him. His photographs, and Betty Jo's, adorned my wallet and the inside of my police hat. Every cop I worked with had to see them. I imagined us having another one or two kids when we could afford, and raising a wonderful and loving family.

By this time, Betty Jo's life had been relegated to housewife and mother. With my mother's credit, my status as a county cop and a little money, we had managed to buy a small house in Miramar, Florida, a new development just west of Hollywood. Betty Jo spent her days shopping, cleaning, cooking and changing diapers. I suppose that was a bummer for a girl not yet nineteen years old. We struggled with money, but raises were on the way.

At 7:30 on a Monday morning, I pulled into the driveway after a long and tiring shift of many reports. The sun now hovered over the eastern horizon, casting long shadows from nearby trees across all the lawns. My eyes were heavy. I yearned for a cool bed with the shades drawn.

Still wearing my uniform, I sauntered to the front porch and unlocked the door expecting to see Betty Jo, sans make-up, in her robe sipping coffee in the kitchen, and perhaps, feeding Bennett in the high chair.

"Hi Honey. I'm home."

No response.

Something was wrong. I shouted again, "Honey?"

Is there an echo in here? Where's Bennett's high chair?

I checked the baby's room. The crib was missing. So was the diaper pail and all his clothing from the drawers. I checked the master bedroom. My clothes hung in the closet, nothing else. She was gone. She took the baby. No note. No explanation.

That morning, my world collapsed. It was like a sudden and unexpected death of a dream. Besides fitting into the world of police and friends, my son and my wife were everything I'd ever wanted. And now, without warning, they were out of my life. I thought about my own father, and how he had been committed to a mental institution, then had died at the age of 42, never to know me and to have a role in his son's life. Just as sad, I never knew him. Now, my own son, whom I adored, would likely grow up in a home without his father being a major force. It was everything I didn't want to happen.

I called and found her at her parents' house. She refused to talk to me. I never knew why.

For the next few weeks and months, I obsessed on drawing her back. I wrote letters on top of letters, asking for forgiveness for whatever I might have done to offend her. I begged her, asking that we keep our family together for Bennett's sake. Gushing from a broken heart, I promised to be better, if she'd only tell me what went wrong.

She filed for divorce on grounds of "Mental Cruelty." I had lost my temper on two or three occasions trying to fix and repair things around the house, and ranted and raved. A handy man I wasn't. But it gave her the grounds. I had never cheated, abused, neglected or mistreated her in any way. My true crime was immaturity.

As I reflected over the years, and in future talks with her after we became grandparents, the matter was cleared up. She wanted more out of life than being domesticated, cleaning house and caring for a baby every day. She wanted more money. She wanted more of the easy life, and access to material things. For her, it would come easy. After all, she was young and beautiful.

It took three months for the divorce, which provided for child support payments and controlled visits with my boy on Sundays only. The event precipitated many of the problems my son and I would encounter in future years.

A year later, Betty Jo, then twenty, married Bill Gertz, a man thirty-seven years old.

I started rooming with George Reincke in a garage apartment, the same giraffe-like friend who spun tires in front of my mother's house in 1955. George had also joined the police department and was assigned full time to the jail. Night after night, George and I cruised the bar scenes, drinking until the wee hours of the morning, lamenting over my loss. Then I'd go to work, and arrest someone for drunk driving.

Something wrong there.

One morning, I overslept. The clock read 6:10 A.M. I was due at roll call at 6:45 A.M. No time to shower. I rapidly donned the same uniform from the previous day and jumped into my car for a fast twenty minute drive to work that should have been thirty minutes. My speed must have exceeded ninety along the highway. The moment I pulled into the station parking lot and exited my car, another car pulled up. A man opened the window and pointed directly at me. "If I had gone those kinds of speeds," he said, angrily. "You'd have put me in jail."

I felt small as an amoeba.

Fortunately, he didn't report me. But he would probably like to know, the confrontation had a lasting effect.

CHAPTER FIFTEEN
A Real Cop

Though I was into my second year on the job, transferring to the North District was like being a rookie all over again. After all, I still knew very little about street policing in a crime-ridden district.

In the next six months, I worked with no less than a dozen experienced officers. Each had their own style, peculiarities and systems. I learned from them all. But no matter what, the bottom line in assessing performance came down to pleasing the man wearing the gold badge, the sergeant. One of those, Sergeant William "Bill" Butler, stood six-foot two and had shoulders the width of a Mack truck. I had heard about the department legend back at the airport. When Butler's shift took over midnights in the north end, crime went down because arrests went up. Thieves and burglars, it seemed, knew when Butler's shift rotated to midnights and they migrated to another county to commit their crimes. Butler had an unwritten edict: Anyone out after midnight who wasn't working, and had no reason to be out, went to jail.

Those were the days when statutes like "Vagrancy" and "Public Drunk" were still on the books, later thrown out as unconstitutional. They gave cops a mighty and arbitrary tool by which to put people in jail at a whim. That was good, for good cops. That was not good for cops who shouldn't be cops.

I learned that a state, county or municipal cop is, singularly, the most powerful person in the United States, who can take a citizen's freedom away on the spot. No one else can do that, not even the president. Fortunately, most did not abuse that power, but some did.

Charlie Black was a good cop, very private. I don't think he liked being assigned a rookie. Smart, quick, slick-tongued, Black had his own agenda, studying and passing tests at the top of the list, his eye on future promotions. He drove, I wrote. And wrote. And wrote.

Bob Windsor was young, big and tough, straight as a beam. He dubbed every citizen, "Neighbor." Windsor was one of those cops who had a traffic ticket written before the violator got out of the car. It didn't matter if they were racing to deliver a baby. No excuses. "Tell it to the judge." If he saw a car slide through a stop sign at 3 A.M., when no other car was in sight, the ticket was written. I think Windsor set the record for writing tickets. The sergeant loved him.

Richard (R.K.) Johnsen took time aside to show me how to fill out forms and handle complicated issues. A weight lifter and private pilot, soft-spoken Johnsen carried out his duties with an even temperament and always handled the public with respect, regardless of race, sex, age or socio-economic class. Everyone was "Sir" or "Ma'am." Skinny and narrow shouldered, Jim Mathers' hair looked like a spiked flat top that grew out too much. Mathers was much like Bob Windsor, racking up those stats to please the sergeant. "I didn't make the law," he insisted with a southern drawl, "I just do the enforcing." Each cop used pet sobriquets for people of the streets. Mathers called black males "Boy". Anyone over the age of fifty was "Mom" or "Pop."

One night, after 3 A.M., Mathers and I were having a dull shift, only two or three cars towed so far and less than a dozen tickets. He cruised down a darkened residential street in north Dade County while I worked on a report, then pulled to the curb where an elderly woman had been staggering along the sidewalk. I looked up and caught a whiff of her alcohol breath when she leaned into the car.

"Come on, Mom. Get in the car," Mathers said, authoritatively.

I got out and assisted her into the back seat where she listed to one side. As we drove away, Mathers notified the dispatcher we had a prisoner en route to jail and instructed me to write the arrest form for public drunk. I turned around, pen in hand. "Your name? Ma'am?"

She crossed her eyes, slobbered and formed a grin.

"Mathers."

I hesitated. "Excuse me? Is that your name?"

"Shore is, Sonny. Mary Jane Mathers. Born and raised."

This had to be the coincidence of the decade. I looked at my partner driving the patrol car, smiling ear to ear. "Jim. She's got the same name as…"

"Yep. I know it."

"Come on, Mom. Get in the car."

"She's not your mother, is she?" *No no. I couldn't be.*

79

"Sure is. Mom's got a problem, see? So I take her in every once in a while and let her sober up in the jail. I'll come down after work and bail her out." He grinned, like he was proud.

Atop the table, the omnipresent bottle of Dewar's. By early evening, she was usually bombed and I had to help her stagger into bed. "Come, Mom, stand up, hold on to my shoulder, you gotta get into bed."

All I could think about was being ten years old, attending to my mother, night after night, being there in her times of need, loving her, and respecting her despite her weaknesses. And here this guy was locking up his mother in a stinking jail cell with common criminals. I tried to imagine throwing my mother in jail. It was unthinkable. I wouldn't care if she murdered the Pope.

Minutes later, we pulled into the jail sally port and helped the prisoner through the sliding barred doors and into Hotel Hell.

I'd once been told that there were cops who would lock up their own mother. I hadn't believed it until then.

* * *

When I started working in a cruiser by myself, I thought I'd arrived in the true world of policedom. On my own with no trainer, no coach, I could make my own decisions and handle calls as I saw fit. Not yet twenty-three years old, I was putting people in jail for any offense I could muster up, just to please Sergeant Butler. The power was incredible.

I had asked to ride the strip, otherwise known as Motel Row, on the beach side. This also included a small residential area on the north end of Miami Beach. I made friends at all the restaurants and other businesses, and patrolled the service road at Haulover Beach where lovers made out at night and girls wore Bikinis in the day time. The strip was one of the least desirable zones among cops because it had fewer crime calls, less action and more emphasis on public relations among tourists. I loved it. It was like working in my own back yard, for it had been my personal stomping ground throughout my teen years. I had worked there at several motels and for Frankie Dio. It was also Bernie's hotbed of bookmaking activity which, of course, I knew nothing about. (ahem)

Girls were everywhere, drawn to a young stud in a police uniform, like flies to fly paper. I was getting laid on and off duty, occasionally twice a day. Sometimes I didn't even know their names.

Midnight shifts were the best. Few calls, a lot of patrol time and an invitation to a popular Jewish deli known as the Rascal House at 2 A.M. every night while they counted their money. Corned beef sandwiches on rye were piled so high, I couldn't get it into my mouth. Strawberry cheesecake was like none other—one slice was as big as some entire cakes. Free.

Early on, I learned that special perks for wearing the uniform were free chow and free movies. When not in uniform, just show the badge. How brazen we were. Warren Greene* was the epitome of brazen. Greene rode solo as motorcycle cop. At times, he joined up with a group aptly named the Wolf Pack. Their job was intensive enforcement in select areas. Each day, Greene ate at the IHOP on Collins Avenue and ordered steak and eggs, free. Until, one day, he invited the entire ten-man Wolf Pack. They all ordered steaks, and then were shocked when the owner presented them with a full-price check. That ended free meals for cops at the IHOP.

Greene was a first class prick. He stopped Bernie for speeding one day along Sunny Isles Causeway, on the way to the strip. Bernie asked Greene if he knew me. The officer had heard of me, but he was writing a ticket anyway, lecturing Bernie along the way. The lecture gnawed at Bernie until he shot back, "Listen, Officer, I ain't feeling too good. I admit, I was speeding. Will you just write the fucking ticket and shut-up." Greene prattled on about traffic safety until Bernie turned white, started breathing heavily, and informed the cop he was having a heart attack. Greene ordered Bernie to drive to the nearest police station, where he would finish writing the ticket. Bernie, in fact, ended up in a hospital that afternoon with heart failure.

* * *

Spotting a suspicious car parked in a remote location—deep into a wooded area—during midnight shift would normally draw the attention of a patrolman, because it might be stolen, abandoned or used in a crime. That often led to the amusing task of catching lovers in the act. It was not really "enforcement." After all, who were they really hurting? But we would usually take an officious stance, as though the sanctity of our pristine county was being violated, then chase them away.

The first time I caught two lovers, I was as shocked as they. Nearly 2 A.M., I spotted a station wagon parked in the dense foliage in the north end, near the bay. I caught a glimpse of the red reflectors as my headlight beams panned the area, then I turned off my lights and slowly drove toward the station wagon. Parked fifty yards away, the voyeur in me didn't want to alert them until I got right beside and turned on my flashlight. Aha! Sure enough, the car rocked like a baby's crib, windows steamed. Through the moonlight, I could see flesh against flesh inside, moving, gyrating, until I wiped the window and turned on the flashlight. Suddenly, they went into a panic, scurrying about inside the car. That's when I realized—these were two men.

One was a boy barely younger than myself. The other was a man in his forties wearing a neatly trimmed beard. I let them dress then stood them outside the car to ready themselves for my police lecture about trespassing, doing offensive things in public, threatening them with a vagrancy arrest, and so forth. In those days, a Florida Driver's license denoted a person's occupation. That was always helpful to cops. In this case, it was even more surprising. The boy's license showed he was a student. The older man?

Priest.

From that time on, I became more wary of sneaking up on lovers. The priest situation, though shocking, also made me feel incredibly invasive, like I was meddling in other people's personal affairs. Perhaps my actions were justified, but there was also something dirty about it. But that didn't stop me. The very next night, I came upon a beige car at the parking lot in Haulover Beach and thought it might be abandoned or stolen. When I shined the flashlight inside, there they were, a naked man and woman getting it on, flashlight or not. For that moment, I felt affronted that they continued on despite the sight of a cop, until I realized why. The man inside fumbled for something in his right hand, then promptly presented a gold sergeant's badge to the window, without missing a stroke. I got the message.

"Yes Sir, Sergeant, Sir. Have a good time, Sir. On my way, Sir."

Names remain anonymous .to protect the author.

CHAPTER SIXTEEN
BamBOOZled

In mid-December, after my training period was over and Sergeant Butler was assigning me as a solo unit, he'd heard that I preferred the tourist strip at Sunny Isles as a permanent riding zone. No other officers were regularly assigned there, so the slot was open. After roll call, he took me aside. Butler was an imposing figure, like being confronted by a Jesse Ventura with hair. "Frank, you ready to work alone?"

"Yes, sir."

"Wanna ride the strip?"

"Yes, sir."

"Okay. But you gotta do me a favor, okay?"

"What's that, Sarge?"

"The Christmas party is coming up. We need some booze."

I thought for a moment, wondering what he was getting at. "Okay. What do I do?"

"You know people on the strip, right? Bars, stores, motels."

Ah. Now I got it. "Yeah. Sure."

"Think you can pick up some Christmas cheer? You know. A little variety?"

Well. It was better than working Liberty City, handling violent criminals every shift, drunken domestics, burglars, juvenile delinquents and shuttling prisoners to the jail.

For a choice assignment, it was time to pay my dues.

At 11:30 P.M., immediately after roll call, I was on the strip pandering to bar owners and liquor stores for whatever "donations" they'd like to give to the local police for Christmas. Two hours later, the trunk of the police car had two boxes full of scotch, bourbon, vodka and gin. And if I was lucky, I could pad my stats with a good DUI arrest.

* * *

December was an important month for Miami Beach. It began the tourist season when thousands fled the cold north for sun and fun during the winter months. As a zone cop, I could see activity in bars, restaurants and motels starting to heat up, with more cars in the parking lots and hookers on the streets. Always packed with locals as well as tourists, The Wreck Bar at the Castaways Motel was a magnet for wolves on the hunt because prey knew the best places to get themselves picked up. The Banana Boat Lounge across the street was another hot spot.

Some of the larger motels had nightclubs, like the Dunes, where *Toots Shelley performed nightly, a fat homosexual comedian who sang and danced on stage topless, tassels spinning from his nipples. Stars like Vic Damone and Connie Frances had appeared at the Newport and Thunderbird Motels. Frankie Dio still owned Dore's Restaurant and Lounge where one of his female acolytes performed at the piano bar.

Off duty, I hung out at a small lounge at the Kimberly Motel, owned by a former prize fighter with a bad eye and a bum leg named Sam Sharkey. The Umbrella Room was aptly named for its array of upside down umbrellas that hung from the ceiling to conceal dirty and unpainted plaster. Booze was cheap for us because Sam loved cops. For entertainment, he employed Larry Lawson, a skinny piano-playing queen with blond bangs who delighted patrons with his brash, risqué music and bold humorous references to his love for men. For Sam, it was a draw, to compete with other lounges on the strip.

I was chasing every skirt between the ages of eighteen and forty, and finding great success. But it wasn't love and companionship I sought. It was conquest. All that anger still lingered inside of me because my dream girl and my little boy had been wrenched from my life. I didn't want to love, and I didn't want to hear any girl say that she loved me, because most of them were down-on-their-luck waitresses and barmaids hunting for a meal ticket. Besides, I had silly visions of a possible reconciliation down the road. Perhaps, I thought, Betty Jo would dump the older man and return to my arms once again. In reality, she'd have nothing of it. She secretly moved to Islamorada in the Florida Keys with my son and her new husband. If I hadn't access to research tools, available to a cop, I might not have found her. She avoided me like the plague, and I didn't know why.

Before donning the uniform for a tour of duty on the graveyard shift, I'd often stop in at the Kimberly for a couple of drinks to kill time. After all, booze was cheap and drinking had become my regular past time I listened to Sam lament about bad business and how wonderful it would be if the state legalized casino gambling. He always wanted me to show him my badge and asked if I could get one for him. Larry Lawson played red-hot mama songs in the background while folks clapped and laughed. I'd stay until ten o'clock, then tell Sam I'd see him later when I was on duty.

I hadn't been riding solo for very long, but I knew every nook and cranny of the strip. Sometimes, when I felt tired and radio activity was slow, I'd park in a remote spot behind the seagrape trees next to the ocean, stretch out and catch a few minutes of sleep.

It was after 3 A.M., when I had awakened from a little snooze, and listened to the dispatcher banter back and forth with other police units on the mainland, having nothing to do with me. In those days, we patrolled with the car windows open because there was no air conditioning. Cool salty breezes from the shoreline helped arouse my senses and I resumed patrolling the main drag, Collins Avenue, on the hunt for good stats.

While cruising southbound, almost in a trance, my attention was suddenly drawn to a pair of headlights approaching northbound at a high rate of speed, weaving left and right, all over the road. As the vehicle zoomed by, I could see it was a light blue Cadillac. I reached for the mike and broke the radio silence, calling it in as a possible DUI chase, then made the U-turn between the median and hauled ass. Adrenalin started to pump. A good chase would always do that.

I accelerated to seventy miles per hour, but lost sight of the vehicle's tail lights ahead. Where did it go? The moment I sped by the Newport Motel, I caught a glimpse of rising smoke in my peripheral on the right. I whooshed by, then saw the Cadillac in my rear view mirror where it had smashed head-on into a telephone pole.

It posed an eerie sight, indeed, because there was no other commotion, no red lights, no sirens, ambulances, barricades, all those elements we usually see after the fact. This had happened almost before my eyes, in the silence of the night, a single smash, and not one bystander.

I screeched backwards to the site, called in the location, asked for an ambulance on a "3" signal (emergency) and rushed out of my car. No one was in the Cadillac except the driver who was pinned behind the steering wheel. Smoke and steam billowed from all sides of the crumpled hood which had impacted against the pole, and I could smell the hot steam. His door was jammed, so I ran around to the passenger side. In the darkness, I saw a lone man, perhaps in his mid-40s, wedged like a vise between the wheel and the seat, moaning pathetically and reeking of alcohol. Blood gushed from his nose like a faucet. "Oh God. Oh God," he murmured over and over in drunken dribble.

Panic raged through me. No time to wait for an ambulance or other medical assistance. It was all up to me. The man was in terrible pain, soaking in blood. I entered the car and asked if he could understand and assist me in getting him out. All he said, repeatedly, was, "Oh, God."

The sudden responsibility of life and death was overwhelming. So lonely, just the two of us, strangers, grappling in the dark, thrust together by circumstance, his life in my hands, dependent on my actions, or the lack of them.

Where was that ambulance? Where was my backup?

I reached across the seat to grab his body. He instinctively reached with one bloody hand and grabbed the back of my neck. Good. At least, he was semi-conscious and able to help. I tried reaching under him, pulling and grunting, to no avail. I could not get a grip because his neck, arms and hands were slippery with blood. This became a very desperate situation as he continued to grope at my neck. His wet bloody touch poured into my very soul. Three minutes earlier, I had been driving around in a quasi-trance in the hope of some new activity to jar the serenity. Moments later, I found myself dealing with an emergency, vital to the life of one human being.

My breathing became labored, heart pounding. This was taking too long. I felt clumsy and frustrated. This guy deserved a cop bigger and stronger than me. The awful tugging continued until I finally freed him from behind the steering wheel. He held my neck until I could slide him across the seat. Drenched now, I could taste his blood dripping across my lips as he leaned upon my head and shoulder. His head bobbed onto my chest, hair matted, drooling, uttering "Oh, God," over and over.

Just the two of us, on a quiet darkened street. "Easy now," I reassured him. "You're going to be okay."

Finally, I managed to lift him from his seat and cradled his body as I lowered him to the sidewalk. From a distant gaze, he glanced into my eyes for a brief second and muttered, "Oh, God," once more. As I started to lay his head down, he gurgled. His eyes became fixed, head heavy. His hand slipped from my neck. Panting from exhaustion, my face was inches from his. I knelt there, holding his head, staring at this stranger. I felt so helpless. He breathed no more.

A man died next to my bosom.

My eyes the last he ever saw, my hand the last touch he ever felt.

Finally, an ambulance attendant stood over me, but it was too late. "He's dead," I said. That was all I could say.

"He's dead. I tried. But he's dead."

Later on, I learned that Bill Morrison had been a local bartender and a recovering alcoholic who obviously had gone off the wagon. He had been depressed over losing his wife to another man. With her went his two kids and his dream of family life.

The direct hit into a telephone pole crushed his sternum against the hub of the steering wheel. Bill Morrison died, literally, of a broken heart.

CHAPTER SEVENTEEN
Conflict of Interest

I couldn't let on that I knew a lot of mobsters. When Sergeant Butler held roll call and read postings about hoods like John Manarite, Guido Penosi and Frankie Dio, I thought about the old days and the dinner parties in Mom's house, my past jobs working for Dio, Bernie's parade of hoods coming in and out of the house, not to mention the protection money being paid to the very top bosses I worked under, whose photos adorned station house walls. Meanwhile, other cops listening to Butler were thinking about a great prize if they could arrest any one of them.

I had maintained my secret well. Yet, my heart came to a stop in the squad room one day at the end of a shift when Charlie Black, bold as ever, announced aloud for all to hear, "Hey Marshall. Some guy named Bernie Stein says he's your stepfather. But I wrote him a ticket for running a red light."

Bernie? Bernie who?

I think Black was watching for a reaction. So I pretended not to hear and went on with my business. Everyone was busy with their own reports and paid no attention.

All I cared about was pleasing Butler. Build those stats. Write tickets. Tow cars. Look for poor Whites, Hispanics and Negroes in dumpy cars wanted on bench warrants. Put people in jail. Insignificant people, that is.

I thought Mike Zarowny was insignificant, even though he was a lawyer. After all, lawyers break the law, too.

I spotted an all-white, brand new Cadillac speeding down Collins Avenue on the wrong side of the street, causing on-coming traffic to veer to one side or another. I blared the siren and he pulled over. Slowly, he exited the car, and stood up. I thought I'd shit. The man was huge. At least a foot higher than me, a hundred pounds heavier and bald as Mr. Clean. One growl and I'd have cowered like a frightened puppy. To my surprise, he was very gentle and polite. Zarowny's breath reeked of alcohol. Staggering and weaving on his feet, he couldn't see straight through crossed eyes. He flunked all the roadside tests. When I laid my hand on his shoulder and told him he was under arrest for DUI (or did I ask him?), he just nodded and said,

"Okay." The handcuffs barely fit around his wrists.

I learned, later on, that Mike Zarowny was well known as a notorious alcoholic who had grappled with as many as six cops at a time in previous arrest situations.

Boy, was I lucky.

But something went wrong. In 1962, an arrestee for DUI had to blow .15 on the Breathalyzer to be considered legally impaired. I figured he would double that, or more.

After Zarowny was taken downtown, I heard that he read a mere .02, legally sober. Very sober! But he could hardly stand up, much yet blow into a balloon. Something was amiss.

Two months later, I stood before a wiry old judge named Jerry Strickland who promptly threw out the DUI charges. As Zarowny walked out of the courtroom, Strickland peered over his granny glasses and asked me from the bench, in front of everyone, "Officer Frank.

Didn't you know who that was?"

I got the message.

The low Breathalyzer reading, I figured, must have been either human error or faulty equipment. It also occurred to me that a *special* relationship may have existed between Zarowny and the drunkometer technician, or the judge. Maybe both.

Not only was I naive, I had become the department's premier cynic.

* * *

I liked Bernie. I admired Bernie. The old man had helped me enormously, and I owed him a debt of gratitude. But working as a cop while holding a secret about my family ties was like being on two sides of a fence at the same time. And that ain't easy.

Early afternoon. Roll call went quickly. Sergeant Butler called me in his office to inform me of a call waiting for me on the strip. A stolen car, used in a robbery, had been found at Haulover Beach parking lot. I was to get over there as soon as possible to relieve the on-duty officer.

Across the bridge on the island side, traffic had backed-up slightly from Collins Avenue. I stopped for the red light behind a string of cars. My driver's window was open. Suddenly, I heard an angry man's voice booming from my left, "Come back here, you dirty son-of-a-bitch! I'll kill ya!" On the sidewalk in front of the Limehouse Chinese Restaurant, I caught a glimpse of a burly man with wild grey hair walking on the sidewalk amid a crowd, waving a small pistol in the air and screaming his lungs out,

"You son-of-a-bitch!" Other men were trying to hold him back.

My God! It's Bernie!

Hair wild, face red, I saw Bernie chasing after a small pudgy fellow who was running as fast as his legs would go toward Collins Avenue, looking over his shoulder like a scared animal. I recognized him as a small-time thief named Anthony Moscardino, better known as Mushky.

Bernie was livid. Out of control.

The whole world must have been looking at me, a uniformed cop in a patrol car sitting directly across from the happening, watching to see what I was going to do. Like an idiot, I sat there stunned and looked straight ahead. Had this been anyone else, I'd have called for a back-up and arrested the man for any one of many charges. But, this was Bernie! Was I to arrest my own stepfather? The man who got me this job? Not a chance. Again, his voice boomed, "You dirty son-of-a-bitch!" I just knew everyone's eyes were steeled to me.

Eyes and ears open, mouth shut.

There was only one thing to do. Pretending to be totally deaf, I turned on my overhead flashers, wailed the siren and headed south on Collins toward Haulover Beach as if on an emergency call, then prayed he didn't shoot the man. If he did, I'd have no choice but to return to the scene.

By the time I arrived at the Haulover Beach parking lot, the hold-over officer, Terry Denisco, asked me why I was speeding there with red lights and sirens blaring. "Hey.

It's only a stolen car, Marshall. Take it easy."

"Oh." I feigned surprise. "I thought you had the robbers too. Sorry."

Whew!

Two weeks later, Anthony Moscardino, alias Mushky, was gunned down on a residential street behind the 163rd Street Shopping Center. The case remains an unsolved whodunit to this day. I guess Mushky must have pissed off a lot of people.

Years later, when I worked Homicide and had access to old case files, I looked up the Moscardino murder and reviewed all the reports. Mushky had been killed in the night with a rifle bullet by someone passing by in a white Cadillac. The prime suspect was a hit man named John Manarite, a well-known mobster who drove a white Cadillac.

John Manarite had been a regular guest in the house of Bernie.

CHAPTER EIGHTEEN
Transition

Being a divorced father was troublesome, indeed, especially when the mother of my son did everything she could to exclude me from his life. After Betty Jo remarried, she and her reconstructed family moved around like nomads, first down to the Keys, back to Miami, to Vero Beach, then Ft. Lauderdale. She never notified me in advance of her moves. If I wanted to visit my boy, I'd have to go on the search for phone numbers, utility records, driver's licenses, traffic tickets and such, just to find her or her new husband, Bill Gertz, a gourmet chef who often changed jobs.

She was indoctrinating young Bennett to accept Gertz as his father and to think of me only as *Marshall*, a man who came to visit once in a while. Nothing could have hurt me more. I was young, but a good dad, loving and attentive. My mother loved her grandson and yearned to be more involved as his life. I sent child support checks promptly every two weeks and paid his medical bills. In her efforts to establish a "perfect family" environment, Betty Jo considered my existence an inconvenience. She got pregnant again and eventually gave Bennett a younger half-brother, John.

Undoubtedly, I still dealt with emotional trauma from the sudden departure of Betty Jo and Bennett in the fall of 1961. Over the next three years, I dated many young women, but had no interest in serious affairs outside the bedroom.

I never realized how easy it would be to score with girls. It certainly wasn't my money; I didn't have any. I rarely took a date to a movie or out to dinner. But the police uniform draped over a young man in his twenties is very alluring. I didn't seek sex, sex found me. I would meet a girl while on-duty, then invite her to my apartment off-duty. But through it all, I found myself sinking deeper and deeper into depression, exploiting females for nothing other than the conquest. While the moments may have been fun, I was not a happy young man. An outcast to my little boy, I was smoking four packs a day, boozing too much, working a job I really didn't want, and had become a colossal disappointment to my mother.

* * *

While standing at roll call one Saturday morning, a pair of rookies from the police academy joined ranks for their first field-observer assignment. One looked hauntingly familiar, but I couldn't place the face in his recruit uniform. Sergeant Butler announced: "Okay, guys, we have a couple of rookies for ride-alongs. Windsor, meet Tony Borowski. He's your partner for today."

We listened for the next name. The sergeant continued, "Frank, you ride with Gary Minium."

Who?

I looked down the line. Gary waved. Sure enough, it was *him*. The bully from North Miami High. The same guy who scared the shit out of me seven years before. The same guy I had likened to Stanley Press. I thought he'd be in prison, not joining a police department.

What a turnabout, I thought. Now here I am, training this same guy, me a salty cop and him a rookie. To my surprise, Gary was amiable and intensely interested in policing. He'd put in a long stint in the U.S. Marine Corps and then wanted to follow in his father's footsteps in civilian police. Until then, I hadn't realized that his father had been a career cop. As it turned out, Robert "Pappy" Minium was one of the most respected police detectives ever, a legend on the department. I had never connected the two names before.

Our careers would cross paths many times, and in one instance, he may well have saved my life.

* * *

After a year working the Airport, and two years of uniform patrol in the North District, I was ready for a change. Police work had its high and low points. I enjoyed the camaraderie. I liked the respect given me by people in general. I thought the fight against crime and evil and helping citizens in trouble was a noble endeavor. All was well, but something was missing. I was not fulfilling my potential. There had to be something better than patrolling in uniform every day, answering calls and hawking decent folks for building stats. That's what bothered me the most.

My stats were waning. Instead of writing lots of tickets, I'd fallen into a pattern of stopping and only warning people for violations, unless they were too severe.

No quota actually existed. Nevertheless, the sergeant used tickets, towed cars and arrests as a numerical gauge for rating performance. Officers who worked the mainland zones made many more arrests a month and wrote hundreds of tickets. The strip didn't yield that many opportunities, but I still managed an arrest now and then, while ensuring at least twenty traffic tickets a month.

In the final days of September of 1963, I discovered I'd only written eight tickets for the entire month, with two days to go. For certain, the sergeant would be unhappy. Time to go fishing.

Sunny Isles Causeway was a two mile stretch of four-lane divided highway between U. S. Highway One on the mainland, and Collins Avenue on the beach. The speed limit was 45. No one went 45. Not even the cops, on or off duty.

At the break of dawn, motorists were coming to work, while tourists were heading out. Needing stats, I'd park in a spot out of sight just around a curve, then go after them as they sped by, never writing anyone for less than 60 mph. In one two-hour period, I wrote seven speeding tickets.

One young man got out of his car, driver's license in hand, and apologized profusely for going 62. Steeled to my duties, I listened, but kept on writing. I'd heard the sob stories before, the points, the insurance, the cost of the fine, going to court, cannot take time off from the job, etc. *Tell it to the judge.*

I could see a young woman sitting in the car. As he reluctantly signed the ticket, I asked where he was heading.

"Well, we just got married yesterday. We didn't have enough money to go on a honeymoon, other than a night at a motel."

I felt lower than whale dung.

He continued, "We're going to the IHOP for breakfast."

"Well, have a nice day," I said before returning to the police cruiser.

I sat there a few minutes, watching the car drive off, knowing I'd just cost this fellow half of a weekly paycheck for doing what everyone does every day on that same speed trap, all because I was in a panic to build my stats and please the sergeant.

I knew the owner of the IHOP where they were going. I stopped at the nearest pay phone and told Mrs. Margarite Harrison that a small light-blue Ford Falcon would be pulling in with a young couple. Breakfast was on me.

* * *

During those three years in uniform, I thought detectives were awesome. They were the real Joe Fridays, who worked incognito, drove unmarked cars, investigated major crimes and earned the respect and admiration of everyone in the criminal justice community. They were the police heavyweights, the leaders who took charge, the best dressed, the smartest and the well-known. Every time I handled a death case, they took command of the scene and dismissed me like an unwanted wart. I wanted to be a detective.

At the end of my shift, I approached Sergeant Butler in his office with a written request in my hand. "Sir, I want to put in a transfer request to Detective Bureau."

He stopped what he was doing, laid his pencil on the desk and looked up at me with an expression of pure disgust. "Frank, you gotta be shitting me. There are twenty other guys here waiting for transfer to detective, and they all have more seniority than you. Forget about it. It'll be five or ten years before you'll be a detective." The sergeant seemed almost offended. Then he asked, as if threatening,

"Are you sure you want to submit this?"

"Uh. I guess not."

My heart sunk. I dreaded working in uniform another five or ten years. There was only one thing left to do.

Bedroom. Flash paper. Tiparillo. Underwear. Telephone.

"Bernie, I think I might resume violin lessons and become a serious musician."

"What's the matter, kid?"

"Nothing really. I just need a change."

"You don't like bein' a cop?"

"Yeah. It's okay. I like it. Well, I don't like it all the time. I don't feel right in some of the things I gotta do. I'd like to be a detective, but the Sarge says I haven't enough seniority."

Bernie waffled his head with that familiar impish grin, cigar in teeth. "So, you wanna be a detective?"

"I've only got three years on the department. They'd never consider me." I hesitated. Bernie grinned.

* * *

Three weeks passed. I was called directly into the office of the weighty district captain, Paul Morgan. "Frank. You're going into plain clothes, the Warrants Bureau, starting Monday. I don't know what's going on here, but I'll find out." I was elated. Sergeant Butler called me into his office later and asked how I pulled it off. "Beats me," I said.

That Monday morning, wearing a thirty-three dollar suit purchased at J.C. Penney's, I showed up at headquarters where I reported to the captain in charge of Warrants Bureau, Noah Scott, the same man who hosted my first day in the old county jail three years before.

Thanks, Bernie.

CHAPTER NINETEEN
Rookie Detective

A deep male voice boomed from behind. "She's gone! The window's open. She's out on the ledge! Get her! Quick!"

Yike!

I ran over to the sash window and stuck my head out. On the sixth floor of the County Courthouse overlooking downtown Miami, there she was, to my right, standing on the twelve- inch concrete ledge, her back pressed against the granite edifice, hands spread, threatening to jump, just like in the movies. But this was the real thing.

Oh shit!

My first day in Warrants Bureau had nothing to do with serving warrants. Part of the job, I learned, entailed the transport and guarding of the mentally ill from various facilities to the courthouse for Incompetency Hearings. Detectives dubbed it: The Nut Detail.

[1]Wanda Mae McGowan was a haggard thirty-four year old schizophrenic who looked fifty-four. That's all I knew about her when we placed her in the empty jury room to wait until the judge called her name. She apparently lifted the sash window and made her exit. My partner, Wesley Harmon (yes, the same Wes Harmon who showed me how to beat the crap out of jail inmates) prodded me, "Go get her, Marshall!"

I broke out in a sweat. My heart skipped three beats.

I dared not let anyone know I had a lifelong problem with acrophobia. The mere view from six floors up sent my head in a tailspin.

"Uhhh... me?"

I just knew my detective career would be over after only two hours in Warrants, at the whim of the same deputy who had thought I was a wimp three years before. Wes could see that I was not going out on that ledge. He flipped his eyes to the ceiling and huffed, "I'll

---

[1] Wanda Mae McGowan - fictitious name

get her from the other side and walk her back to your window, then you pull her in, get it?"

"Got it!"

The portly cop went to an adjoining courtroom, stepped onto the ledge, then sidestepped his way toward the woman. She screamed something about jumping while she inched away from Wes. He pursued and she kept moving away, but in my direction. A group of curious pedestrians assembled below, looking up. I raised the sash as high as it would go. Sure enough, she came in front of my window and in one swoop, I grabbed her by the waist and hauled her in. Good thing she was small. I don't think I could live with the thought of dropping her.

Saving a life was one thing. Averting a heart attack was another. Boy, was I glad that was over. *That's it. I'm going back to playing violin.* From that time on, I saw Wes Harmon in a new light. He may have been a brutal cop, but he did risk his life to save another's. There's much to be said for that.

* * *

I had wondered about all those television shows, movies and novels depicting street cops slugging it out with bad guys every day, engaging in shoot-outs, surviving a kill or be killed arena where guns and violence were a constant presence. During three years in uniform, I never shot anyone nor fired my weapon on duty. Neither did I seriously injure another person. I was quite happy over that. Most subjects, I found, did not resist arrest, provided they were treated with some degree of dignity. Some were not as cooperative, which required physical force usually amounting to grappling and arm-twisting.

That is not to say that police did not have to apply extreme methods at times. I happened to be lucky. Besides, I rode the strip, where violence-prone calls were less prevalent than on the mainland.

I first encountered the office secretary as I arrived in the Warrants Bureau that November morning in 1963, a pert pony-tailed blonde with an hour-glass figure who stood no more than five feet tall. With an engaging smile, Grace Cantrell led me to the office of Captain Noah Scott, the same man who first hosted me at the old

County Jail in 1960. Then I met the rest of the staff and went on my first "nut detail" with Wes Harmon.

For the next two years, I became a virtual statistics machine.

The main job of a Warrants Detective was to serve arrest warrants that had been filed by citizens or by other police agencies, or to locate fugitives from other jurisdictions. It was great fun, hunting for wanted subjects using the clout of a sworn police detective, delving into private phone and utility records, driver's licenses, past infractions, job history and family records. Where I once made three or four arrests a month, I now made that many in a day. Often more. Charges covered the gamut, ranging from Breaking & Entering, Robbery, to Worthless Checks, Fraud, Auto Theft and other less than violent offenses. The most serious charges, like Murder and Rape, were handled by the investigating detectives from those units.

I was trained by experienced detectives, like Frank Celinceon, one of the "connected" old-timers who ended up in prison on corruption charges three years later. Frank and I were serving a warrant in a house one day when we heard the television news announce that Kennedy had just been shot. That wasn't the only killing that took place that day. We would learn later that a grisly murder of a small child took place in the southern regions of Dade County that same afternoon, a case that taxed the department's resources beyond its limits.

Warrants Bureau detectives were not only used for serving warrants, transporting prisoners to court, and handling "nut details," we were a ready resource of manpower if and when needed for any other department needs.

The day after the Kennedy assassination, I was told to report to Homicide.

Me? Homicide?

The body of Loreen Thorbahn, age 10, had been found in a remote area of South Dade, lying face down in a wooded area, her pants pulled own, and her head crushed by a blunt object with a circular pattern. She was last seen alive walking home from Coral Reef Elementary. A media blitz followed, overshadowed only by the Kennedy killing.

The community was in an outrage.

This affected me not, until I was assigned as part of a special fifty-man squad of investigators ordered to follow the thousands of leads that streamed in following the news release.

I couldn't believe it; I was working in Homicide! These were the star cops of the department, and now I was working along side of them. My heart raced with anticipation. The first morning, detective captains like Pat Gallagher and Sam Billbrough stood before the assembly issuing orders and information in the squad room. I had heard of them, like surreal icons, but now they were real before my eyes. Then, there was Detective Sergeant Raymond Beck, the lead investigator, handling the most important leads, the same persnickety sergeant that pissed off uniformed cops at the airport three years before. Now a fabled homicide detective, Beck stood before the group articulating all the important points of evidence. Tall, thin and with dark wavy hair, Beck had the presence of a movie star and spoke with the diction of a trial lawyer. He was immaculate. I was impressed.

"The child was struck on the side of the head with a blunt instrument creating a round concave wound to the skull the size of a silver dollar. It appears that the subject then masturbated over the body. Bear in mind, ladies and gentleman, that another body was found in south Dade three months ago, of another little girl, only she was fully decomposed. Her name: Cheryl Armel. We are considering this a possible serial killing."

The audience of fifty plain-clothed cops listened closely.

"The victim was starting to decompose, her flesh partially eaten by insects. Rigor had come in and out of the body." *This is so cool.* "Tire tracks on the scene indicate the subject may have driven a truck. The tracks have wear patterns that can be identified. We also have information that a suspicious light blue station wagon had been seen hanging around the school, driven by a white male."

Ninety-nine percent of the leads amassed by call-ins would probably be irrelevant, but the case was too important to pass on any one of them. Thus, the huge number of investigators. Teamed up with a skinny pencil-nosed chain smoker named John Vermilye, my job was to interview one citizen after another, check out tags, search vehicles, research known sexual predators and work twelve hours a day. I was certainly one of the least important detectives, but I relished the experience.

Shortly after seven o'clock on a clear night in South Dade, John Vermilye and I heard another detective unit over the radio announce that he had a light blue station wagon in view, occupied by a white male who was refusing to pull over. We were not far away. John headed toward the neighborhood called East Kendall. Other nearby units announced they were on the way also. Then we heard one word screamed over the radio, a word that invariably produces that power surge of adrenalin: "Chase!"

Sure enough, when we reached U.S. Hwy One and Southwest 156th Street, we spotted an unmarked police car turn a sharp right, its blue light flashing atop the dash, siren wailing, heading north on the highway directly behind a light blue Ford wagon. I set the portable blue flasher on the dash and we took pursuit directly behind. This had to be the suspect, we thought. Why would he be running? We imagined ourselves nabbing the child killer, true heroes of this important investigation.

Affectionately nicknamed, the B'nai Brith twins, the initial chase car was occupied by Detectives Jack Kahn and Joe Kogan, both Jewish, both respected cops. (Jewish cops were a rarity.) Within minutes, at least four detective and two uniform cars were involved in the chase, one long string of cars traveling at high speeds while frightened motorists pulled off the side. The chorus of sirens wailed on.

The subject hung a left, west bound on North Kendall Drive, then a dirt road under construction for miles, being widened to accommodate the burgeoning population growth. With a perennial cigarette dangling from his lips, Vermilye reached speeds up to ninety miles per hour. Every five blocks, we crossed north-south arteries that were elevated above the level of Kendall Drive, giving the chase a roller coaster effect, up and down, up and down, airborne after each avenue crossing, headlight beams undulating. We kept our eyes focused on the chase car before us while I felt like a rag doll plopping up and down, side to side, heart racing, hoping this would be over soon. In 1963, seat belts did not exist.

Finally, after twelve long minutes and as many miles into the uninhabited, the station wagon hung a sharp right. We all hung sharp rights. Then, a sharp left. We all hung sharp lefts. Now into dark and desolate farm country, the B'nai Brith twins suddenly pulled off into high weeds. We stopped directly behind. The station wagon had missed a turn, slid into the watery ditch and turned on its side. Other cars pulled in behind us. Red and blue flashers illuminated the area. John and I ran to assist. Our heartbeats must have doubled.

Jack Kahn lost control. Cursing at the top of his lungs, he stood atop the side of the vehicle, reached into the driver's window and started pulling the man out of the window by his ears. The fellow yelped in pain. "You son-of-a-bitch!" Kahn continued hollering, his face red, until a more even-tempered Joe Kogan physically pulled Kahn away and ordered him to calm down. After seeing the phalanx of police cars, the man surrendered with his hands up. Kahn and Kogan took the fellow downtown, where it was determined he had nothing to do with the Loreen Thorbahn killing. To this day, I don't know why he ran from the police. But it was an exciting event, indeed, one in which I learned much about the difference between a leader and a follower. Kogan was a true leader who stepped in to quell the fray instead of joining in. His actions made a lasting impression. As my career unfolded, I would see instances in which the absence of a good supervisor on a scene led to disaster. If all sergeants were like Joe Kogan, terms such as *police brutality* and *corruption* would almost be rendered obsolete.

After two weeks of night and day investigations, the primary homicide detectives came up with a suspect named Herbert Lee Evans, a lawn spray man whose truck had been spotted in the neighborhood. While following leads, two auto theft detectives had checked on several lawn spray companies, examining the tires of their trucks, when they found what appeared to be a possible match. After the truck was impounded, the tires were matched to the scene impressions, positively. Traces of Loreen's blood were scraped from under the gear shift lever. A steel pony wrench, used for hydrants, was found in the truck. The rounded end, shaped like a donut with a hole in the center, matched the skull wound like a jigsaw puzzle. And Evans' palm print matched the bloody latent on the girl's shirt.

Hustle bustle prevailed throughout the second floor of headquarters, as the Detective Bureau boiled over with excitement. John and I were dismissed from the special squad, no longer needed, but I remained fascinated by the case, hoping one day I'd work in Homicide.

I'd heard that the suspect was in the building being questioned in the Interrogation Room. John Vermilye arranged for me to watch part of the process from an adjoining room, through a glass one-way mirror, tape recorders rolling. There he was, the killer, sitting alone in the tiny cubicle, a tall fellow with puppy dog eyes who looked no different than a friendly super market clerk. I wondered what had twisted his values, what it was he could not control or overcome, for he surely had not envisioned murder and rape as his lifelong ambition.

Clad in a white doctor's smock, a gangly homicide detective named Wally LaPeters entered the room to sit with Evans. The name, *Dr. LaPeters*, had been stitched over his pocket. His first words to the suspect were, "Hello, Herbert. I'm Doctor LaPeters. I'm a psychiatrist, here to help you."

Cool.

Those were the days before Miranda warnings, and such actions are probably why they now exist. Other detectives, including Ray Beck, needed the darkened room to look on, so I didn't stay long. Certainly not long enough to hear his entire confession, which included the killing of young Cheryl Armel three months before.

Evans spent the next thirty-five years in prison until his death from natural causes in 1988.

CHAPTER TWENTY
Finger Charlie

When it came to important police matters, more decisions were made over coffee and pastry in Finger Charlie's Coffee Shop than in any other place on the department. Located on the second floor of Headquarters, this was a tiny order-at-the-counter café where everyone from the lowest rookie to the highest department brass, including uniform, detectives, communication, records, crime lab, training, administration and intelligence, met and came to know each other. Without it, there would not have been a forum for informal discussion and, perhaps, many cases might never have been solved.

Its now-infamous name was derived from the proprietor, a loudmouth blind man with disgusting habits who knew everyone in the entire building by name. Who would dare to complain about a blind man? Wearing his perennial dark glasses, Charlie hailed from The Bronx, drooled incessantly, and groped women using blindness as an excuse. He would walk down the hall with his stick in one hand and his palm extended in the other, just in case an errant breast got in its way. "Oh, sorry, ma'am." He always knew when the girls were near, just like he knew the sound of money.

The coffee shop was full of employees one morning when a coin fell to the floor in the far corner. Charlie could tell everyone's voice and where they were sitting. "Hey, Chuck Harbolt, your dime is on the floor." We were amazed.

We were also amazed that Charlie was able to pour soft drinks from the fountain without spilling a drop, because he'd hold the cup under the dispenser with his index finger dipped over the lip, sensing when the cup was full. Thus, his nickname: Finger Charlie.

One morning, I was drinking coffee, smoking and chatting with other detectives when my sergeant/supervisor, Phil Lindsley, poked his head through the door and motioned me away. "We got a lead on this guy," he said, holding up a mug photo of a black male. "Supposed to be hanging out in Overtown. Escapee from a chain gang in Georgia. Armed Robbery. Let's go."

His nickname was "Eyes" because the subject had eyes as big as cue balls. Phil wanted to cruise the streets to see if we could spot the man. I went along, figuring this was going to be like finding a needle in a haystack. After all, who ever nabs a wanted criminal just from a photograph?

It didn't take long. Just a few blocks from downtown Miami, in a predominantly black business neighborhood, we pulled to the curb. I looked at the photo one more time, then spotted "Eyes" sauntering across the street, then down the sidewalk, all alone. It had to be him. There couldn't be two people who looked like that. The man had a pair of boingers like I never saw before, no eyelids, just eyeballs.

"Let's get him!" Phil said. Now, this was a real dangerous guy, and I did worry, but dared not let on to Phil.

From behind, we followed, conspicuous as hell, two white guys in business suits walking in "The Hood". That was as much undercover as wearing a uniform and blowing a bugle.

"Eyes" was not a big fellow, which made me happy. I couldn't imagine tackling some guy the size of Hulk Hogan.

We got within two steps of him. My heart raced. Phil motioned, "Now!" Without a sound, Phil grabbed him from behind in a bear hug and pressed him against the store front, while I linked his hands together with my cuffs. Then I pulled a .22 caliber pistol from his waist band. From there, quickly to the unmarked car at the curb and to the jail. I was amazed at how fast and easy it went, no resistance, no crowd, no wrestling or fighting. He denied his identity, but fingerprints confirmed it. He was definitely "Eyes."

One might ask why I tell this story. After all, nothing really happened other than a routine arrest. It's no different than a duffer golfer telling his story about a hole-in-one. Catching a criminal on the street from a photograph has about the same odds, or maybe less. And we did it. Yea!

* * *

In two years of working warrants, I made about one thousand arrests, nearly all of them working alone. That would be unheard of in today's police world. In retrospect, it was plain crazy. But the department resources did not keep pace with the demand for services, and cops often were called upon to risk their lives without back-ups.

Rarely did I have anyone resist or try to run, except on two occasions.

I found a little Spanish fellow wanted for a pair of worthless checks that had been filed by department stores. He was meek and timid and I saw no need to put the handcuffs on. We chatted in the car all the way from West Miami to the newly built County Jail until we stopped at a traffic light near downtown. Suddenly, he opened the car door and bolted off, running like a deer in the woods. I had already notified the dispatcher I had an arrestee in the car, heading for jail, so it was all on record. This could be an extremely embarrassing situation, sure to end up in a disciplinary report.

I bolted after him on foot leaving the car at the traffic signal. I couldn't let him get away. He ran between buildings, I ran between buildings. I kept him in sight, across streets, between cars, knocking over garbage cans, leaping fences. Bear in mind, I smoked almost four packs of cigarettes a day, and the attempt at running was short lived. Gasping for air, I stopped, unable to keep up. He kept running. There was only one option left. I knew it was against policy, but I took out my gun and fired one shot into the grass, in front of a church. From a hundred yards away, the little Latino came to an abrupt halt and shot his hands so high in the air, I thought he was going to fly.

There's one that didn't get away.

Then, there was the pervert, wanted for a number of indecent exposure charges. We'll call him Rupert. After some research, I learned he was living with friends at a small house in Opa Locka, a low-income, blue-collar town northwest of Miami.

The house was like a large square concrete cube, never painted, graffiti on the walls, and a single door at the center, up two steps. The neighborhood smelled of garbage. Houses had no landscape, other than sandy lots and weeds. I knocked. The door opened. A tall, dark-haired white fellow with facial blemishes asked what I wanted. I showed my badge. "Are you Rupert?" I asked. He nodded.

"I have warrants for your arrest."

As Rupert stepped out onto the landing, I expected a simple surrender, a handcuffing and a short ride to the jail. Not to be. Rupert suddenly pushed me away and started running around the house. I ran after. And after. Rupert ran nowhere, except around the house, looking at me over his shoulder while I chased him on foot. I felt like an idiot. The soft sandy yard was like running on a beach. After four stupid revolutions around the house, I was totally exhausted. Rupert just kept on running. I didn't dare fire a shot with everyone looking on. The neighbors must have been laughing while I nearly passed out, gasping for breath. Rupert eventually ran off in straight line, north into the business district. I got on the radio, huffing and puffing, advising the dispatcher of the situation. Uniformed police cars arrived to assist, but Rupert was long gone.

There's one that did get away.

Rupert was apprehended two weeks later by two other Warrants detectives who were forewarned of his fleeing nature.

* * *

I came into Warrants Bureau in November of 1963. That's when I met tiny Grace Cantrell, the secretary with the hour-glass figure. Six months later, on April 10, 1964, we were secretly married during lunch hour by a local Justice of the Peace named Ralph Ferguson. Judge Ferguson was a short, squatty bulldog of a man who once played offensive tackle for the Miami Hurricanes and drank scotch, and lots of it. All the ceremony cost was a bottle of Cutty Sark.

Grace had just been divorced and had a small boy, age two. She flirted, I flirted. She obviously liked me. I was tired of the on-going litany of meaningless relationships, and yearned for love and family life. Grace was the most efficient clerical worker I'd ever seen, lightning speed typist, and a whiz at administering the bureau. While Captain Scott took credit for running a tight ship, it was Grace who deserved it.

I don't think we were really in love. Rather, we were in love with the concept of love, wishing for the right person to come along, and then deciding, intellectually, that we loved each other. We had all the right ingredients, youth, virility, morals, smarts, and availability. Why not? Besides, I had grown impatient, rooming with George Reincke for two years. Nice guy. But, not my type.

That afternoon, after we got back to the office from the judge's chambers, the rumor spread that we'd just been married. Captain Scott called me in his office. "Is it true?" he asked.

"Yes, sir."

"Well, then. Get the hell out of here and have a honeymoon, you idiot."

"Yes, sir."

CHAPTER TWENTY-ONE
Violins to Violence

The marriage with Grace took off like a rocket and fizzled like a popped balloon before it ever hit the clouds. My mother didn't like her any more than she liked Betty Jo. Actually, Mom approved of very little I had done in my life at that point.

No one cheated. We didn't fight. Once married, Grace's interest in sex became obligatory. We were like two strangers who woke up married one day and discovered we weren't right for each other. We had nothing in common, other than police department activity. I did enjoy the envy of many other cops who would have liked a roll in the hay with my trophy, but trophies are hard and cold, and they don't necessarily care for you like you care for them.

Nevertheless, being one-time losers already, we tried to make it work. If only we had learned how to communicate. If only we had chemistry beyond flirtation. If only we had not been so impulsive.

Meanwhile, that old familiar *burnout* had crept into my job attitude. Working Warrants Bureau had become easy, but there was nothing to continue holding my interest. No challenge. No future. Older detectives worked it like a mundane assembly line and I could see myself in twenty years doing the same thing, day after day. I had taken my first sergeant's test without studying and failed miserably. I didn't want to do this for the rest of my life.

My off and on visitation relationship with little Bennett, now four, struggled along with difficulty because his young mother still lived in a dream world, making sure I did not interfere with her ideal family situation. She taught him to call me "Marshall," instead of "Dad." Whenever I called, he was in the bath, or busy eating, or out playing. While I considered legal recourse, there was really little I could do. Betty Jo had taught him to love Bill Gertz as "Dad."

Depression is not a good thing. It can spiral a person's life into the pits, and I knew that. I also knew that my biological father had been diagnosed a manic-depressive and paranoid schizophrenic, and I thought about his genes raging through my blood. I needed to take control.

Time for a change. At twenty-six, I realized Mom had been right all along. My true destiny lay in the world of music. My second marriage was dead. My career was at a dead end. I made a momentous decision. On a balmy July night in 1965, I looked up Artie Canonico at Miami Beach's Eden Roc Hotel where his orchestra was performing. After the show, past midnight, we sat in his car and talked for over an hour, each of us chain smoking and sipping from his flask of scotch. I didn't want to stay a cop. I wanted to play in symphonies and perhaps, even solos. With great humility, I asked if he would resume giving me violin studies. He said no — unless I was dead serious and willing to put in hard work.

I was.

I thought about how pleased my mother would be, but I wanted to keep it a secret for the time being. When Christmas came, five months away, I would surprise her with a private concert, one she'd never forget. I could just imagine the look on her face and the tears of happiness. For once, I would make her proud.

I always kept a key to her dance studio, which was vacant every evening after 6:00 P.M. With terrazzo floors and mirrored walls, the acoustics were perfect for practice. Practicing at home was out of the question, with Grace and her little boy there watching television. We were barely speaking at this point, and I'm sure she was happy to see me out of the house during the evenings.

For the next five months, the routine was the same; serve warrants during the day, eat dinner out, secretly practice violin at night, two, three, sometimes five hours at a time, alone in my mother's dance studio. That time remains among the most rewarding and fulfilling memories of my entire life, as though I'd discovered that my violin had become my best friend. I thrived on the music. If anyone could see, I might have looked like a total idiot pacing the terrazzo floor in front of floor-to-ceiling mirrors, deep in concentration, ranging my sounds from weeping Gypsy strings to high-flying scales, then embracing Sarasate, Beethoven and Mozart. It was like breathing again.

Some friends who knew were amused and stopped in occasionally for a private concert. I also met George Wolf, another violinist who rapped on the window one night, and we became musical partners. We remain good friends today. Mr. Canonico came to the studio one night a week to give his lessons. He was quite pleased with my progress. I never played better. He thought, finally, I had grown up, and I was going places with music.

I often stopped at the IHOP in North Miami Beach. That's where I met Joan Simms. Dark haired, pug-nosed, sultry, about twenty-three, this waitress was the object of every male customer who entered the restaurant. I could not take my eyes off her. A feisty southern belle and lover of country music, Joan was born and raised in Miami, married to a construction worker, and had three small kids.

We connected. Both unhappily married, we knew the relationships were going nowhere. I felt no guilt whatsoever. I didn't know what Grace was doing in the evenings, nor did I care. And she probably figured I wasn't being faithful either.

I made arrangements for a rendezvous with Joan in a friend's apartment. That was the beginning.

Little did I know, this young vixen would become a major player in my life.

* * *

December 1, 1965, was a day that might have ended everything, save a fraction of an inch.

The fugitive warrants for twenty-two year-old *Jack McKnight indicated he came to Florida from upstate New York, fleeing charges of auto theft. He had no history of violence. His girl friend was a woman fifteen years his senior, with a child.

Phone records and utility bills in the woman's name gave us a probable address. Detective Bob Lamont and I checked out the old apartment building near downtown Miami and saw that the suspect's vehicle was parked outside. This was to be a routine arrest, but one that required two men because of the fugitive status.

Bob and I were peers, about the same age, both transferred into Warrants from the North District. He had a reputation for being a good cop, but a hot-head at times.

The old stone building was probably built in the 1940s. We knocked on the door to the second story apartment. A blonde woman open it a crack and asked what we wanted. Because we'd heard that a child was inside, our guns were not drawn.

I showed my silver badge. "Sheriff's Office, ma'am. We have warrants for Mr. Jack McKnight."

"He's not here, I'm sorry."

We knew better. I showed her the warrant. "Please let us in, ma'am."

"No!" she shouted, and started to close the door. Lamont pushed it open. We charged inside. Lamont ran down the hall to the left, as I checked behind the door. That's when I heard the woman scream, "Get out! Get out!"

I turned. Weeping hysterically, the woman stood across the living room waving a small rifle like a water hose in my direction, with a little boy holding on to her leg.

Whoa! Yike! Caught in a sudden trap, I didn't know which way to turn. I thought of pulling my revolver, but she'd surely shoot me on the spot. She screamed over and over, "Get out! Get out!"

I thought this was going to be my moment of death. "Get out! Get out!" Lamont was out of sight.

I said, "Okay. Okay."

There was nowhere to go but back out the door, leaving Lamont in danger. I was no James Bond. Neither did I have a choice. My heart raced. I decided to run outside, draw my gun and return quickly. As I turned, I heard a *POP!* The moment I stepped out the door and began reaching for my gun, I felt a tingle in my upper, inner thigh. I touched my pants. My hand was full of blood.

My God! I'm shot!

But, I had left my partner alone in there. I had to do something, fast. Revolver in hand, I limped back into the apartment and saw Lamont grab the barrel of the one-shot .22 caliber rifle, disarming the woman on the spot. Jack McKnight was already handcuffed in the back bedroom. He surrendered without a struggle, as we had expected. What we hadn't expected was the wrath of his girl friend.

Had the trajectory of that barrel been a centimeter higher, the bullet would have rendered my life over at the age of 26. (And Grace would have been happier as a widow than in marriage, with all the benefits due the surviving spouse of a law enforcement officer killed in the line of duty).

An ambulance brought me on a "3" to the emergency room of Jackson Memorial Hospital. Because I am allergic to penicillin, the only way they could disinfect the wound was to inject hydrogen peroxide directly into entry with a syringe, and let it drain out the exit wound. I screamed so loud, a nurse fainted. I never experienced so much pain in my life.

Later that afternoon, homicide investigators arrived at my hospital bed to take a routine statement. Standard operating procedures. As the entourage walked into the door, the lead detective was none other than Sergeant Ray Beck, the same man I admired in uniform at the Airport and watched with fascination during the Thorbahn murder investigation. He said my actions were proper, and that they had arrested the woman who shot me.

While the statements were being taken, hospital staff members gathered around in fascination. The story was in the news. I felt like a celebrity.

During my five-day stay, Grace never visited the hospital. Neither did I expect her. But a young LPN who looked on during the statement was very impressed. Each day, she checked in on me every hour on the hour, chatted for long periods, and rubbed my back with alcohol. Great hospital, I thought.

Wracked with grief, my mother visited daily and eventually picked me up the day I was released. She wasn't feeling well at all. And that worried me.

A woman named Eunice Molter had fired that rifle. Without consulting me, the State Attorney's Office accepted a plea for aggravated assault and had her sentenced to two years.

* * *

On a cool Thursday, one week before Christmas, I came to Mom's studio before she closed and asked her to stay a little longer before locking up. "Why?" she asked.

"You'll see."

Shortly after six, Artie Canonico showed up, violin case in hand. Stunned, she asked, "Artie? What are you doing here? How nice to see you. It must be over eight years now."

I could see she hadn't caught on yet. They embraced and talked a few minutes about their families. Then she realized this was a special day. "What is going on, please tell me?"

The maestro and I took seats in the center of the studio floor and began playing a Mozart duet. I played first violin (melody), he played second violin. I watched her from the corner of my eyes, and saw her hands to her face, tears streaming, lips quivering. I played my heart out. I never played better. I had disappointed her so much for so long, it was time to make it all up. When the duet ended, the audience of one rose to her feet, applauding and crying at the same time. "What a wonderful Christmas present," she said. "Since when did you...?"

The evening was as I had wished. I finally made my mother happy. And I had made myself happy. My new career would be blossoming soon, so I thought.

Mom lay her hand to her head and asked if I had any extra aspirins.

I never saw it coming.

CHAPTER TWENTY-TWO
Ordeal

Brain tumor

Two weeks after the new year rang in, Bernie called me at the house asking that I come over and help with Mom. She'd been having severe headaches, dizziness and constant nausea, so bad that she vomited everything she ate, sitting on the bathroom floor holding the toilet bowl in agony. Somehow, through the Christmas holidays and since, she had managed to hide her suffering.

Her family doctor had diagnosed her with an inner ear infection.

When I arrived, Bernie took me aside and explained how serious the condition had become. Mom resisted going to a hospital, but now it was beyond her decision. From the edge of the bed, she held her head into her hands, weeping and delirious, her gray roots showing prominently through thick and straggled auburn red, all that glamour reduced to pitiful suffering.

The day after she checked into the hospital, she went into a coma. I never saw Bernie so stressed. We were all confused.

Her dance studio was in high gear with 110 students on the roster, ages six through twenty-six, and a huge recital scheduled for the middle of May. Parents had already paid for costumes and future lessons. Routines had to be choreographed and practiced. There was no one to run the business, but me. But I had a full-time police job serving warrants, a waning marriage to sever and a little boy I was trying desperately to be a father to. My violin studies would have to go on hold for a while

At twenty-three, pert Betty Palumbo was the star student of the studio entourage, the same girl with whom I danced jazz routines back in my teens. Already an assistant teacher, she agreed to work as the primary instructor for all classes until my mother got well. I'd handle the business end.

Mom remained in a coma for five days until Doctor Ken Luxenberg, a one-eyed neurologist, explained that she had a tumor at the back of her brain. With medicine, she had come out of her coma, as if she'd come back from the dead.

I stood by as the doctor explained her condition and her need for surgery. She wept, then asked if the tumor was malignant.

"We won't know that until we go inside and see," he said.

"Okay," she said. "Let's get it over with."

When he left the room, she motioned with a waving hand. "Well, I guess my life is now in the hands of *Cyclops*."

Bernie was not handling this well. He became bedridden at home claiming that he felt weak and dizzy when he stood up, and out of breath. His son, Jerry, was in the military overseas, and his daughter Phyllis, now seventeen, was in her senior year in high school. She began staying at home to help her father during the crisis.

Meanwhile, I tried desperately to reach Betty Jo for a visit with Bennett so I could bring him to the hospital for Mom. She adored her grandson. That's when I learned that Bennett had been diagnosed with a serious heart murmur and needed surgery. "No exertion," she said. "Visits will have to wait until next month sometime."

Life spiraled into disarray.

I paced outside the operating room, alone, for eight hours on the day of Mom's surgery. When the doctor came out, he announced the tumor was malignant. My mother was going to die. The stark realization hit me like a truck. I could not imagine my mother *dead*.

"She'll go home and improve for a while," he said.

"Then the tumors will form again, and she'll regress."

"How long?" I asked, my eyes welling.

"Three to nine months."

I felt the weight of the world on my shoulders that afternoon. There was no fixing this, no turning back, no remedy. I was going to watch my mother suffer a painfully slow death, this rock of a woman who had loved and sacrificed for me all her life, and whom I had disappointed terribly. Grace was in the kitchen when I arrived home. After telling her the news, I went into the bedroom and sat on the edge of the bed and broke out sobbing. Grace stood near to me. Though we'd not been close, I thought she might console me in this moment of need. I had no one else. I'll never forget her words: "What's the big deal? Everyone has to die sometime."

The next morning, I packed my things and moved into my mother's house. Later that same day, Doctor Basso checked Bernie into the hospital with heart failure. This time, it was no charade.

Later that week, I filed for divorce. My task was to take my mother home two weeks after surgery, make sure she was comfortable, give her steroid shots every four hours, twenty-four hours a day, to keep the brain from swelling, then feed her, give her shots of scotch, plenty of cigarettes with the healthy filters, just love her and give her hope. She repeatedly asked what Cyclops had said about the tumor being malignant or benign. I assured her it was benign, that she going to live and get well and dance again, and run the recital in May. I could not imagine telling her that her life was over. I wanted her to enjoy her final weeks and months as though there was hope. I wanted to see her smile again.

When I brought Mom home, Bernie remained in the hospital. He was not recovering very well. He had lost weight, his face sallow, strength gone.

Thanks to an understanding boss, Lieutenant Ed Janofsky, I managed to maintain my job in Warrants Bureau, working most of the day, assigned cases only in the north end so I could periodically stop in for my mother and for Bernie while on duty. Mom was now able to teeter on her feet, her head in a turban. I made her meals, helped her to the toilet, cleaned her bed, gave her shots, and spent more time talking with her than I had in the previous twenty-six years.

Betty Palumbo ran the studio operations. I stopped in every day to keep the books and handle the banking.

Bernie needed money. Several *customers* and other seedy associates owed him huge sums of cash which could only be picked up in person. From his hospital bed, he dispatched Phyllis—now 17—to make rounds for collection, using his car. I suppose he could have asked me, but even in his darkest of times, he kept me clean from involvement on his side of the fence.

Nevertheless, this was a dangerous job for a young teenage girl to be doing alone. For four days, when I got off duty, I helped Phyllis collect the array of payments owed to my bookmaker stepfather. Most were reluctantly cooperative, not very happy about coughing up money owed on loans and bets. One guy was a total jerk, screaming nasty epithets at Phyllis and me, then throwing five hundred dollars in cash at us to pick up. I thought, surely, we'd end up in a fight or maybe even shot. How would I explain that to Lieutenant Janofsky?

During the chaos, I stayed in touch with my grandmother in New York City, and Mom's sister, Aunt Frances. They were the only family I had left, and with the burdens that now befell me, I had hoped for assistance. Such would not be the case. My grandmother, then 77, eventually came down by train to stay one week, as a final goodbye to her eldest daughter. Frances elected to stay in New York. A judgmental sister, she thought my mother had lived the wild life, smoking, drinking, and carousing. She showed little sympathy. Whatever the reason, no one would help.

Mom suffered a setback with returning headaches.

The doctor said to bring her back to the hospital for another week. She occupied a room on the fourth floor while Bernie was on the second floor. That same week, my boy, Bennett, then five, was checked into Jackson Memorial Hospital for heart surgery to close a small hole between the ventricles of his heart.

I spent an entire day pacing floors at Jackson Memorial Hospital during Bennett's operation, while eating my guts overhearing Betty Jo and her new husband telling doctors and staff that they were the boy's parents, ignoring me. The surgery was a success. But the times were certainly harrowing, with my mother and stepfather in separate hospital rooms with terminal conditions, and my son undergoing major heart surgery, all at the same time.

Once she stabilized, I brought Mom home again and resumed the twenty-four hour care, still holding the job and taking care of the studio. Because of all the stress and the need to finish her senior-year studies, Phyllis moved into a friend's house, leaving Mom and me completely alone. We notified the Marine Corps that Jerry's father was terminal and likely to die very soon. They arranged for emergency leave. Jerry was home within three days, staying at the house, a self-absorbed egomaniac. (In my humble opinion)

Grace had quietly moved out of our house and in with her parents. The marriage that never was, would soon end. We never spoke again.

Two nights after Bernie had been moved to Intensive Care, I stood alone with him at his bedside. Phyllis and Jerry were downstairs in the waiting room. Now rail thin and hardly recognizable, his face had broken out in lesions and he smelled rancid, like a rotting carcass. I thought about 1949, when my mother slapped me before seeing Willie Strauss, my other stepfather, in his deathbed.

"Your father is dying," she said, with fire in her eyes. "Don't give me any more trouble."

Looking at Bernie, so many things went through my head. I wanted to hug this man, and thank him for being the only real father I truly knew, who took me on as though I were his son, who guided my life into stability and prosperity, and who made sure I remained an honest cop amid a sea of corruption. I thought about the road trips to upstate Florida, when I drove him to the prison once a month to visit his convict friends, who laughed at my stupid jokes, and who told me stories about the old days in the streets with famous gangsters, paying protection money to politicians and cops. This man, who had said he knew no other life but the con game, but insisted I keep my nose clean. What a man. If only he'd grown up in a different environment.

As Bernie's head sunk into the pillow, barely breathing, he managed a glance up to me and asked for a sip of ginger ale. I held the paper cup as he sipped from the straw. When I replaced the cup on the table, I looked down again. His mouth had fallen open, eyes closed. It was over.

My eyes, the last he ever saw, my hand the last touch he ever felt.

After I rode down the elevator, I saw Phyllis and Jerry kidding and laughing. They saw my face, and the laughter came to an abrupt halt. "Come upstairs," I said, somberly. Inside the elevator, Phyllis asked what was wrong. When I could not answer, she went into hysterics.

The Bernie story had reached its conclusion.

Later that night, I poured my mother a double glass of Dewars before telling her the grim news. Perhaps she was affected by the medication, or the brain trauma, but she only shrugged. "Well," she said, "I knew he'd leave me. I guess I'm a widow again."

The next morning, at the house, I caught a glimpse of Jerry trying on his father's sports jackets and jewelry, posing before the mirror. I restrained my impulses.

For the next three days, I hired a full-time nurse to care for Mom while I attended Bernie's funeral in New York. That's where his sisters, brothers and older kids were living. All so familiar, the black clothing, the wailing, the yarmulkes. All that was missing was Mom.

Days later, Jerry returned to the Marines, while Phyllis stayed at her friend's to finish her schooling without interruptions. As always, I was alone on this journey.

As Mom's hair started to grow out, I tried helping her with a dye job, but failed miserably, leaving her with pink-orange hair about one inch long around her head. That's when I bought her a dark auburn wig to satisfy her vanity.

For the next three or four weeks, we talked hours at a time, planning trips to Europe that would never be, about playing violin and piano together in the future, and of her dance recitals, her past in show business and her future as a single woman again. She seemed to improve, taking her own baths, watching television, even playing a few notes on the piano now and then. But as time passed, just as the doctor had predicted, she started to regress, teetering on her feet, speech slurring, eyes unfocused. She began dropping her drinks and her cigarettes, rambling on about nonsense, and then defecating in her bed. I wanted to keep her at home as long as possible, to prolong her life, to give her back what she had given me—Love.

"When you love someone, always be there, no matter what, especially in the hard times."

One day, I found her holding her head in her hands. I knew we'd crossed over the bridge, from life toward death. The headaches were returning, and no medicine, no steroids would help her. The tumors had reformed in full force. She became delirious. I couldn't care for her at this point and returned her to the hospital.

At the end of May, thanks to Betty Palumbo, the studio's recital went off perfectly. When I told Mom about it in the hospital, she didn't know what I was talking about. Instead, she reached out into thin air trying to grasp something that wasn't there. Then she went into a final coma. Doctor Luxenberg (old Cyclops) said he could keep her alive for a couple months with medicine, if I wanted. I told him, "No." It was time to let her go.

In the early morning hours of June 3rd, I'd been sitting near her bed while her breathing had grown so loud, she sounded like a braying mule. She had lost two of her front teeth and her face had developed lesions, just like Bernie's. She also reeked of that same rancid odor I remembered from Bernie's death bed. I closed the hospital room door, so other patients wouldn't be disturbed by her raspy noises. I'd become accustomed to the rhythm of those breathing sounds, having heard them all night long. Then, while I sat in the plastic chair half asleep, I awakened a the deafening sound of silence. Her breathing had stopped.

I felt so alone.

Services were held two days later. A gathering of about fifty showed up. Many of her friends were there and a few of mine. Phyllis and Jerry, the kids she had step-mothered, were absent. Her mother and her sister were also not there for her, or for me.

As I reflected, I think my friends would have been more involved with me in the whole ordeal, but they thought that others were filling the support role. They just didn't know.

I lost control. Now it was me with the contorted face, weeping until I could not breathe, consumed in grief. I don't even know who was sitting near me. All I remember was driving home after, entering her empty house, and sitting, and crying until my stomach hurt. I couldn't imagine a world without Vivien. No longer would there be someone I could call Mom.

Once a glamorous showgirl herself, vivacious Beatrice LaVerne operated her own dance studio on Miami Beach and was a longtime friend of my mother's. As I sat in my mother's Florida room later that day, a car pulled up outside on the gravel drive. Beatrice stepped quickly up the walkway and entered the house without knocking. When she saw that I was alone, she came and sat next to me, and said some really nice things. I remember collapsing into her lap as she stroked my head. During those few comforting moments, I realized how much I had missed human contact.

Four days later, my divorce was final.

My mother, Vivien. c. 1935

Sonia and me, Arcady, NY 1949

Me and my violin, age 16

Dancing a lá Peter Pan with the Palumbo Sisters
(1955)

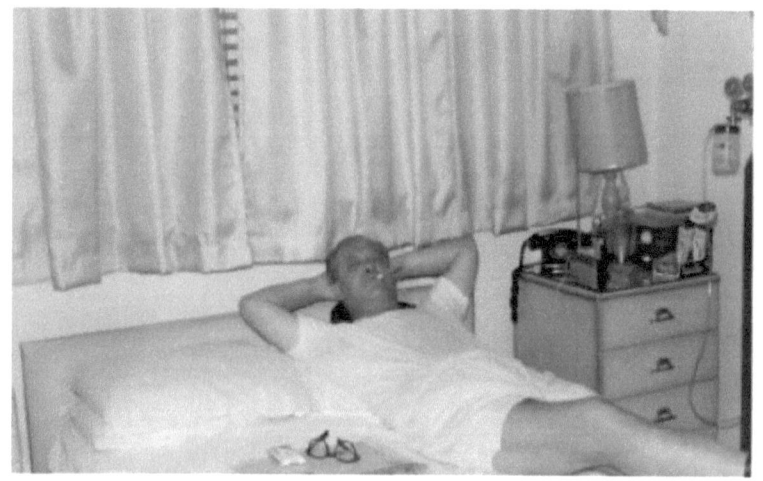

Stepfather, Bernie, hard work
(Note cigar and oxygen tank)

Mom and Bernie, c. 1958

Rookie cop, 1960

CSI Commander – Hard work (1975)

The witness told me to stick it in my ear.
(1972)

At a recent book signing. Back to Violins.

CHAPTER TWENTY-THREE
Taking Out the Garbage

Outside of physical requisites—food, clothing, shelter, etc.—I believe the most essential need for any human being is love. It is the nourishment of human emotion. Those who are without love often turn to God, like convicts in prison who feel abandoned by the outside world.

Kids who grow up with love and nurturing usually become stable and secure human beings. Children who grow up without love fill our prison systems.

When people have love in their lives, its value often goes unappreciated. Love is one of those unseen, unscented, untouchable entities that many fail to treasure, until it doesn't exist.

The death of my mother, and the ordeal of the preceding six months, turned my life upside down in many ways. I could cope with grief and stress and responsibilities. I could live without playing violin and without seeing very much of my little boy. I could handle the job I didn't want as a cop. But I couldn't bear the thought of living without love.

As long as my mother existed, there was at least one human being on earth who loved me unconditionally. The love of girlfriends and wives, and relatives had either been temporary or at best, superficial. I felt sympathy from others, but love from no one. Mom was gone.

Love—was gone.

Imagine being on a large ocean liner when the ship sinks. Everyone is dead but you, and you are floating in a lifeboat that has no oars in the middle of the ocean.

I really did think about rolling overboard. A tall glass of whiskey in one hand, my .38 revolver trembling in the other. After all, my second marriage failed. My son had been converted into the son of another man. My job meant nothing. My ambition to resume music studies died when Mom died.

Instead, I thought about Joan Simms, that voluptuous dark-haired waitress from the IHOP with whom I'd enjoyed a few rolls in the hay. I called her up. After all, we had made love together. Sure enough, she'd been divorced. And, she was available. We met. We did "it." I gushed over hearing her say three words that I craved: *"I love you."* Three months later, she and her three little children moved into Mom's house with me. (Randy, age 9, Annette, age 7, Russell, age 4)

I had love in my life again. Multiplied by four.

* * *

When I got back to work, I was shocked to learn I'd been transferred to Internal Affairs. That was pretty cool, a new assignment, and a prestigious one at that. I don't know how or why it was arranged. After all, Bernie was now dead. But I reported to the third floor office with great enthusiasm.

I thought I'd be working under cover, checking out dishonest cops, and probing complaints about police brutality and corruption. Not so. I spent the next two months running backgrounds of applicants for palmist licenses and gun permits—not very exciting. But I thought that was a good thing, making sure anyone who wanted to carry a gun was checked out by police, to make sure he or she wasn't a nut. That entailed a complete investigation, including checks of credit reports, rap sheets, driving records and interviewing employers, friends and neighbors. A far cry from the non-standards of today.

Meanwhile, the department was in crisis. Corruption expose`s saturated the newspapers and television media with stories about Sheriff Tal Buchanan and his cronies, Manson Hill (Chief of Detectives) and Leslie VanBuskirk (now the Police Division chief) the same two guys who took payoffs from Bernie, plus Maxie Berman, the tough detective sergeant who brought me to take the police test, and others. If Bernie was alive, he'd have been devastated to know that his connections went down the tubes.

After six weeks in I.A. I was notified to report to Criminal Intelligence. Wow! That's with the big boys, the heavyweights of the department. How did that happen?

This was the mysterious brain trust of police investigations, where real undercover cops dug up dirt on well-known criminals and disseminated information throughout the department. They conducted surveillance, intimidated mobsters, busted organized crime figures and made them flip on other hoods. Criminal Intelligence enjoyed a special enigma, for no one really knew what was going on behind those doors. Everything, was confidential. Mysterious. Interesting.

So I thought.

The unit was being run by Maxie Berman, one of the cops under scrutiny by the press and the FBI for corruption activity. Nevertheless, the unit continued to operate as though nothing was wrong. I figured, because of my connection with Bernie, they thought I could be trusted. I would never have worked there if Bernie was still alive. Now, it didn't matter.

The first day I walked through the doors of Criminal Intelligence, I felt like I was entering the hallowed halls of the CIA. Inside, all I saw was four or five desks crowding a small office with glum-looking detectives sitting there reading newspapers, talking on the phone, or doing crossword puzzles. A second smaller office was in the rear, but I was told not to go in there.

Under obvious stress, Berman moved furtively in and out of the office smoking one cigarette after another. He rarely talked to me. "You'll work with Larry Schum," he said with that strained New York accent. "He'll tell you what to do."

Okeydokey.

A skinny chain-smoker from New York, Schum had more nervous tics than anyone I ever knew. My training was relegated to searches for important newspaper articles, cutting them out and placing them into associated files. That became my job. Cutting articles from newspapers every day for the next month.

Meanwhile, I watched the anti-communist paranoia unfold as Hilmer Erickson, a detective on assignment, ran up and down the department's stairwell wearing a fake beard, sneaking in and out of the building and into that mysterious back room where he was plugged into a telephone talking to newspaper reporters. He looked like a character from Laugh-in.

I was told to study my book, *None Dare Call It Treason,* by John Stormer, an anti-communist paperback that suggested half of the U.S. Government were conspirators trying to dismantle democracy. According to Hill and Berman and others, our own county government was rife with communists. One of the goals of the

Criminal Intelligence unit was to ferret out and expose them. Little Hilmer Erickson, who was plucked from the police academy with little or no experience as a street cop, was sent to infiltrate meetings of civic groups, in churches, town halls, etc., and then report back to Maxie Berman, who in turn, reported back to Van Buskirk and Manson Hill. The paranoid inner circle of police echelon under scrutiny by FBI and the media tried their best to sidetrack those investigations by labeling government officials as anti-American. If any of the county commissioners, or other notables, took a liberal stance on issues, they were immediately tagged a communist and reporters were secretly fed that information.

But, my job—as Bernie often said—was to watch and listen, and keep my mouth shut. That was easy for a newspaper clipper.

As the media bore down with daily stories, and the FBI led a relentless probe, the department's reputation went into shambles. Under a cloud of cynicism and suspicion, honest police officers throughout the department suffered tremendous hardship maintaining respect and cooperation from local citizens.

Manson Hill was smooth, but he was also brazen and sloppy. One day, while sitting in a detective's car, he didn't know the mike button was stuck in the "on" position. That's when everyone on police radio overheard him talking to Captain Richard Gladwell about taking payoffs.

Days before that, Hill and his wife were at Hialeah race track when a woman spotted a diamond bracelet on Mrs. Hill's wrist. The woman went hysterical. It was her bracelet, stolen in a burglary just weeks before.

Hill was known to be in cahoots with various and sundry shylocks, fences and thieves, under the guise, naturally, of obtaining intelligence information. Included among these was Lefty Rosenthal, whom I'd seen sitting in Hill's office on two occasions. A Las Vegas based movie was made about Lefty twenty years later, called Casino. Robert DeNiro played his role.

Meanwhile, I managed to get out of the office one day when Larry Schum and I were ordered on a stakeout. I thought this was going to be exciting. Our job was to watch a houseboat from across the river on 77th Street, near where the Playboy Club was located, and not far from that Italian restaurant where I played violin until the shots rang out from the kitchen. I really didn't know what we were looking for, other than to make notes about what cars came and went. Who knows? We were probably shuffled out of the office by Maxie Berman for ulterior reasons.

The stake-out turned out nothing, though I did learn that Larry Schum was a thief. Either that, or he was testing to see if I was a thief. Before this, all I knew about Schum was that he was a friend of Berman's. That, alone, was enough for an indictment.

"Hey, Marsh," he said, in his nasal New York accent. "Let me tell ya, how I make good money. Maybe you wanna go in with me, like a team?"

"What's that, Larry?"

"Ladies purses. See? They put them down around the swimming pools, next to the lounges when they go in the water. It's easy. Just walk by, take the purse, later on you pull out the money, then dump it in a garbage can."

"Really?"

"Yeah. One of us can be a spotter, then other takes the purses. Wanna go in?"

I didn't know what to say. I certainly did not want to be a purse snatcher, but I didn't want Schum or his cronies to mistrust me. If I pacified him and agreed, he might drive directly to The Fontainebleau Hotel where I'd find myself in a compromising position, and perhaps even go to jail. If I said no, he'd think I was a rat, and my Criminal Intelligence career would be short lived. Maybe, because of my known connection to Bernie, he figured I was a crook like everyone else. There certainly was no one to report him to, especially Maxie Berman.

"Uh, Larry, that's not my style. Thanks for the offer, anyway."

"Hey, Marsh. No sweat, buddy."

Whew!

* * *

Like most people in my social milieu, I had a low opinion of garbage men in 1966. They were usually poor, black and uneducated, and they smelled. I'd always lived in a segregated society, with a segregated mentality. Garbage men worked at one of those unglorified but necessary civil service jobs that folks like myself would never think of doing.

My perspectives changed in the summer of 1966. The county's waste collectors union went on strike.

A small group of scabs (union busters) agreed to work, and they were subjected to threats of violence. Garbage pick-up had to continue. To protect the workers, the county ordered every garbage truck in Dade County manned by an armed police officer until the strike was over.

How thrilling. My stint in Criminal Intelligence was plenty to brag about. I been reduced to a newspaper clipper, (and nearly recruited as a purse snatcher) and now I was being sent out to ride shotgun on garbage trucks.

Six A.M. sharp, I reported to the Waste Management facility in West Dade and boarded the truck. Whew, did it smell. A large, black fellow drove, while two more blacks rode the rear platform. This was mid August, the height of summer in South Florida.

While times have since changed for the better, garbage cans in 1966 were made of galvanized metal, much heavier than the plastics of today. And residents kept their garbage cans in back yards, usually two each, requiring the workers to walk behind every house and carry the heavy cans to the truck for disposal.

One of the workers stood no taller than five foot, four inches, but he was built solid and strong, like a fireplug. The men worked non-stop, laughing, jiving, never missing a step, back and forth, hustling every minute of the day with the exception of a fifteen minute break for a fast sandwich and a drink. Their goal was to finish by 1:00 P.M. and take the rest of the day off.

I'd never seen human beings work so hard, while maintaining an upbeat attitude. To me, they were friendly and cordial, happy I was there. By the day's end, they surely smelled, just like anyone would smell working that hard under a hot Miami sun for seven hours.

The assignment lasted three long days. I'd never want to do it again. But it did leave me with a new found respect for *Sanitation Engineers*.

From there, I thought I was headed back to cutting newspapers. I was wrong.

CHAPTER TWENTY-FOUR
Homicide

In August of 1966, the proverbial shit hit the fan. The media went into a scandal frenzy. Sheriff Buchanan and his cronies were indicted for various and sundry charges, along with a myriad of thugs from the world of organized crime. Seems that Bernie died just in time. His greatest nightmare would have come true, Doc Basso or no Doc Basso.

The department was left without leadership. A select cadre of high ranking officers were appointed periodically as interim heads until the county commission could arrange a special election that would return the sheriff's position from an elected post, to an appointed director. They used Buchanan as an example of why elected police officials could not be trusted. With a police director reporting to a county manager, the central government of Dade County would take over controls of the largest police agency in the southeast United States.

Everyone in the Criminal Intelligence Unit—about five of us— were under scrutiny, because authorities, and the media, assumed we were all one big family of crooks. But it wasn't true. A detective sergeant named Ray Haar, an honest journeyman cop who eventually served over thirty years on the job, was put in charge until a new director could sort out the good guys from the bad.

For me, it was time to get out of there. I didn't want the new department hierarchy to think I was *one of them*. I submitted a transfer request back to safe haven: Warrants Bureau.

Affable Richard Plager had just been promoted to Major of Detective Bureau replacing Manson Hill, who was on unpaid suspension pending trial. Many considered Plager an oddball who marched to the tune of a different drummer, an accountant by night, a cop by day, and an I.Q. somewhere in the stratosphere. He walked funny, like a rag doll, and talked like stand-up comic at a Jewish vaudeville show. I'd seen him around the hallways, but never once said hello. I didn't even realize he knew me.

"Report to Major Plager's office," Ray Haar barked one morning. "I don't know what it's about."

I shrugged. What would the new chief of detectives want with me?

Plager sat me down at the table which extended from his desk, waffled his head and smiled with a shit-eating grin. "Hey, Marshall, how would you like to work Homicide?"

The question stunned me. Visions of Sergeant Ray Beck and all the other well-dressed dicks flashed through me head, the Thorbahn case, bodies, crime scenes, the department elite. Me? In Homicide?

"Well. Yeah, sure. But why are...?"

"If you want to work Homicide, you'll work Homicide."

Yes! But I couldn't figure it out. Why me?

Plager summoned Captain Lou Spaeth, head of Homicide, to come into the office. Spaeth had the looks and stature of a movie star, tall, confident, immaculate suit, dark wavy hair speckled with gray at the temples. The moment he walked into Plager's office, he gave me a dirty look. Plager announced, "Hey, Lou. Meet Marshall Frank. He's your new homicide detective."

Spaeth's face turned blood red. "Godammit, Dick, you know who I wanted."

Plager waffled again, and smiled to me. "Marshall, leave the room, okay?"

As I waited in the secretary's office, Spaeth's angry voice could be heard three blocks away, ranting and raving. I thought about opening the door and saying, "Forget it, it's okay." But then, I knew this might be my only chance ever of working in Homicide. If the captain didn't want me, I'd have to prove my worth. Obviously the loser in the argument, Spaeth burst out of Plager's office and barked,

"Follow me." As we stepped lively down the halls, he turned and waved a finger, "Remember, Frank, everything you do here is critical. Don't forget that."

I didn't. The mere thought that I had to perform in a critical environment piqued my incentive further. I wanted this.

It was the first time I'd been inside the homicide office since the massive Thorbahn case, three years before.

There they were: Bob Laws, the hunter, Bobby Jones, the boyish genius, Jay Huff, the string bean, C. T. Clark, Mr. Meticulous, and Ray Beck, the articulate prima donna I'd admired since I was a rookie.

Spaeth turned me over to a crusty old cigar chomping lieutenant named John Esty, toothless as old Sergeant Craver, and said to him, "Here's your new detective. See what you can do."

Esty had nothing to say to me. If ever I felt unwanted, this was it. But I had nothing to lose, everything to gain. Esty called Ray Beck into the office. "Ray, this is your new trainee. Make a detective out of him."

That was the day that my job morphed into a career. Why Major Dick Plager selected me for Homicide, and stood up to strong resistance, remains a mystery to this day. Ray Beck would later tell me that I had developed a reputation as a slick report writer, a prerequisite for Homicide. Somehow, though, I figured Bernie must still have been looking out after me, even in absentia. And, just as he always warned, I didn't ask questions.

* * *

In the beginning, all was bliss in my household, with three kids to play daddy to, and a beautiful young woman who craved sex as much as, or more, than me.

The kids were gorgeous. Randy, the oldest, was ninety percent deaf. He had been attending a school for retarded children in North Miami, basically a class of miscellaneous handicaps in various form, and a waste of time. I helped Joan enroll him at the Florida School for Deaf and Blind in St. Augustine.

Annette was the apple of Joan's eye, a beautiful dark-haired girl who yearned for family stability and a father.

Russell was the youngest, a four-year-old boy who spoke with a strained voice and uttered the funniest and most innocent comments ever to come from a child's mouth.

Joan was happy to see me in Homicide because I was happy to be there. Much of what I'd dreamed of—short of having Bennett in my life—had come true in a matter of months. Love. Family. A trophy girl friend.

Acceptance by the department elite. It was like having played ball in the minors, then drafted by the New York Yankees. I made it into the major leagues of policedom.

Joan wanted attention. Lots of attention. Joan wanted sex. Joan wanted nice clothes, and nice furnishings, and the best of foods and restaurants. I wanted to give her all of these things, but a paltry paycheck had its limits.

The concept of overtime pay, in 1966, was just that: A concept. No one thought about extra pay for extended hours. We worked cases to the bare bones, no matter the hours, because that's what was required. I could not earn any more than I earned. I wanted no more failures.

I proposed. She accepted.

On May 19, 1967, Ralph Ferguson, the same bulldog judge who presided over my marriage to Grace three years before, performed an informal ceremony in chambers, all for the cost of another bottle of Cutty Sark.

* * *

I was lucky to be assigned the best trainer a new detective could ask for. Ray Beck put his heart and soul into teaching. First, and foremost, the Medical Examiner's Office. "The autopsy is the core of evidence in a murder," he said. "It's important that you work closely with the pathologists." And so we did. Standing around decayed bodies and watching autopsies now took on a new dimension where I saw beyond the unpleasant and worked with new goals. *How did this man die? Where are the pieces of evidence? What's the trajectory of the bullet? What are the stomach contents? Are there any defense wounds? Check in the nose, mouth, ears, anus, fingernails, toes, crotch,* for anything that might yield evidence.

Next, he introduced me to every Major Crimes prosecutor at the State Attorney's Office where I received indoctrination on the importance of presenting a complete and thorough case file.

We spent hours in the Crime Laboratory talking with forensic scientists about trace evidence, hairs, fibers, blood and body fluids, ballistics, handwriting analysis, tool marks, tire tracks, photography, polygraph and more.

CHAPTER TWENTY-FIVE
Deciphering Death

I remained under Ray Beck's wing nearly two months before I handled my first case alone. I wondered how Captain Spaeth felt after learning that Beck had given the thumbs-up sign to Lieutenant Esty, saying I'd made the grade. I was, indeed, homicide detective material. I made the team.

Just as in the case of little Rolando Arguello who drowned in Miller Lake, my only real problems were in dealing with family, friends and loved ones of deceased people. Dead bodies, gore, blood, the stench of decay, stomping around in swamp, working a street scene in a driving rain, sweltering under a noon Miami sun, were all unpleasantries, but nothing could compare to the emotional drain of handling the assembly line of broken hearts, for they were always there, case after case after case. That was an integral part of the job, rarely depicted in newscasts, motion pictures and novels.

And while homicide detectives are often acclaimed for investigating murders, I learned that the greatest part of the job was not murders, but death cases of all kinds, including unattended natural deaths, accidental deaths and suicides, all in the interest of eliminating any possibility of foul play. In my first month with Ray Beck, we investigated three rapes, four natural deaths, two suicides, five accidental deaths—including a lightning strike—and not a single murder. I sat in on a major murder trial prosecuted by Gerald Kogan, who later became the Chief Justice of the Florida Supreme Court in the 1990s. Those kinds of things taught me the art of investigating a crime scene, identifying evidence, working with forensic experts, legal issues dealing with search and seizure, interrogation, and using all the department's resources as needed.

As part of my arsenal of field equipment, Beck suggested I carry a small bottle of Old Spice cologne and a spare handkerchief with me at all times. They came in handy when I worked my first case alone.

Living as a widower in a mobile home park, an old retired jockey named [2]Jake DeMauro smelled a foul odor emanating from Mrs. Whittle's trailer next door. It had been a very warm day in November. The unmistakable stench cloaked the entire park. I wondered why someone hadn't called sooner.

The small mobile home was sealed, windows and doors locked. That indicated a self-contained incident, most probably not a murder. I knocked a few times, for show, but we all knew that was futile. I needed assistance from the maintenance man who used a crow bar to pry open the front door. That's when the hoard of flies blasted from inside to outside, like something from a horror movie. Once inside the darkened room, it was difficult to see anything through the thickness of flying insects. The maintenance man gagged. Onlookers gathered on the street, covering their faces with towels. I brought out my handy Old Spice and hanky, covered my face, took a deep breath and stepped inside.

This was one of those days when the old cliché held true. *It's a tough job, but somebody has to do it.*

Jake DeMauro said she was a cranky old widow who had lived alone for many years and minded her own business. No friends. One surviving daughter living in Maine. Few other sources of information.

She lay on the linoleum floor, fully dressed, her body blackened and bloated beyond recognition. No signs of a gun or other weapon. Suicide was doubtful. No note, no drugs.

There were many possibilities. She may have fallen and hit her head. She may have had a heart attack. My job was to sort through her belongings, search for clues and get her shipped to the morgue for an autopsy. I tried to perform a brief physical body examination, but the stench was too much to bear. My shoes were sticking to the body fluids that had not yet dried on the floor.

One clue did it. In searching the house, I discovered a bottle of scotch had been smashed and lay in pieces inside a garbage can in the kitchen sink. Dried blood covered some of the shards. Next to it, a dust pan lay on the floor with smaller pieces of broken glass still inside.

---

[2] Jake DeMauro – fictitious name

Mrs. Whittle was, indeed, smashed. Her blood alcohol level was .32, three times the drunk driving threshold. The Medical Examiner found a small cut in the top of her forehead. By all indications, Mrs. Whittle staggered with the bottle in hand, fell and cut her head. As she tried to clean up the mess, she continued to bleed. And because her blood had thinned from so many years of heavy drinking, it lost the capacity to coagulate. From a small cut, she collapsed on the floor in a stupor and bled to death.

When the death was classified as "accidental" the $10,000 life insurance policy ballooned into a $20,000 benefit for her daughter.

This was a small case, unworthy of newspaper print and insignificant to the department. But it validated my worth as a new homicide investigator, putting pieces of a puzzle together, working with forensic scientists and reaching an important conclusion.

* * *

Everything did not always go so well.

On a Sunday just past noon, the on-duty shift lieutenant sent me down to Goulds to investigate the death of a woman in a private home. "A probable natural," he said. Sounded easy enough.

Goulds was an unincorporated district in the rural south of Dade County comprised entirely of poor black residents and a few small black-owned businesses, such as grocery stores, barber shops and garages. Annie Mae Fowler* was a mammoth woman who weighed over four hundred pounds. She had just returned to her small wood-frame house with friends and family after attending church services. Like every Sunday, they all gathered for snacks, sodas and tea, about eight or nine of them, mostly women.

While they were talking in the living room, one of the ladies noticed that Annie Mae had laid her thick head back against the top of the sofa. They all continued to laugh and talk, not realizing that Annie Mae was dead, until Mrs. Tucker laughed aloud and slapped Annie Mae on the knee. Annie Mae did not respond. Mrs. Tucker stood up, indignantly, and walked into another room. The initial caller told the complaint desk officer, "Could you please send someone to pick up a body?" as though we were Animal Control being asked to remove a snake in the grass.

Upon arriving, I was amazed to see the small house abuzz with friends and relatives still gathered around, sipping tea and sodas like nothing had happened, while the huge body of Annie Mae Fowler sat in the middle of the sofa like Buddha staring at the ceiling in a death gaze. I asked everyone to leave.

The investigation was the easy part. What lay ahead was getting Annie Mae out the door and into the morgue van, inappropriately referred to by some as the "meat wagon."

In those days, morgue wagons were not equipped with high-tech gurneys. The drivers were usually thin weirdo-looking guys with big eyes and bushy eyebrows, who never spoke unless spoken to. After all, who would really aspire to such a job, transporting dead people around, all sizes, shapes and... ugh... conditions.

In this case, the attendants would need the assistance of the uniformed officer and me. This was a very sensitive moment, because we had to take Annie Mae from the couch, lay her on a stretcher and cover her with a sheet. The four of us would each take a corner and carry her from the house to the van, while neighbors, friends and relatives stood outside watching. It was like trying to lift a hippo. But we managed.

Then came the somber trek from front door, down the porch steps, across the yard and into the wagon. A dozen bulging eyeballs looked on as I held my end of the stretcher rod with two hands. So did the other cop. It could not have gone worse. Annie Mae listed to one side, and before we could adjust her, she rolled over and onto the grass like a giant sack of potatoes, face down.

The crowd erupted into a chorus.

"Eeeiiiiggghhh!"

"Oh, Lordie! No, Annie Mae."

"Ahhhh.... Yiiiieee!"

"Dear Jesus, poor Annie Mae!"

If ever there was a time I could crawl under a rock and never come out, this was it. All I could see was a sidewalk full of white eyeballs staring at me. Yes, we managed to get her back onto the stretcher and into the van. I disappeared from Goulds, not to return for a very long time.

* * *

It was nice to feel loved again by my new wife, and by Annette, Randy, and little Russell. While the new marriage enhanced my life, the relationship with Bennett was at an all time low. I still tried to arrange visits, but Betty Jo remained ever evasive. When I phoned, Bennett, then six, was not permitted to call me "Daddy". He whispered "Marshall" with his hand cupped over the receiver, then, "I'm sorry, my mother's here. I can't call you daddy." During one rare weekend visit, he brought his baseball glove. I noticed his name was written on the inside, "Bennett Gertz." When I confronted Betty Jo on the telephone, she said it was important to her family unity. She asked if I would permit Bill Gertz to adopt. The answer: "No."

As per court order, Joan's ex-husband was supposed to pay child support, but he often reneged or made partial payments. Neither did he visit with the kids very often. Sensing a new found charge of fatherhood, I offered to adopt them all, thereby relieving the natural father of support obligations. The only stipulation, was that he'd step out of their lives. He agreed. In the sweep of a judge's signature, I became the father of four, not one.

* * *

I hadn't realized then, that I had probably chomped into far more than I could chew. While I reveled in my new role as a homicide detective, and new father of three, and husband of one, my private craving was for pockets of solitude, to be alone sometimes, to write into a daily journal, to play my violin and my piano whenever I felt the need, and to reflect on my family's life. I had enclosed the carport into a small music room, a replica, in fact, of that little closet room at the Silver Palm Hotel where I could be totally alone and cuddle my blonde doll when the rest of the world was in turmoil. It was a place I could be me, not who I was supposed to be.

After a long night of handling a house fire where I picked up the charred remains of a little girl from the rubble, I came home deep in thought, hoping to find space and solitude in my little music room. At 12:30 A.M., I sat at the baby grand piano to play a quiet rendition of Fur Elise when the door opened. It was Joan. "Aren't you going to pay any attention to me?"

Yes. Of course.

CHAPTER TWENTY-SIX
Unjust rewards

In the winter months of 1967, the war in Viet Nam raged on with nearly a half million American soldiers fighting for democracy. We all chilled at the daily reports of deaths and casualties. Another casualty, of sorts, was the heavyweight boxing title which had belonged to Muhammad Ali, who was now stripped of it because he refused induction on religious grounds.

I might have been one of those casualties had I been called up before my discharge date. Fortunately for me, my Marine Corps reserve unit got the summons to ship out just months after I finished my obligation. Close call.

In the wake of the corruption scandal and with the support of the powerful *Miami Herald*, county management convinced voters to change the department head from an elected position, to an appointed one. They also changed the agency's name from The Sheriff's Office to the Public Safety Department. After a nationwide search, a former FBI agent named E. Wilson Purdy was hired to clean things up, change the tarnished image and professionalize us all.

And that he did. Purdy was a staunch no-frills outsider with no ties to existing personnel or local politics, other than the County Manager who hired him. Heads rolled. Demotions, promotions and transfers gave new breath to a demoralized staff. As for me, I only wanted to be left alone, to work in Homicide.

At the time, all homicide detectives held the rank of sergeant, while I was at the bottom of the pecking order, still a patrolman. I'd taken two sergeant's tests before but never cared about being promoted, always figuring my police job was only temporary. I never studied for the test. Homicide changed all that. Now I had to match up to these guys. After work every day and night, I boned up on administrative orders, legal issues, crime scene procedures, forensic science, and police psychology hoping to make the list high enough for promotion. Some 400 officers took the test. I came in twentieth.

Immediately, the top six were promoted, leaving me at fourteenth, with no vacancies. The list was good for one year, before it would expire.

* * *

It was a cool Sunday morning when I got the call from Headquarters that a dead woman had been found near a lake in Southwest Dade. By this time, I'd worked solo about two weeks handling simple DOAs. Homicide cases were given to the more experienced detectives, though I was often summoned to help with area canvassing, transporting witnesses, and so forth.

Only two detectives worked on Sundays. Bob Laws, whom I'd known from my uniform days, was following up a major whodunit that happened the previous week. He was unavailable. I was it.

Mary Ann Mosely lay supine on the bank of a rural lake under a pine tree, her caramel bronze skin glistening in the morning sunlight, eyes fixed in that now-familiar death gaze. She was pretty, full-breasted, thin and in her early twenties. The uniformed officer who cordoned off the scene had determined the probable identity of the victim from a missing person's report that had been filed the night before by her mother, not far from there. According to the report, Mary Ann had a violent argument at 1:00 A.M. with her common-law husband, who took her out of the house and forced her into his car. She had not been heard from since. Her description matched the deceased perfectly.

This was my first opportunity to play detective with a bonafide murder. The responsibility felt awesome. I wanted to do everything right. Between the fine preliminary work of the uniformed officer, the mother's statement and the assistance of a crime scene technician, my job was made easy.

First, the scene. Photographs were needed from all angles. I ordered aerial photos by helicopter to depict the scene as it was on death day, in the event they were needed for trial. I had been indoctrinated to keep court in mind at all times. *"Everything you do here is critical."*

Tire tracks were imbedded in pockets of dirt that led to the pine tree. The tracks could be traced all the way back to the paved road, about two hundred feet away. The technician thought they might be identifiable. He took angular pictures, then made plaster casts. It reminded me of the Loreen Thorbahn case, and I hoped for the same positive results.

I examined her in detail. Her body was in full rigor, indicating at least six to eight hours of death. Bluish lividity had settled in her back. I looked at my watch: 9:45 A.M. She was last seen at 1:00 A.M. Conclusion: Probably killed shortly after being forced into the car. The technicians bagged her hands in order to take nail scrapings later in the morgue. I looked into her eyes, wondering if there would ever be a way of capturing that last moment of sight.

Petechial hemorrhages—tiny blood spots—coated the whites of her eyes, a sign of asphyxiation. Fingernail marks on her neck indicated what I already thought. Strangulation. The Medical Examiner would later discover a broken hyoid bone in her throat.

I interviewed the fisherman who found the body, the victim's best friend who knew the history of violence between Mary Ann and her husband, and her mother who actually saw the fight the night before. Formal statements before a court reporter would be taken later. But time was of the essence. I had to find Jimmie Lee Warren* first.

That was easy. The victim's friend knew that Jimmie Lee hung out at a local garage where the locals gambled. I asked the uniformed officer to accompany me, in the event I needed a back-up. After all, Jimmie Lee already showed violent tendencies. There were no other detectives working.

Prepared for the worst, I entered the mechanic's bay of the darkened wood-frame gas station to find three young black men sitting around on folding chairs, smoking, giving me the evil eye as though I was the enemy. I showed my badge. "I'd like to talk to Jimmie Lee Warren," I said. The tall fellow in the middle stood up and spoke in a soft but arrogant tone. "I'm Jimmie Lee. What can I do for you?"

"Can we go outside?"

"Sure," he responded, as though he had nothing to hide.

Once outside, I asked if he was the common-law husband of Mary Ann Mosely. This would confirm that I had the right man. But the evidence, at this point, was strictly circumstantial. The mother had witnessed the argument and the violence confirming that he was likely the last person seen with the victim. No other evidence linked him to the crime, yet.

"Yes, I'm with Mary Ann. What's the problem?" He acted innocent, as though he knew nothing.

"Mary Ann is dead, Jimmie."

"What? You're telling me my wife is dead? That can't be?"

Denial! I had my man, but the task was now more difficult. I wanted to interrogate him, but the new Supreme Court rule stemming from the Miranda case in Arizona required that suspects be advised of their rights before questioning. If I asked him any questions at this point, about the argument when he tossed Mary Ann into his car, etc., the answers might not be admissible. If I questioned him here, arrogance before his friends would cloud the atmosphere. I was at a disadvantage. If I told him he was a suspect, he would probably not cooperate. If I could arrest him, he'd have no choice, but to be in my custody—away from South Dade—for the next several hours. Time for a decision.

He did not resist. The presence of a uniformed officer certainly helped, physically and psychologically. When told he was under arrest for murder, he whined and complained, but turned to the wall and assumed the search position, one that he knew quite well. Jimmie Lee had been arrested several times for an assortment of misdemeanors, and one felony burglary for which he did time.

I wanted a confession. The case was not solid enough for a sure conviction. I saw Jimmie Lee as my first attempt with hard interrogation in a murder case.

I once watched Ray Beck—the ultimate cynic—interrogate a suspect picked up in the rape of a child. Contrary to the movie images of cops standing around brow-beating a suspect, Ray took a different approach.

"Become his bosom buddy," he said. "Kill 'em with kindness. It works every time."

Now at headquarters, I had Jimmie Lee Warren on my turf, in my control. I didn't ask any questions in the beginning, just sat with him, offering cigarettes, soda, patting him on the shoulder as though I understood his sorry dilemma. I had to give him his Miranda warnings, but I also knew he didn't have the capacity to truly comprehend when I asked, "Do you understand all these warnings?" As long as he signed on the dotted line, I had full license to ask any questions I wanted. He signed. I'm sure he thought that a refusal would be a sign of guilt.

Here I was, this lily-white classical violinist who never knew a black person in his life, a well-groomed racist who knew nothing of the black culture other than the dark side, sitting with an ex-convict who was raised and role-modeled in the streets of South Dade, living a life of crime, seeing police as the mortal enemy. Two humans from two ends of the socio-economic world, locked by circumstance in a moment that would be vital to each. I wanted something from him; a confession. He wanted something from me. Freedom.

Alone, both of us smoked one cigarette after another. I asked him about his family, what sports he played, then segued into talking about Mary Ann, and why they argued the night before. That was a key, to get him to admit that. So I posed it not as a question, but as a fact, and simply asked, "Why?"

"She'd been a bitch," he said. "She mess around with another man. How would you feel if your wife?"

I stayed focused. I inched closer in my chair, my knees touching his. I lay my hand on his shoulder, "I do know how it feels," I said. "Believe me, Jimmie, I know exactly how you feel. I'm sorry that happened to you." I think he had expected to steel himself against tough questioning. Instead, I offered him sympathy.

He looked at me with eyes that cried out for understanding. The time was ripe. Strike now. "Jimmie, tell me how it happened."

He started to weep. I lay my hand on his shoulder again. "She started hitting on me. I had to defend myself.

So I put my hands around her neck."

I had him! "Then what?"

He finished off the entire confession in every detail, including the carrying of her body to the lake shore. Now, it was time to validate the confession. I needed a witness. I needed to formalize. He thought I was convinced that the killing was in self defense, though I hadn't said that. When the court reporter was called into the room, he readily repeated the entire statement.

I swabbed his hands, scraped his fingernails, took his pictures, and booked him into the County Jail for First Degree Murder. Crime scene to booking to dictating the entire report, took all of twelve hours. Case closed.

I was now a full-fledged homicide detective.

The next day, I received praises from a number of detectives, including Ray Beck, Lieutenant Esty, Bobby Jones and of all people, Captain Lou Spaeth.

Yes!

* * *

I'd just returned from the Justice of the Peace court after testifying at a preliminary hearing. Captain Spaeth called me into his office. He had news I didn't want to hear.

"You're being transferred, Frank."

My heart plunged. "Why?"

"Purdy has instituted a new policy. Only detectives who hold the rank of sergeant may work in Homicide.

You've done a great job here, but you're still a patrolman. I tried, but I can't help you." It was gratifying to know that Spaeth had taken on a new respect for me. Surely a far cry from that first day. "Let's hope enough vacancies open up for sergeant, " he said. "You're a good cop, Frank. We want you back."

CHAPTER TWENTY-SEVEN
Back To Homicide

There are wonderful things to say about innocence. At the tender age of four, my newly adopted son, Russell, had an impish nature about him. I wished I could have been as endeared to my natural son, Bennett. Russell reminded me of a younger *Dennis The Menace*, always saying and doing the most outrageous, giving us belly laughs that linger to this day.

At a crowded beach outing one Sunday, Joan and I were lying on a blanket when my darling little boy ran up holding his crotch in anguish. "Mommy, Daddy, I have to pee."

Being lazy, and the rest rooms far away, I told him, "Uh, son... go on down and... shhh... pee in the ocean water.

It's okay."

With that, Russell followed directions explicitly, and stood at the end of the surf, pulled his bathing suit down to his ankles, and proceeded to boldly urinate into the breaking waves for all to witness. From then on, I remained very careful how I worded things to my son.

* * *

The transfer back to Warrants was utterly demoralizing. For five months I had worked with the best, the sharpest, the most respected cops in the department.

Through no fault of my own, after proving myself, and doing a good job, I'd been shit canned back to the world of mediocrity.

Another five new promotions chipped away at the sergeant's list, leaving me hovering at number nine on the list, with no vacancies in sight. But there were rumors that Purdy was going to ask for more positions in the budget. That would be a good thing. Hopefully, those position would come before it was too late. I didn't want to take another test and then wait another year. Or worse, not score well enough.

Midnight shift with week-days off was even more difficult, because it disrupted the home life, forcing me to sleep during the day when everyone in the family was up and about. But I could also spend more time with Joan and the kids on regular days off, going to beaches, swimming pools, parks and games.

The relationship with Joan went well, at first. After all, I'd met a woman who loved to be loved. She was beautiful, pert, squeaky clean and looked nice on my arm, a great trophy, to be sure. Joan also had expensive taste, enjoyed fine clothing and the best of foods. I called often, gave gifts, wrote poems, and sent flowers. I tried to give her all she asked for.

She wanted one thing of me that I could not always provide: Time.

* * *

While back in Warrants, the guys across the hall in Homicide must have felt sorry for me, for they were always bringing me along to death scenes to help out.

Bob Laws looked like a football quarterback, tall, broad shouldered, close-cropped hair, articulate, and smart, especially when it came to analyzing a crime scene. I was bored and sitting alone in the Warrants Office at 2:15 A.M. when he suddenly walked in, "Marshall, there's a DOA on the Tamiami Trail, a mile west of Krome Avenue, laying right on the road. Some dog is guarding the body. You wanna come along?"

"Sure."

An adrenalin rush came over me once more, en route to a probable murder scene, knowing that this experienced detective held me in enough esteem to summon my assistance. As it turned out, there was little assistance I could render, other than moral support.

The scene was like something out of a Stephen King novel. In the middle of a cool night, under a starlit Miami sky on the edge of the Everglades, we arrived to find a half dozen police and civilian cars off the side of the road, all with headlights burning. Laws parked directly behind. Squawking police radios were the only sounds of the night. As we stepped lively to the center of attention, we saw the man's body lying face down on the pavement, spread eagle, his head centered in a large pool of blood. The crowd had formed a circle, about ten-foot radius from the body, while a full grown Doberman Pincher lay on the pavement guarding his master, lapping blood, sneering, menacing anyone who dared to take one step closer.

A small amount of traffic was building in each direction. Laws, the Homicide Investigator, was now in charge. He had determined, from other witnesses, that the victim had had an altercation with another driver on the two-lane highway, which somehow ended up in a shoot- out. The other suspect was still at large.

The first order of business was getting to the body, but the dog stood in our way. Animal Control officers were summoned to the scene, but they were ineffective. The dog outsmarted them every time they tried to noose the animal Stun guns, or dart guns, were not available.

Laws was an animal lover and avid hunter, and I could see the dilemma in his eyes. But time was fleeting by and the investigation had to begin. Laws had but one option left. Reluctantly, he returned to the trunk of the detective car, removed a 12 gauge shotgun, and told the crowd to disburse.

I couldn't see, but I could hear. The shot fired. The dog squealed. A second shot fired, and the dog squealed louder, and harder. Then, a third shot. Silence.

I felt sick to my stomach.

Laws was visibly disturbed. Later, he would endure cynicism and degradation from ignorant critics within the department. I know, to this day, he never got over the trauma of that moment.

* * *

For another two months, I was assigned to work in a squad called Special Enforcement. This was a group of ten or twelve casually dressed undercover cops, who reported to headquarters at 9 P.M., then roamed the county during the midnight hours in unmarked cars for no other purpose than looking for and harassing known criminals. It was the closest thing to "proactive" policing I'd ever seen. The squad had originally been headed by Lieutenant Charlie Black, the cop who broke me in when I went to North District Uniform. But now, he had been transferred up to Criminal Intelligence, leaving the squad to a sergeant

Robert "Pappy" Minium, the father of Gary Minium. Bulldoggish and intense, Minium was considered the ballsiest supervisor in the history of policedom. A stand-up guy, and no-nonsense.

It was also a compliment just being asked to work there, because these guys were hand picked from the best cops in the entire department My performance in Homicide had served my reputation well.

I often rode with Bob Windsor, a tall oak tree of a man about six years older than me, the same taciturn cop who had those tickets written before the violator got out of the car. *"Tell it to the judge."* Windsor was a tough detective who took his job seriously, all business, rarely smiled, but enjoyed the respect of all others, on both sides of the fence.

Routine activities for any given night were to target known jewel thieves, burglars, gamblers, pimps, fences, or any organized crime (O.C.) figure, follow him around, scare him to death, stop him, search his car, then find something wrong, like bald tires and have it towed. We could also put them in jail for driving unsafe vehicles or other trumped up charges, all in the interest of trying to squeeze information or pressuring them to cease criminal activities in Dade County. We also hunted for individuals wanted on active warrants.

Figures like John Clarence Cook, a notorious jewel thief, were constantly being tailed, and they knew it. A known fence, Dolores Costello lived in a big waterfront home on Keystone Point in North Miami with her lover, Brian Perez. She and her customers received attention from Special Enforcement on a regular basis. Big Tony Esperti, a bent-nosed, Mafia-connected brawler was always causing trouble for the mob with his brash behavior. Esperti's short boxing career had come to a halt in the third round of a 1961 fight by a promising young fighter named Cassius Clay. There certainly was no shortage of target mobsters to harass. I just hoped I'd never be in a position to deal with any of Bernie's old friends with whom I once dined and entertained.

While we probably violated people's rights in record numbers, the underworld sure knew who we were and often took their business elsewhere, like up in Broward County where the Ft. Lauderdale Police could deal with them.

Though I rotated partners from time to time, one I'll not forget is Marshall Holt, a small-framed, smooth-talking redhead who once sold automobiles for a living. I worked with him four or five times, doing what we all did best—putting hoods in jail. Around 2 A.M. one slow and boring night, Holt drove over to Eastern Shores, a new development of upper middle class homes not far from the beaches. There, he stopped across the street from a two-story house which had no neighbors, and turned out the lights. I didn't understand what he was up to, but I figured it was time to just have a cigarette and chit chat about women, police, thugs and sports.

"See that house right there, Marshall?" he asked. I puffed my Pall Mall, one of eighty I'd smoke that day, and looked over. A half moon glowed softly over the street, which had one burning lamp at the end of the block, about a hundred yards away. I thought he was going to tell me about a thief who lived there. He continued. "I've been in that house. I know where they keep the jewelry."

"No shit?"

"No shit. And furs, too. Minks. These people are loaded."

"No shit?"

"Bracelet and a broach, diamonds and emeralds.

Must be worth twenty grand."

No shit?" *What is he getting to?*

"You and I could do this job, and be in and out of there in five minutes."

Job? What job? I puffed my cigarette again.

"They're socialites. We watch for when they're not going to be home. We keep the car running, lights out, down the street, while I slip the glass sliding doors. We get in and out of the bedroom in seconds, with twenty grand in our hands."

"We do, huh?"

"Are you in?"

The question dumbfounded me. He must have wondered why I took so long to answer, but I was trying to sort the reality of this. Was he really an active burglar himself, looking for a partner in crime? Why me? Did he think I was a crook? Did he know I had been connected by family to the mob? Or was he testing me, to see if I'd bite the bait? Or was this a test of trust? After all, nothing in policedom is more important than being a "stand-up" guy. Translated, that means you never tell on another cop for anything. Then again, Holt may have been assigned by Pappy Minium to see if I was really a thief? Was this all a ruse?

I may never know the answer to those questions. I flipped my stub out the window, and looked over to Holt.

"Ah. Not my style, Holt. I'll take a pass."

"No sweat, Marshall. Just thought I'd ask."

And that was that.

Marshall Holt went on to serve several years in other assignments before moving on to another vocation. As far as I know, he was never fingered as a crook nor caught in any acts of dishonesty.

* * *

By the end of July, the day before the list expired, an amended budget had been approved for enough promotions to reach me on the list along with four other cops. I felt exhilarated that day in the office of Director E. Wilson Purdy, receiving the revered gold badge from the top man himself. Now I had reached the level of my mentor and idol, Ray Beck, and so many others for whom I'd developed so much awe and respect. I suppose that also included ornery, toothless, Earl Craver, who thought I'd never make it as a cop. I'd have politely rubbed it in his face, but he had already retired by then.

Within a day of being promoted to sergeant, I was back in Homicide. Capt. Spaeth was true to his word.

CHAPTER TWENTY-EIGHT
Whodunit

Weekends at Detective Bureau were barren, at best. One Shift Commander, usually some over-the-hill lieutenant, worked the desk answering phones, logging cases and dispatching detectives as needed. Each unit (Homicide, Robbery, Auto Theft, etc.) deployed one on-duty detective on Saturday and on Sunday. Senior investigators did not work weekends unless they were following up a hot whodunit.

Now back at the bottom of the pecking order, I was assigned as the only investigator in Homicide this Sunday morning, there to handle any simple DOA that came up. If a major homicide occurred, they'd send the on-call man from home and I'd serve as an assistant.

That's the way it was supposed to work.

Sunday morning. 10:00 A.M. Miami already started to sear under a rising September sun. "Marshall, just got a call, there's a dead body out in the Everglades, lying in a ditch," said the lieutenant. "Start heading out, see what it is.

I'll send the Crime Scene Unit."

Bodies in an Everglades ditch rarely, if ever, equated to a natural death. I prepared myself for a long day ahead.

Carrying a .22 caliber rifle, a hunter and his boy had been walking along a dirt road a half-mile south of the Tamiami Trail (Southwest 8th Street), two miles west of the last trailer park before reaching the infamous sea of grass. There, amid the vast span of wild life, they spotted the body of a nude male lying face up in a watery ditch. It would be a moment he and the child would never forget.

Neither would I.

As I steered my car from the paved road down the dusty trail, I could smell the rotting carcass from my open window before I ever saw it. A cloud of dust formed as I parked the car half on the dirt road and half into the marsh. I took the names and information from the man and boy and let them go on their way, leaving me alone with the corpse for the next fifteen minutes until the crime scene technician arrived. It was an eerie feeling, indeed, just me and the unknown dead man out in the wilderness.

I removed my jacket, loosened my tie, and rolled up my sleeves. Within the thicket, ever wary of alligators, I pushed the foliage aside to see the partially decomposed body lying on his back, hands drawn up in a pugilistic position, his eyes and mouth eaten away by insects leaving a ghostly appearance with bared teeth and open sockets. A scorched, marbleized veneer to the skin of his legs, hands and stomach gave me reason to think an attempt had been made to set the body on fire.

I looked closer, then gagged from the stench. Soon, I adjusted and continued, using the handy-dandy handkerchief doused with Old Spice. From my little experience and knowledge and judging from the heat and outdoor elements, I figured the man had been dead about two days.

Four circular wounds about the size of silver dollars were visible on his torso, from his chest to his stomach, indicting shotgun blasts at close range. I imagined the killer dropping the naked body, standing over him beside the ditch and firing those shots. Shell casings would eject to the right. Sure enough, to my right, deep into the thicket, there they were, four twelve-gauge casings. The crime scene technician arrived, took pictures, and began collecting samples of evidence, foliage, dirt, tire tracks, and of course, the casings, one of which yielded a visible print on the brass edge.

I reported back via radio, and informed the Shift Commander this was a whodunit, to send out the on-call man. I'd stand by. Ten minutes later, the Shift Commander raised me again, and said that Lieutenant Esty had been contacted at home and that I was to handle the entire case.

It must have been an important football game that day, leaving a major whodunit to a detective who had never handled one before. The sense of responsibility was incredible. Knowing the command level had bestowed that much trust, I was determined to prove myself.

These were the days when the detective and the crime scene technician did it all at the scene. No Medical Examiner responded, no battery of cops, no State Attorney arrived to log a field visit to a crime scene.

I sketched, wrote copious notes, ordered aerial photographs, and had the body taken to the morgue in a black bag. The next day, I assisted Dr. Brian Blackbourne, a tall, lanky and very young Assistant Medical Examiner with the autopsy, holding implements and digging for evidence inside the decomposed carcass of this unknown man, checking his stomach contents, and locating another four previously undetected .32 caliber bullet holes in his body. Somebody really wanted this man dead.

Other detectives had case loads that were mounting, and the omnipresent problem of daily DOA cases which needed handling left me alone to follow up on this new case. For a time, the office would not assign me any other death cases.

Being assigned a first whodunit in Homicide was like being called up from the Yankee reserve bench to be a starting pitcher. One or two poor performances, and those starting assignments would become distant history. I had to do this right.

Seven fingers of the corpse yielded enough fingerprint ridges for identification. The victim was a thirty-two year-old thug from Broward County named Joseph Jerome (Jerry) Springer, a nightclub owner and small time hustler who'd been arrested for minor vice crimes and drunk driving charges in the past. He ran the Show Club, a topless bistro in Dania, just south of Ft. Lauderdale, where dancing girls were required to wear pasties, except for a separate hidden bar behind the building where an extra surcharge permitted special guests a view of live nipples on parade.

That Monday night, with the support of Lieutenant Esty and Captain Spaeth, I and four other homicide detectives descended on the night club to check everyone, interview all the employees and search the place where Springer lived, a motel apartment just a mile down the road.

As we stood in the darkened parking lot discussing the strategy, Captain Spaeth asked me, in the presence of everyone else, "Okay, Marshall. You're in charge. What do you want to do next?"

Squidgie had come a long way from being seen as a *fairy*. I couldn't let on that I was in awe of the moment or that I felt overwhelmed. Two detectives were sent to Springer's apartment. Another two were assigned to interview hookers, strippers, bartenders and any guests on the premises. I talked with Russell Golden, Springer's diminutive and legitimate business partner, and big, affable George Datz, the bouncer, Springer's long time childhood friend from Pittsburgh.

According to them, Springer was last seen alive at the club early on Friday night, when he left for an errand, due to be back in a short while, but never returned. Oddly, Springer's car was still in the parking lot, so he must have taken off with someone else. One person of importance, but not available on the scene, was his girlfriend, Linda Pierce, a twenty-five year-old Madam, who ran a string of her own hookers. She was known as The Black Widow, because two other boyfriends had turned up dead in years past. This made three.

During the next four days, newspaper stories in Dade and Broward Counties carried a series of articles about the spectacular new whodunit. Organized Crime had been leaving its mark in South Florida with a litany of murders and expose`s connected to the mob.

Information poured in about Jerry Springer. The Broward County Sheriff's Office had an entire file on Springer and the tawdry activities at the Show Club. At their request, I met with Captain Cecil Stewart, the head of Vice, and his assistant, Sergeant Howard Metzger, a tall pot-bellied redneck who I figured was loyal acolyte to Stewart, but not much of a cop. Now in his fifties, the gravel-voiced Stewart had once been a West Virginia trooper. He still wore his gray hair in a military flat top.

I learned that everyone hated the hot-shot Jerry Springer except for his partner, his trusted old buddy George Datz, and probably, Linda Pierce. Other than them, Springer had pissed off enough customers, hoodlums, lawyers, hookers, and politicians to form a list of suspects five pages long. He was a homicide victim waiting to happen.

One good example was his relationship with the town police chief, Monty Smith. Homely and fat, Smith frequented the club, (as part of his duties, of course), enjoyed free booze, and cautioned Springer to knock off the secret titty room in the back, or else he'd have to close the place down. To that, Springer asked if he'd like one of the girls to do some special favors for him. Smith couldn't turn down a deal like that. "But, don't think this gets you a pass, Jerry," he told Springer.

Two nights later, Monty Smith, a married man, enjoyed a tryst with a buxom brunette in a small local motel up the road from The

Show Club. What he didn't know was that Springer had rigged the next room up with a peep hole and a movie camera.

The next time Chief Smith came into the club, Springer displayed three still photos taken from the movie frames, of him having sex with the brunette. "Leave me alone, Smith. Or I'll drop a thousand of these from an airplane all over Broward County. Understood?"

"Understood."

* * *

Captain Cecil Stewart located Linda Pierce and arranged office space in Ft. Lauderdale for me to conduct the interview. I figured she was the key to solving this case. She knew Jerry Springer better than anyone. I also figured she may have been involved somehow.

I was struck by her long neck, short dark hair, her sullen expression and a tight, thin, nearly flat-chested body. "Pleased to meet you," she said, extending her hand from her chair. Sultry in a tight-fitting black dress, pearl necklace, crossed legs and black pump shoes, Linda seemed remorseful, interested and said she wanted to help, but didn't know who had killed her lover. She and Springer had dated over a year, and she was aware of his many enemies, just as Cecil Stewart had told us about. "Jerry pissed off a lot of people," she said. She had last seen him earlier that Friday evening, before leaving the club to take care of business. She would not elaborate on what "business" that was. Basically, the first interview with Linda Pierce told me nothing I didn't already know.

Cecil Stewart and Howard Metzger continued to share file information and lead me in a number of directions that might yield clues or suspects. But as the first week wore on, working sixteen hours a day, writing reports on top of reports, I realized I had a bonafide whodunit on my hands, with no hard evidence or information leading me to any suspects or witnesses.

The fingerprint on the shell casing turned out to be partial, not enough for identification. The burning and marbleizing of the victim's body was caused by gasoline and a match. Had Springer been dumped into a dry bed of grass instead of a watery ditch, his body would have burned beyond identification, other than, perhaps, dental records.

My new wife, Joan, was supportive. She had left a note of encouragement for my first major case. I tried to call often.

Otherwise, coming home meant nothing more than a few hours of sleep and hustling back out the door. An approved weekend visit with Bennett had to be canceled.

All the guys in Homicide encouraged me, offering to assist if they could break away from their own cases. Captain Spaeth seemed amused at my doggedness, and said, "Why don't ya take it easy, Marshall. You'll probably never solve this kind of case."

While my world was absorbed with murder case and family, the department moved along with the cleanup under the thumb of E. Wilson Purdy, who had just appointed Major Charles O'Connor to be the new head of Detective Bureau. O'Connor was a friendly fellow who looked more like a Sunday minister, nearly bald, and considered by the rank-in-file as not the sharpest knife in the drawer. Detectives demeaning referred to him as "Nipplehead." But he had the one quality that was more important than anything to Purdy. He was honest and trustworthy. Smarts didn't matter. What Purdy didn't know, or didn't care, is that it mattered to the detectives and field supervisors, to be working under someone who couldn't find a clue if it were pasted to his eyeballs.

Because I'd been up to Broward County a number of times by myself, at all hours of day and night, talking to possible witnesses, acquaintances, mobsters, showgirls, and the staff at the Show Club, I received a call one day from Lieutenant Esty telling me to report to Nipplehead." Marshall, I don't want you working up in Broward County alone any more. I'm assigning Dick Ward to assist you."

That was great. About my age and size, even tempered and more cerebral than the average cop, Ward and I had gone through the police academy together and got along well. We interviewed dozens more people, including Linda Pierce, but got nowhere. Linda didn't want Cecil Stewart, or other cops, to know she was talking to us so much, so our meetings were clandestine. We spent lots of petty cash from the Detective Bureau till at North Lauderdale restaurants, bars and lounges, listening to her ramble on about pure nothing. As I looked back, I think she was gathering more information from us, than we were from her.

Finally, Nipplehead said we were spending too much money. "Why don't you just buy a bottle of booze and take her to her apartment?" he said.

"Well, sure, boss."

She had a loft apartment. I got drunk. Ward got drunk. She stayed sober. We fell asleep on the couch, still in our suits and ties. At early dawn, we drove home, without a clue as to who killed Jerry Springer.

Whoever said writing memoirs would be free of embarrassment?

CHAPTER TWENTY-NINE
The Squad

My Homicide colleagues were like an engaging group of characters from a cop movie, full of personality, diversity and passion. They became like a second family. In some ways, they were my first family because I spent more time with them than I did at home, with my mind absorbed in cases day and night, especially the Springer murder. I had adopted an attitude that no murder was perfect, that every case could be solved, it was just a matter of finding the right clues, or the right people, and handling it the right way. Captain Spaeth's words haunted me, *"You'll probably never solve this kind of case."*

Meanwhile, I had to go back into rotation, handling suicides, accidental deaths, naturals and in some cases, rapes. That was okay, each case honed my skills. I accepted each assignment eagerly, knowing I'd learn more and more, and become a better investigator with each case.

Illegal abortions were also investigated in Homicide by a resident expert named Sergeant Ray Wertis, a New York implant who preferred working alone. We all knew why. He spent more time at Hialeah Race Track than he did working abortion cases. Wertis was the only cop I ever knew in Miami who wore a fedora.

Charles (C.T.) Clark was, in my opinion, the best all-around homicide investigator I ever knew. About ten years my senior, with piercing blue eyes, strong nose and thinning hair, Clark had the poise of Ray Beck, the smarts of Dick Ward, the crime scene evaluation skills of Bob Laws, the balls of Lieutenant John Esty. He was also the best interrogator I ever saw.

In one of his cases, a young black school teacher named Patricia Rooks was found dead at home by her husband. She'd been raped and strangled. All signs (two coffee cups, two brands of cigarettes) led Clark to believe the intruder was known to the victim, perhaps even an old acquaintance. Clark dogged the case, researching her entire life, including every name in her high school yearbook. After two dozen interviews, one of those old school chums, [3]Anthony Bell, agreed to come into the office to answer some questions. There was a method to Clark's madness. As Clark chatted and asked routine questions, he offered Bell a cigarette. Bell said, "thanks," but he had his own brand, Benson & Hedges, just like on the crime scene. Then Bell made a fatal mistake. The killer's cigarettes in the Rooks' house had been partially smoked and bent over two times in the ash tray, an interesting habit. Sure enough, he smoked half the cigarette and bent it twice. Clark had his man. Thirty minutes later, he blathered a confession.

J. K. (Kermit) Russell was a type A personality (like myself), hyper, intense, quick-stepping, energetic and smart. His manner and physique reminded me of movie star, Jimmy Stewart. The son of another career detective, Russell's birthday and mine were two days apart, but he had made sergeant before me. Russell was one of those edgy detectives who needed to stay busy, taking on DOA cases and homicides as fast as the lieutenant would assign them.

H. Marvin Pittman was a pillar of integrity, transferred into Homicide from the rural regions of South Dade where he had developed a reputation as a hard-ass and energetic patrolman. Of course, that translated to building stats, but he seemed to enjoy the respect of cops who were also respected. That meant a lot. Earlier in his adult life, after his beloved wife had survived a life-threatening illness, Marvin had an epiphany and turned to God for his source of strength and motivation. But he never imposed his religious leanings upon others.

Mike Coon was the squad maverick. Blond, crew-cut, Mr. Macho stood no taller than I, (almost all the detectives were taller and bigger than me) but was built more like a fireplug, with strong arms, a broad chest and a cocky gait. Coon was reliable, good for a back-up, because he loved to mix it up if you needed help. He had a reputation for bulldog tenacity when working a whodunit, to the point that he rarely worked any other cases.

John Henry Ford, around C.T. Clark's age, was best known for his hyena-like laugh. He, too, was an honest and hard-working cop who earned the admiration of all. In those times, I never knew a bad homicide cop. Not that it had anything to do with it, but in 1967, there was no ethnic diversity. We were all white. All non- Hispanic.

---

[3] Anthony Bell - fictitous name

All males. And there were bigots among us. Sometimes, we worked up to one hundred hours per week without mentioning the term, *overtime*. It was not part of the vocabulary. No one thought of extra pay for extra time. Cases got worked in the field, from the office, and often from home, when they needed to be worked. If that was too much to ask, then we could leave Homicide. With paychecks the same every two weeks, we worked for the stimulation, for the camaraderie, the importance of it all and the honor of just being there.

Throughout my career, Lieutenant Esty would remain imbedded in my mind as one of the best supervisors I'd ever known. Face lined like dried leather, this cigar chomping, toothless stork of a man stood up to anyone in support of his people, if he thought he was right. And he was smart, he gave time and attention to those who needed help, and he cared. His field supervisory duties came to an abrupt halt one rainy day, when he raged into an argument with his boss. Major "Nipplehead" O'Connor was admonishing Esty about the status of personnel and cases, when the lieutenant suddenly removed his cigar from his teeth and flipped it on Nipplehead's desk, saying, "Go fuck yourself, Charlie. Find yourself another lieutenant." Being discharged from his duties on the spot, Esty was no longer entitled to a take-home vehicle. He walked ten miles all the way to his house in Hialeah.

Afternoon shifts were manned by a smaller group of great detectives whose main duties were to handle DOAs, and any homicides that were cleared on the spot, like domestics or suspects in custody. Whodunits required a call-out from one of the regular day detectives. Among these, were Wayne McCarthy, a smart, robust man who could think on his feet as well as any. McCarthy went on to head up Homicide as commander in his latter years. Bob Dwyer, a New England transplant, was also an intelligent smart young detective but with a drinking problem. He remained as a journeyman investigator for several years until he got caught up in sexual deviation problems. After his departure from Homicide and his legal problems cleared, Dwyer rehabilitated himself and went on to a law degree, but he could never get a job as a lawyer.

John "Tiger" Lewis, hustled cases along with the best of them on afternoons. With a dry sense of humor, John had an unimposing, casual demeanor, not the stereotype of a cop. But when he got mad, he got real mad. Thus, the nickname. John went on to become a chief of police in two major Florida departments.

The squad *paesano*, Frank Mussoline, one of my best friends, sometimes handled three or four death cases a night, racing from scene to scene, loving his work, never complaining, always holding his own.

I must also credit the right arm of any investigative unit without whom it could not function; Clerical employees.

In Dade County, the name, "Betty Cousins," and "Homicide" were associated like a bun to a hamburger. She kept it all together, especially the keeping of records long before we knew how to spell "computer." She worked as the head secretary for over thirty years, answering phones, logging cases, inputting case patterns and peculiarities such as modus operandi, victim and suspect profiles, typing reports and administrative data, virtually the rock upon which every detective relied for guidance, structure, and information. The wife and then the mother of suicide victims herself, Betty never received the recognition she deserved.

Always on the ready line, Court Reporters took dictation for long and copious reports, and statements from witnesses and suspects. They have always been a vital and integral part of the homicide investigation process. Without them, case files might never have passed the prosecution muster. Stella Southern was a gray-haired grouch who could type on an electric IBM as fast as you could talk, without an error. While dodging flirtations from half the men in Detective Bureau, petite, blonde Jeanne Volk, added grace and charm to a busy office, taking an interest in the cases as much as the men. Pleasantly plump, Frances Essa, capable and hard-working, was best known for a nasty habit of stopping the proceedings—with a little smile— lighting a match during a statement to cut the smell of involuntary flatulations. Charlotte Stemple suffered polio from childhood and walked slowly with a lame leg, yet she overcame her handicap and remained as one of the best court reporters over a span of twenty-five years.

Lieutenant Esty remained in Detective Bureau, but only as the afternoon shift commander, answering phones and dispatching detectives to their calls. In his place as the new field lieutenant in Homicide, a young lean quiet-spoken fellow named Chuck Harbolt, transferred down from the North District, a man everyone knew as unshakably honest and loyal to his people. Yet, the tragedy that would befall Chuck Harbolt will later touch my heart in a special way.

Also promoted to handle the administrative matters in Homicide was former detective, Bobby Jones, who made lieutenant on his first try.

Sometime in the fall of 1967, Detective Bureau Major Charles "Nipplehead" O'Connor resigned and took a private job outside the department. We were all shocked when the new replacement was announced was made. From Criminal Intelligence, and only 32 years of age, Lieutenant Charles Black, the same high-energy cop I rode with in uniform, who had headed up Special Enforcement a year earlier, was elevated above two dozen department captains to take over Detective Bureau where crooked Manson Hill once ruled. Obviously, Purdy trusted him.

The detectives were happy. After a year of an inept leader at the Bureau's helm, we now had a man everyone trusted and admired, who could find a clue pasted over his eyeballs and would stand-up for his men, yet remain loyal to the department.

Things were good.

CHAPTER THIRTY
Shades of Bernie

I slept deeply. During the first week of Lieutenant Harbolt's new position in Homicide, (as the story is told) I was the on-call whodunit detective. I awoke from a dead sleep when he called me at 3:00 A.M. and proceeded to relay all the data about a dead body that was found behind a bar in South Dade. When he finished giving me all the information, he asked, "Got it, Marsh?" Harbolt listened.

No answer. "Marshall. Did you get the information?"

The next sound he heard: "Uuuugghhhkkkkk".

"Marshall! Wake up!"

"Uuuugghhhkkkkk. Uuuugghhhkkkkk."

"Marshall...please. Just, hang up the phone."

In those days, unless both parties hung up, the phone line remained open. Chuck Harbolt had to put on his clothes and drive to a pay phone to call out another detective.

* * *

By the end of October, I'd worked the Springer case to death, and still didn't know who killed him. But I had shored up the respect of fellow detectives by showing my willingness to work and help others, by my determination, and the excellence of my reports. Because I could type and write fairly well, other detectives often asked me to help with their reports. The squad now accepted me among the department's finest.

One of those late night phone calls occurred at 1:15 A.M. on the morning of October 31. A shooting at a popular restaurant and bar in North Bay Village called, The Place For Steak, had left the body of a well-dressed middle-aged man lying on the foyer floor. The municipality of North Bay Village, a link between Miami and Miami Beach, was known for its two-mile strip of bars and hangouts which were a safe haven for Mafia.

Slick, gray-haired, Tommy Altamura was a midlevel Mafia lieutenant who ran illegal gambling and prostitution on Miami Beach and resided next door to the Place For Steak in a waterfront high rise. Wearing a gray sharkskin suit, he strolled over to the restaurant at 12:30 A.M., stepped inside the foyer, lit a cigarette and looked around. A band was playing on the stand behind the crowded bar, while patrons on the dining room side chatted and ate sixteen ounce filet mignons. Shots rang out. Tommy went down on the spot. Patrons, men and women, left their drinks and tables, and darted out the front door in tandem, tripping over the body along the way.

One night, during my rendition of Autumn Leaves, sharp staccato sounds suddenly burst into the air—Pop!-Pop!-Pop! They came from the kitchen area. People in every direction jumped from their tables.

The suspect, a large burly man, fled out the front door in front of a hundred patrons, entered his car and drove away. By the time local police arrived, only four patrons remained as witnesses, plus employees. A hundred people, at least, stampeded out the door.

When I arrived on the scene, one hour later, the night Shift Commander had already authorized the removal of the body to the morgue, which did not please me, but it was too late to complain.

Tony D'Amico was a fumbling North Bay Village cop who once worked for my police department, but left under dubious circumstances. When he arrived on the scene, he spoke to four out-of-town businessmen who had been sitting at the bar. They witnessed the entire incident. Before I got there, he had already transported them to headquarters.

My arrival was met with a kitchen helper swabbing the blood from the foyer floor. A crime scene tech took an embarrassing photo of me scratching my crotch. I spoke with employees, who were of little help. According to the North Bay Village Police chief, the four men gave excellent descriptions of the killer, so precise, that we all knew who it had to be. They said the gunman had been standing at the bar talking to a girl who was seated. Two minutes later, they saw him under the bright lights of the foyer, pointing a gun at the head of Altamura, then firing five shots. In the midst of a hushed nightclub, the killer boldly strolled back to the bar, grabbed his girl- friend's arm and took off on foot.

Based on the description,—bent nose, huge girth, ruddy face— we were certain the killer was Tony Esperti, the same hood that we worked in Special Enforcement. According to street information, Esperti was known to be in an on-going dispute with Altamura.

I interviewed eleven employees, waitresses, bartenders, band members, etc. No one saw anything.

As I learned later, D'Amico held a conversation with the witnesses while en route to headquarters. One of the men remarked, "Wow. Come to Miami, and the next thing you know, we're witness to a murder."

D'Amico responded, "Yeah, not only that, but a Mafia murder, too."

When I met the four men at headquarters, they were sitting together in one room, a basic no-no in the realm of murder investigations. Never allow witnesses to be accused of collaborating or getting stories straight. Nevertheless, by the time I was able to isolate them and, in light of the blunder by D'Amico, their memories had seriously faded. [4]Forest Simpson, a consultant from Philadelphia, had given such a detailed description of the killer at the scene, that it matched Tony Esperti exactly, down to the scar on his face. At headquarters, after his tête-à-tête with Tony D'Amico, his memory lapsed and the description became vague.

During the night, intelligence officers searched for Tony Esperti and his known girlfriend, Audrey Fowler. She had been in the restaurant that same night. Finally, they contacted Tony's attorney, Louie Vernell, who surrendered him at 9 A.M. that morning.

When Tony was brought into Homicide in handcuffs wearing an oversized tee shirt, I saw a huge man, ruddy, angry, menacing, a man easily imaginable as a hardened killer. I was the lead investigator. They sat him down in a side office where I took over. We were alone for a very few minutes. Perspiration dripped from his face. I had developed good skills at interrogation, but I figured this would be a waste of time. I had to try. "Hey there, Tony."

I was shocked at his response. "Yeah. Hi ya doin', Marshall." Then he winked.

He knows me?

Mob lawyer Louie Vernell was known to cops as a little grease ball with a habit of nervously twirling his curls at the front of his hairline. In the office, he made one demand after another, insisting we release his client, and all that. A thought occurred to me to swab

---

[4] Forest Simpson - fictitious name

Esperti's hands, in case he still had traces of gunpowder. That would be great evidence, if it rendered true.

Vernell objected and asked to talk with Esperti. We allowed him two minutes. Then, with the lab technician standing by with wet cotton swabs, I ordered Tony to extend his hands. He refused and stiffened. Three other detectives and I grabbed his arms and legs. He pulled away violently and was slammed to the tile floor like a lassoed steer. People scurried away like ants from an anthill. Betty Cousins screamed and fled the office. Lou Vernell paced and whined. As Tony writhed and pulled, we held his arms and legs while the lab tech tried in vain to swab his hands. But he was too strong, and resistant. Finally, I decided to apply a bit of "excessive brutality" and leaned my knee into his groin with all my weight. He groaned in pain. Swabs were taken.

Later that morning, one at a time, we marched all four out-of-town witnesses into a line-up room using five look-alikes from the jail to stand beside Tony. Like a joke, Louie Vernell was there objecting to everything. Three of the four businessmen chickened out and recognized no one. The fourth, a gutsy little man from Haddonfield, New Jersey named Charles Dore, pointed directly at Tony Esperti and said, "That's the man."

The next day, forensic analysts confirmed that a flake of gunpowder had been recovered from his right hand. Yes! We had a case.

* * *

Two weeks later, I learned why Tony winked and uttered my name, as though he knew me.

In one of those rare quiet moments at home, I received a call from Guido Penosi, a name from the past, an old comrade of Bernie's with whom I'd broken bread numerous times at the house during the '50s and early '60s. According to police files, Guido was a ranking mobster, but I didn't know exactly what role he played in organized crime. All I knew was his general manner, the shifty gait, gravel voice, New York accent. He wore thick horn-rimmed glasses, his dark hair slicked back, and always spoke in soft tones. "Hey, Marsh, how ya doin' kid?"

Oh shit! Do I really want this call? "Hey, yeah. Hi there, uh, Guido, how are things?"

"Hey, listen. Thought maybe you'd like to come over the house for dinner tomorrow night, Sarah's fixin' a nice Italian dinner. Bring your wife."

A million thoughts ran through my mind. The last thing I needed was some intelligence agent sitting outside of Guido's house taking tag numbers and there I am caught in a trap. But I was curious to know what this was all about.

I agreed to come the next night, but alone. Before I headed for his house, I figured I'd cover my ass by calling Captain Spaeth at home to let him know my destination and why. I bypassed the lieutenant because, the fewer people that knew, the better. This was the first time I revealed any past mobster associations to anyone on the department. Now, no one could say I'd done anything wrong. Spaeth seemed amused and ordered me to keep him informed.

Guido lived in an upscale but modest home in Sky Lake, twenty miles north of Miami. I'd been there before. I was greeted with warm hospitality by his wife, Sarah, who then ushered me into the billiards den. Guido closed the door and took a chair close to mine. He spoke in muted tones as though someone was listening through the door. He made me a scotch, then touched my knee, like we were old buddies. First, a few nice questions about my family, then, "Marsha, I just wanted to talk about Tony. You know."

Ah. I was right. The Esperti matter. Now I knew where this was going. I nodded.

"I hear Tony is in big trouble. This true?"

"Yeah, Guido, he really fucked up bad."

"Too bad. Think there's anything we can do for him?"

I couldn't believe this. Was I in a Mafia movie or what? "Not really, Guido. He was really stupid, doing that in front of a hundred people."

"I hear you got gun powder from his hand. True?"

"Yes. That's true."

Guido leaned over and lowered his hand, with five fingers extended, sending a message. "Anything we can do with that? You know. Things do get lost."

Here I was being bribed for five dollars, or maybe five hundred. Even five thousand. Who knows. All I could think of was the consequences of turning this down. He thinks I'm connected. If I refuse, what happens next? After a little thought, I figured Guido was just doing his job as a loyal hood, but down in his gut, he didn't really give a shit about Tony. Just going through the motions.

"Sorry Guido. It's air tight, all signed for. Wish I could help you. Nothing I can do."

Dinner was delicious.

CHAPTER THIRTY-ONE
Suicide

The gruesome act of anyone wishing to terminate the only life he/she will ever have, and then carrying it out, conjured up more fascination in me than did the act of murder. Perhaps it is a macabre side to my nature, but I think not. Rather, I wanted to understand how, when and why people reached the edge of an emotional cliff, as I had done more than once in my life.

Suicide results from a myriad of reasons: general depression, terminal illness, anger, reprisal, desperation, drug and alcohol dependency, shame and financial ruin. But the common thread that prevailed in all, was that a human being who had lived twenty years, forty, seventy, or only ten, decided to deliberately self-murder, and garnered the courage (or the cowardice) to do it.

Throughout my seven years in Homicide as a first line investigator, I handled more suicides than homicides. On each and every scene, I stood for a few moments in solitude to absorb the deep emotional pain that must have consumed that human being before taking the final step. In some ways, I even admired them. Other times, I had to hold back tears. I tried to envision their final moments, what they were saying, doing, listening to, crying about. I wondered how long they had been reaching out to others, hoping for solutions and finding none. Were signals ignored? Could it have been prevented? Did they truly understand that death was irreversible?

One couple, for certain, knew what they were doing when they embarked on their final journey. Well-to-do residents of Surfside, married for fifty-five years, they had been bonded by love from youth to eternity. One could not, or would not, live without the other. She was seventy-nine and riddled with terminal cancer. Within two months, she would be gone. He'd be alone for the first time since their teen years. It was unimaginable. They were found, huddled together in the back seat of a Cadillac Sedan DeVille, enclosed in their garage with hoses leading from the exhaust to the opening in the car window, the ignition key turned on with an empty tank of gas. I imagined their final kiss, and the warmth they felt passing on as they had lived, as one. It was a sad scene, but a joyful one as well.

The elderly were the most proficient and thoughtful at killing themselves. [5]Sam Gorman was 68 years old. He called the Communications Desk and shocked the complaint officer. "Would you please have someone come out and pick up my body?"

When police arrived, it was too late. Sam lived in a trailer outside the city limits of Miami. Inside, his nude body lay crumpled in a shower stall with the water running, and a short-barreled shotgun at his side. One load of birdshot had been fired under his jaw. Crimson water stained the shower walls, but most had run down the drain. No mess for the living.

Sam had laid out a black suit, white shirt, tie, black dress shoes and socks, on the living room couch. On the end table, three pieces of paper: 1) the name of his funeral parlor, 2) the name and address of his sister in Virginia and 3) the location of his will.

But why? Neighbors said Sam was spry and in good health.

It had been long planned. On the kitchen wall, a calendar was open to that exact date (September 15) with a notation inscribed in blue ink, *The End*. Atop his little desk in the bedroom corner, another desk calendar was secured open with a rubber band, but it was displayed to September 15, from the previous year. The page had yellowed. On that page, he had written, *The day my wife died*.

Happy anniversary, Sam.

[6]Jorge Rodriquez, only thirty-five, a refuge from Cuba, was found in his garage, hanging by the neck from a leather belt, his tongue protruding, and a half-empty bottle of Tequila atop the shelf. His wife had left him two months before.

[7]William Kilmer, in his twenties, was found inside in the back seat of his automobile one morning, parked at the edge of a baseball field. He had used a double-edged razor to carve his arms and neck into forty-five gaping folds of flesh, making one wonder how he could have actually carried that out. The razor was found submerged

---

[5] Sam Gorman - fictitious name

[6] George Rodriguez - fictitious name

[7] William Kilmer - fictitious Name

in the pool of blood on the floorboard. Like so many other suicides, there was the booze on the front seat—courage in a bottle.

[8]Mary Coolidge, 44, had just been released to her parents house from a mental facility, diagnosed with schizophrenia. She wanted to fly. And so she did, directly off the Haulover Bridge into the frigid water where the ocean meets Biscayne Bay. Homicide/Suicide was common, usually resulting from fits of temper during arguments. One example, was the Latino and his cheating wife, who had a violent argument before he finally plugged her with six shots from a .38. One of those was directly into the vagina. When he realized what he had done, he sat in the corner of the room and put a bullet into his own temple. Better than Death Row. But nothing was sadder than the young, desperate woman who was found on the beach at daybreak one morning, lying on a blanket and embracing her baby boy, both dead from gunshot wounds.

[9]Billy Ray Harmon lost his cool one day when he came home to find a wife and a girlfriend conspiring against him in his own house. He soaked up a few beers, then went berserk, stabbing one in the living room, then cornering the other in the bedroom, slashing her throat. Then, he lay atop the bed next to his wife, draped his leg across her corpse, and plunged the knife into his own heart. A small Yorkie Terrier in the back yard must have gone crazy. It was found dead, hanging by its leash over a barbeque pit.

I believe that children who kill themselves don't really understand suicide, or that death is an eternal nonexistence. Many think they'll reawaken, like from a dream, and then revel in sympathy. Or they'll just watch from aside, like a ghost, all the fallout that parents and friends will suffer as a result. Either way, I did learn that adults should take their kids seriously if there is any hint of such intentions.

[10]Danny Fishbein was only eleven when he shot himself with his father's .38 revolver. Imagine the imprint left on his mother for the rest of her life when she arrived home to find his body crumpled in the closet. Danny left a heartfelt note, essentially stating that he couldn't match up to his father's expectations, that he felt he could

---

[8] Mary Coolidge - fictitious name

[9] Billy Ray Harmon - fictitious name

[10] Danny Fishbein – fictitious name

do nothing right. The note was also Danny's version of a last will and testament, bequeathing his goldfish to a special friend, and other toys to school chums.

It got closer to home, when thirteen year-old Lori Batson shot herself in the temple with her dad's .22 pistol. Lori was the daughter of Ann Batson, Joan's sister, my niece by marriage. She was discovered by her mother lying supine atop her parents' bed. Ann had no clue why.

It was an eerie feeling, indeed, standing over her corpse at the Medical Examiner's Office, the same child with whom I had often shared holidays and family events.

During cleanup the next day, Joan discovered a crumpled piece of paper in the closet floor. On it, Lori had written a weepy note.

Joan handed me the note, which—according to rules—should have been entered into property as evidence. Revealing it to Ann and Eddie Batson may have burdened them with an unnecessary sense guilt for all time. I set it on fire then flushed it in the toilet. Her parents are now deceased. Because other relatives are still living it would serve no good purpose to air the contents of that note here.

I picked up another detective's report one day, and noticed the name of the victim, Joseph Strauss. I looked closer. Sure enough, it was Uncle Joe, the brother of my stepfather, Willie Strauss. He had shot himself in the head, leaving a succinct note, "I don't want no cancer."

As degenerate as it sounds, homicide detectives and crime lab technicians—calloused by the repetition of it all—often found themselves irreverently cracking jokes during a crime scene investigation outside the presence of the public. One fellow had hanged himself from a tree in a dense wooded area near Crandon Park. He wasn't discovered for over a week. In his decomposition process, the man had partly mummified, leaving his skeletal teeth completely bare, and his body had elongated by gravity and softening tissue. Two detectives (who shall remain unnamed) stood on each side of the dead fellow, put their arms around him and had a picture taken as though it were a reunion. They nicknamed the corpse: "Stretch."

Some suicides were deceptive by their very nature. I investigated at least three sexual erotic hangings thinking, at first, they were nothing more than self-imposed deaths choreographed to entertain the living. In reality, they were not suicides at all.

One, for instance, was an award winning biochemist who was visiting Miami on a business trip, leaving a wife and two kids at home in Peoria. He was discovered hanging in a Holiday Inn motel room by a maid, surrounded by porn photographs of young boys. Completely nude, the forty-four year-old man had rigged the bathroom door allowing himself to hang by a necktie, cushioned by a small towel, while wearing a woman's pink bra. A large rubber dildo hung from his penis by a shoelace. While rock music played from a cassette, a tripod mounted video camera recorded the event for posterity. Mr. Horny had apparently performed this stunt many times. Experienced homicide detectives had seen it before and learned about it during seminar classes. The intent is for the victim to enter into a sense of euphoria by cutting off flow to the carotid artery, reaching orgasm then loosening the noose before his weight settled too much.

This time, it just felt too good to be true. Ruling: Accidental Death.

Working with the Medical Examiner's records and our own police files, I took my own time to conduct unofficial studies trying to understand the phenomenon of suicide, logging times, dates, methods, motives, sex, race and age. I found it odd that hangings were more prevalent among Latinos. Many who committed suicide were descendants of others who did the same. Women often resorted to overdoses of drugs while men preferred more violent and certain means, like guns and knives. Strangely enough, of two-hundred suicide cases in 1968, only one was black.

In 1969, Municipal Court Judge, Henry Arrington had been the first black admitted into the Miami Yacht Club. Facing mortgage foreclosure and IRS problems, he shot himself dead, the only black that year to commit suicide in Dade County. (Interestingly enough, while blacks once comprised less than two percent of all suicides in the 1960s, they now comprise over ten percent. So much for evolving into mainstream America).

During my thirty years as a police officer, I knew at least ten cops who killed themselves. It could be that police officers become inured to death and feared it less. Or that they are, by necessity, decision makers who know how to fearlessly get things done and over with. Either way, cops are as human as anyone else, suffering from an array of depression, hidden instabilities, alcoholism, illness and broken hearts.

Larry Schum—the detective who tried to lure me as a purse-snatching partner—had long suffered from advanced emphysema and put a bullet in the roof of his mouth. Hilda Clancy had just resigned from the department, depressed. She killed her four-year-old son, and then put a bullet in her own head. Gary Windsor, a young detective, had blown his entire savings on gambling and was hopelessly in debt. He couldn't face his wife. Gunshot wound. Bud Irwin was a scar-faced detective married to Bunny Yeager, of Playboy fame. Killed himself inside his car. We never knew why.

Gus Campbell was the pudgy ex-fighter and longtime deputy whom I first met when he operated the elevator in the old County Jail. He'd been married and divorced twelve times, surviving the first eleven divorces quite solvent. Not the twelfth. Now retired, Gus took a job as an armed security guard at the Castaways Motel, on the strip where I once patrolled. Old, alone, busted out and depressed, Gus sat on a bus bench in front of the motel and shot himself in the head.

Long after his retirement, the department's premier underwater recovery expert, Ed Zehnder, could no longer deal with runaway alcoholism. In his idyllic little cabin in Ocala's National Forest, he took a shotgun, kneeled before his startled girl friend, jammed it under his chin and checked out with one blast.

Eddie Stone was one of the best Crime Scene Technicians the department ever had. A religious and moral man, Eddie was in the wrong place at the wrong time when he stood witness to an act of brutality by a police officer against a handcuffed arrestee. The subject made a formal complaint. Eddie was called to Internal affairs to give testimony. Eddie loved cops, loved his job and loved his God. Buried in conflict, he knew his testimony would result in the dismissal of that officer. But he would never lie under oath. He blew his brains out.

Known for his quiet tone and wrap-around sun-glasses, homicide detective Wade "Slick" O'Keefe sauntered like The Fonz, from Happy Days. He loved his job. He also loved his wife. The two—job and marriage— were not compatible. She accused him of loving his job more than her. To prove his love for her, he quit, and went back to working heavy construction equipment. A year later, she acquiesced, and he returned to the badge and was assigned back in Homicide. It was no use. She was going to leave him anyway. Slick came to work one day, signed reports, handled paperwork, then left the office. No one suspected anything was wrong. He stopped and bought a bottle of gin, went home and wrote an effusive goodbye letter to his wife, his handwriting becoming more illegible with every gulp of gin. Then he removed the mirror from the bedroom dresser, and placed it on the floor against the wall. He sat on the carpet in front of that mirror and watched as he inserted the muzzle of his revolver into his mouth.

Slick was my friend. Slick was everyone's friend.

CHAPTER THIRTY-TWO
Dual Life

Russell was not yet five years old when he watched with fascination as garbage men romped behind the house and started lifting the two galvanized cans. The bigger of the two men noticed the boy standing there. "Hey there, boah. What are you gonna be when you grow up?"

"I'm gonna be a policeman, just like my daddy,"

Russell responded, proudly.

The huge black man stopped and peered at the child. "Oh yeah?"

Russell stuttered and stammered, then said, "Uh, no, I really want to be a garbage man."

* * *

I was married to the job. Homicide work was not only fascinating, but obsessive. Intoxicating. I lived to succeed. To be the best. I lived for that acceptance I'd hungered for since the age of eleven. Sometimes, I'd wake up in the middle of the night, thoughts rambling about the Springer murder, or another case, then pace the floor. An idea would come to mind at 2 A.M., and I'd dress and drive up to a Broward County night club or restaurant and talk to a potential witness. Joan would ask, "Where are you going?" I'd dismiss the question, give her a kiss, and head out.

I admire those homicide detectives who were able to balance job demands with their family lives. Some had patient wives and kids at home who waited for whatever little time their husbands and fathers could offer them without complaint. Some had wives who were professionals in their own right, with their own job demands. That seemed to establish a balance. Others had serious domestic problems. Some remained single. Then there were the detectives who managed to work a lighter case load, milking three or four murder investigations a year to the last drop, avoiding new cases until they had no choice. The bulk of the office case load would end up in the hands of more gung-ho detectives who would take on as many as possible.

For me, and the likes of Kermit Russell and Dick Ward, it was not unusual to handle twelve murders a year, five or six rapes, plus eighty or ninety other death investigations (accidental, natural or suicide), an occasional abortion, police shooting, or a jail inmate rape, all of which fell under the purview of Homicide. On top of that, we all lent assistance to fellow detectives in the bureau, when they were loaded down with a hot new murder and extra manpower was needed. Reciprocity expected. Regardless, these cases consumed huge blocks of time, not only in the search for evidence, interviewing witnesses, and travel outside of town, but in the mundane tasks of itemizing personal property, attending meetings, working with forensics, and writing report after report. Somewhere in the midst, as a detective's work load mounted, so did his demand for appearing at depositions, pre-trials, and court trials. Each cop was also required to attend a number of routine training days a month, outside of Homicide, plus qualify once a year at the range. (By this time, I'd become an average shot, no longer quivering with a gun in my hand.)

Joan wanted more time as a complete family. She wanted more love making time. I doled it out in dribs and drabs. Joan started to make demands. She worked at IHOP by day, took care of kids by night and waited for whatever morsel of time I had to offer. I visited with Bennett, by the grace of his mother, once or twice a month. By this time, I felt more like one of those part-time Big Brothers than his father. Bill Gertz had become his father. When I learned that he had been enrolled in school as Bennett Gertz, I was furious, but helpless.

While I knew that Joan and the kids needed my attention, I felt the need for solitude outside of the job, even if for a few moments. I often stopped at a bar on the way home, just to sit, and smoke, and drink, and think. Coming home, it seemed, added to the pressures rather than relieving them.

Joan wanted to redecorate, fix the house, buy furniture. I dreaded her expectations. Not so long before, I'd been needy for the love I finally acquired, and now I thirsted for pockets of solitude. Sometimes I wished I could just come home to my little room and play piano or violin. (I hadn't taken it out of the case since my mother became ill.)

Fights broke out, usually over money issues or her want for more of my attention. I began pouring giant cocktails, to numb. As pressures mounted, I lost control, and went into rages, spewing anger, shouting, cursing, breaking furniture.

Once, Joan locked herself in the bedroom door and refused to open it. I charged down the hall like a bull, blasted through, splinters and all, screaming, defending, demanding, then running out to the car and driving away for a few moments of peace.

George Reincke joked that when he'd come over for a social visit, he never knew what he'd find in the trash heap, a twisted lamp, splintered end table, broken door, smashed television set.

Of this behavior—and other aspects of my life—I am not proud. But I cannot tell the story without incorporating a little of the dark side.

* * *

The more people razzed me about the Springer murder, the more I was determined to solve it. Captain Spaeth laughingly offered to buy me a steak dinner if I ever closed the case. Other guys offered to help, time permitted, if I needed it. Dick Ward was no longer my regular partner in deference to his own case load. Under strict orders not to venture into Broward County alone, I sought the help of anyone who would just ride along. C.T. Clark, Bob Laws, Marvin Pittman and Mike Coon were among the detectives who volunteered to help, always uncompensated. When all else failed, I scooped up my friend, George Reincke—now in Warrants Bureau—as a stand-in partner.

But the Springer murder had become a conundrum of seedy personalities, varied motives, corrupt politicians and suspicious cops. From Russ Golden, Springer's partner, and George Datz, his buddy, I learned he owed big money to bookmakers (not Bernie), had pissed off a number of mobsters, was paying off the city of Dania, had threatened to kill a patron, and was mired in the middle of a love triangle outside of his relationship with Linda Pierce. In short, I had two dozen suspects, but not a shred of evidence.

Captain Cecil Stewart of BSO Vice continued to feed me information and seemed helpful. But as time went by, I began to realize most of the information was either invalid, exaggerated, or simply not true. Then, I learned through another interview with

Linda Pierce, that she was at police headquarters in the company of Captain Stewart and Sergeant Howard Metzger on the night of the crime, at the approximate time Springer was first missing. Strange, indeed. Allegedly, she told Stewart she had a feeling that something bad was going to happen to Jerry Springer that night. When pressed, this was based on nothing more than a hunch, no facts, no information. I didn't believe her.

According to Stewart, he and Metzger held her there at the office for several hours asking questions instead of proceeding to the Show Club to check things out in person. I began to realize, I'd been had. Now I was sure, Stewart was somehow involved in the murder, either directly or indirectly, and had been deliberately leading me on wild goose chases for months.

My relationship with BSO turned to ice when I asked that Stewart and Metzger take polygraph tests. They agreed, but insisted on an independent examiner of their choice.

On the day of the examination, I arrived first at the home office of Warren Holmes, a well-known polygraph expert in Miami. We sat a few minutes as I briefed him on the particulars of the case, and why I asked for the polygraph. I was then asked to sit in the waiting room.

Ten minutes later, Cecil Stewart arrived with his pudgy acolyte. Just down the hall, I watched and listened as the greetings took place. "Hello, Warren. Good to see you.

How's the family?"

"Just, fine, Cecil. It's been a long time. Good to see you, too. Come on in."

They passed the test.

* * *

Our department had one polygraph examiner on staff, an aging pee wee of a fellow named Kenneth Schorr who reminded me of a high strung Mr. Peepers, a wimpy television personality from those days. After a number of cases, I learned that the machine was really not a lie detector at all, but a stress indicator. In determining deception, it was only as good as the quality of its examiner. The ideal goal for an examiner was to obtain an admission. Of all, that was the best result. Declaring someone a liar based solely on the charts was iffy at best.

An inept interrogator, Schorr could operate the machine and pose perfunctory questions, but his weak persona posed no threat to someone who might be lying. To young criminals, blacks and whites, he was laughable. To hardened killers, he was laughable. Even to some detectives, he was laughable.

In one instance, Kermit Russell and his partner had been watching the polygraph from outside a one-way mirror. They figured they'd play a joke on Schorr. When the little man returned outside after conducting a test, he asked the detectives a question they had anticipated. (he never could make a decision) "What do you think? Is he lying?"

Kermit told him, "I think he's lying, absolutely."

The other detective said, "I think the man is telling the truth."

Scratching his head, Schorr wrote his final report: "Inconclusive"

I used polygraph mostly as an interrogation tool, not as an end-all to find out if someone was lying. With Schorr, I often sat in and conducted the follow-up interrogation, because I didn't have confidence in him. As long as polygraph testing was an enigma to any witness or suspect, it could be used effectively as an object of intimidation. It was not the charts that proved someone a liar, it was the admissions gleaned based on the charts.

It worked best after my partner (Gary Minium) and I had arrested a suspect in a Liberty City rape. [11]Herbert Andrews was an imposing black man in his mid thirties who stood at least six-foot three, and had arms the size of my thighs. The woman claimed they had met at a bar where he offered to take her home. Then, he forced himself upon her in the parking lot against her will, threatening to kill her if she screamed. All evidence pointed to his guilt, including lipstick stains on his shirt, his make and color of car, and a witness at the bar who corroborated seeing them together. She had been taken to the hospital, where tests proved the presence of semen in her vagina. All the pieces fit. We had probable cause.

Herb Andrews sat in the Homicide office wearing handcuffs, waived his Miranda rights and insisted he was innocent. I'd heard that before, a hundred times over. But something about Herb tha made us listen. He was adamant.

---

[11] Herbert Andrews – fictitious name

He did not want a lawyer. He pleaded that we check things out further.

While Herb remained under guard at headquarters, we went back into the field, located the victim, and asked that she take a polygraph. That's one of those questions with only one right answer. After all, why wouldn't she? If she refused, suspicion would point her way.

An hour later, Kenneth Schorr had her strapped to the chair. The needles flew off the chart at the hot questions. I took over the interrogation. Instead of accusing her, I simply asked, "Why did you not tell the whole truth about this?"

She looked around the room.

"It's okay, Nellie Mae. We understand you might have an issue here, but we need to know the whole truth."

She looked around some more.

I looked her directly in the eyeballs, the most intimidating technique known to man. "You see, we know you lied. And you know you lied. So, let's make up and be friends."

"Okay. I thinks I pointed to the wrong man. But I was raped, you hear?"

Nellie Mae was charged with making a false report.

Herb Andrews was released before ever being booked, a good example of an innocent man who was willing to talk instead of hiding behind a lawyer. He was the only man in my entire career I ever unarrested.

* * *

Just as Joan and I were about to make love, the phone rang. "Please, don't answer it," she said.

"I have to. I'm on call." She turned over on her side to face the wall, her pug nose turning red with anger. I picked up the receiver. "Newborn baby found in a dumpster, Marshall. You're it. See you on the scene."

CHAPTER THIRTY-THREE
Trials And Tribulations

Six months after we arrested Tony Esperti, amid a firestorm of local publicity, the trial began with old Judge John Kehoe presiding. The sixth floor courtroom was like something out of a classic 1940s movie, oak railings, twelve man jury box, high ceilings, checkered tile floors. I'd sat in this courtroom many times before watching trials. This was the first time I was the lead detective.

News reporters and television cameras followed us everywhere. I could say they were a nuisance, but in truth, publicity added excitement to the whole affair. I loved the interviews, the television news accounts of the trial, the morning *Miami Herald*, the pictures, and the hoopla.

Al Sepe headed the prosecution team. Italian, short, confident, cocky, he reminded me of Bernie's cronies. With his suave good looks and charismatic personality, he should have been a movie star. Wiry Dave Goodhart was his assistant; nervous, high strung, he looked like a skinny owl, black hair, turned down nose, and never a smile on his face.

Lou Vernell headed up the defense, assisted by a young blond mob lawyer named Bill Moran. Together, they reminded me of a typical Mafia lawyers in the movies, with all the nuances, accents, shifty bodies and threatening glances.

The trial lasted two weeks. As a key witness, I was not permitted in the courtroom. Employees of the Place For Steak testified how they saw and heard the shots, but could not identify the shooter. Fortunately, Charlie Dore, the out-of-town witness, held fast and pointed directly at Esperti. He was not intimidated by the defense. The speck of gunpowder on Esperti's seemed to seal the case.

At the last minute, the defense team came up with a surprise witness who said he saw the shooter—unidentified—enter the foyer from the restaurant side, not the bar side, just before the shots rang out. If so, they said, the shooter could not have been Esperti. The prosecutors were furious that this witness was not revealed to them during pretrial motions. So intense was the anger, a fist fight broke out in the courthouse during a break between Goodhart and Sepe, Vernell and Moran.

But Sepe had it all figured. No one saw Esperti just prior to the shooting and it was entirely plausible that when he spotted Altamura enter the foyer, he took the back route through the kitchen and out into the restaurant side. That would have validated the new defense witness, yet still convict Esperti as the killer.

Sepe was magnificent in closing arguments, pacing before the jury box, reciting the case from his head without looking at notes, re-enacting the murder before their eyes, feigning a gun in his hand, slamming his foot down to give sound to the shots, so effective that the jurors shook in their seats each time he stomped. "And then, ladies and gentlemen, this man, this vicious killer, walked up behind Tommy Altamura and with malice aforethought, fired five shots into his body... BANG... BANG... BANG... BANG... BANG." Filled to capacity, the courtroom sat electrified as Al Sepe charged the jury with the responsibility to find Tony Esperti guilty as charged.

The jury deliberated two days. As history would tell us, eleven jurors had reached a quick verdict. One man held out, refusing to convict. Mistrial. Lest we not forget the element that was on trial here.

A year later, a new trial was held after a change of venue, in Bartow, Florida. Esperti was convicted, and sentenced to life in prison.

(In a twist of irony, Al Sepe and David Goodhart, would eventually become Circuit Judges, only to be caught in a multi-judge sting taking kickbacks for favors. They each served time in federal prison.)

* * *

One of the most important tools of a homicide investigator is his notes. One never knows from the onset of a case, just how complicated it may become, or how long it will take to reach successful closure. While working a whodunit, the "lead sheet" is essential. As ideas come to mind, as clues are known, new names, and information unveils more mystery to the case, a To-Do List helps the investigator to stay on track and not forget little things down the road. As Ray Beck told me, the smallest, most unsuspecting of leads, can surprisingly solve a case.

Still obsessed with the Springer homicide and working at least twenty extra hours a week, besides my regular duties in rotation, I was starting to get discouraged. Three hundred leads on my yellow pad had already been followed in vain, with another hundred to go. Not to give up, I came across a name, Honey North, scribbled on the sheet only because I'd heard she was one of the strippers who once worked at the Show Club. Other than that, I knew nothing about her.

Before seeking her out, I did some research. Honey North worked for the infamous Zorita—the snake dancer—at her strippers club on Collins Avenue's Motel Row where I once patrolled as a uniformed officer. I also learned that she was living in a lesbian relationship with another woman named Gail Bishop. Gail was the daughter of Jim Bishop, a renowned and popular columnist for the Miami Herald. (In 1968, the term "gay" still meant "happy.")

Because the bar was in Dade County, I needed no partner, so I headed out one evening for Zorita's Club. There, Zorita introduced me to Honey North, dirty blond hair, innocently pretty, pug-nosed, designer glasses. A Puerto Rican stripper danced on a stage behind the bar as the music blared so loudly, it was nearly impossible to hear. I asked Honey if I could talk to her about the Springer murder. She said she knew nothing about it and to leave her alone. Then, I played my trump card. After all, being a lesbian in 1968 was not so acceptable as it is today. "Well, do you know Gail Bishop?"

Honey North riveted her posture, looked at me astonished, and became visibly nervous. She knew that I had done my homework. She wanted to protect her lover, and her lover's father. "Okay, I'll meet you outside the club somewhere quiet. But I don't know nothing about

Springer's murder, okay?"

"Okay."

Thirty minutes later, we sat at a table in the back room of the Rascal House restaurant, the most famous Jewish deli in South Florida. I offered a cigarette, she accepted. I said very little, except to watch her body language. She began to tremble, unable to hold the cup of coffee with one hand, lips quivering. I couldn't believe this was all because I knew she had a lover named Gail Bishop.

By now, I figured I'd stumbled on to something. As we talked more in dribs and drabs, she admitted having worked at the Show Club, even at the time the killing took place. She knew Jerry Springer well, saying he was a son-of-a-bitch, wise guy with no manners, who pissed off everyone around him.

She was definitely rattled by my presence. I felt it was time to go for the jugular, but very carefully. *Tell, don't ask.* I took a shot. "You see, Honey," I said, after a long drag from my Pall Mall, "I know you know who killed Jerry Springer."

When she dropped the cup, I realized I had her. A strange feeling came over me. After fourteen months, I was about to solve the murder of Jerry Springer. Inside, I quivered with anxiety but didn't dare let on. It was important to go slow, patronize this woman, make her feel safe. Honey shivered some more, looked all around the room as though the killer might be listening. She glanced up at me with pleading eyes and choked the words, "I didn't want any part of this."

Oh my God, is she going to tell me she did it?

"I know, Honey. I understand."

Before the night was over, and with a promise to protect her from evil, she told everything. Honey North was bi-sexual, and besides her female partners, she'd been the girlfriend of Russell Golden, the slick half-owner of the Show Club. She was on stage dancing when she heard muffled shots fired from the back office. The music continued. She dared not stop. Springer was never seen again.

Early that next morning, Russ Golden was in a state of hysteria blathering to her about his involvement in the killing. He swore her to secrecy lest she be killed herself. Jerry Springer was shot in the office by none other than his best friend, George Datz, the bouncer. Russ was not there, and didn't participate in the murder. But he did walk into the room—unsuspecting—shortly after, and saw Jerry's body lying on the floor. Datz ordered Russ to help him put the body into the trunk of his car. Russ dared not refuse. That's where it ended. Datz took off and returned to the club hours later, with Jerry Springer lying in a watery ditch somewhere in the Everglades. Meanwhile, Russ, 35 years old with no criminal record, was petrified of Datz, and now found himself as an accessory to murder.

Honey North's testimony was pure hearsay and useless as probable cause to arrest. I needed Russell Golden.

After fourteen months and hundreds of interviews, I had established a friendly relationship with the man. I called and asked that he come down to the office, something important to discuss with him. I wanted him on my turf. He arrived wearing his customary turtle neck shirt and plaid sport jacket. Chuck Harbolt and C.T. Clark listened in from outside the door. We exchanged pleasantries, but I could see he was concerned about this trip to the homicide office.

I didn't want to waste any time. I lit a cigarette and posed the same statement I posed to Honey North. "Russ, I know you know who killed Jerry Springer."

The words stunned him. He looked behind his shoulder, though he knew we were alone in the room. Sweat beaded on his brow. His eyes shifted, left and right, then stared at me with guilt written over his forehead. He pretended that he didn't know what I was talking about, but I peered into the pupils of his eyes, and told him over and over, "Russ. I know. You know. It's time to stop the bullshit, or you will go down the tubes also. I'm waiting."

The local line buzzed. It was Chuck Harbolt, whispering to me, "Go slow, Marshall. You got him, but go slow."

Two minutes later, Russ Golden cracked. He was deathly afraid of George Datz, and asked for whatever protections we could give him. I told him that Datz wouldn't know he talked, until after he was in jail.

I had me a solved whodunit.

There had been an on-going feud between George Datz and Jerry Springer, but Russ didn't know Datz was capable of murder. When he stepped back into the office that night, he almost fainted when he saw Springer lying on the floor next to the door, blood oozing from his shirt. Datz was holding a .38 revolver with a crude silencer attached. Russ panicked. Datz ordered him to shut up or he'd kill him too. Then he helped put the body in Datz's trunk.

The next day, he and Datz stood on a street corner in the town of Dania, Florida, talking about their strategy, how and what they'd tell the cops if Jerry was reported missing. Datz never thought they'd find the body. While they stood there, Datz took the silencer from his pocket and tossed it into the sewer drain.

Arrest warrants were drawn up. Marvin Pittman and I went to the Show Club the next night, with a number of forensic criminalists and caught George Datz completely by surprise.

"You are under arrest, murder one."

How sweet it was.

* * *

As a follow up, I asked the Dania Public Works Department if they could assist us by digging through the sewer drain, just in case that silencer was still there fourteen months later. After an hour of digging through sludge, there it was, coated with dirt and grime, but a silencer nonetheless. Russ Golden had told the truth.

* * *

Besides Al Sepe and Dave Goodhart, I had established a close working relationship with a number of fine prosecutors. Among them, I. Richard Jacobs stood out as the only lawyer I ever knew who could go into a pretrial or preliminary hearing without ever looking at a file, then shoot from the hip and win every motion or ruling he went after. Thin and wiry, Jacobs had an eye for the ladies, ever distracted by a passing skirt as I tried desperately to brief him on a murder case in the two minutes allotted. But he was a powerful force before a jury, often bringing them to tears in his summations.

I wanted one of these guys to prosecute George Datz. They refused. Since the murder actually occurred in Broward County, thus the case belonged in Ft. Lauderdale.

In helping to prepare the Broward State Attorney's Office over the next six months, I sensed their prosecutors weren't particularly sharp or as dedicated as I was accustomed. A month before trial, the elected State Attorney resigned, leaving his vacancy to a temporary prosecutor until a new election could be held. The assigned prosecutor in the Datz case also resigned. The case now shifted into the hands of a newcomer who, to my disappointment, took very little time orienting himself to the intricate details of the case.

Meanwhile, folders from the giant Springer case file became mysteriously missing from the Homicide office. Betty Cousins, whose integrity was unquestioned, maintained all files in a locked cabinet which was accessible only to Homicide supervisors and the shift commanders who worked the evening and midnight shifts. Two weeks later, those folders suddenly reappeared into the case file again. Truly a mystery.

Broward County prosecutors insisted that Russell Golden take a polygraph. He did. He passed. Then they wanted Golden to submit to truth serum. He agreed and appeared at a doctor's office where he was administered sodium amytal. That was an interesting experience to watch, seeing him in a state of drowsiness, slurring out the same consistent story he had told before. Passed.

Datz hired defense attorney, Jack Nagley, famed for his ill-fated defense of Jack "Murph The Surf" Murphy who, along with an accomplice, had just been convicted for his part in the knifing murder of two young women at Whiskey Creek.

With the new team at the prosecution table, the trial began amid another onslaught of daily television cameras and newspaper reporters. Again, as a key witness who knew more about the evidence, witnesses and principals than anyone, I was not allowed in the courtroom. During breaks, I tried to consult with the young prosecutors, but they avoided me. I had a bad feeling about this. When I finally took the stand, I awaited key questions, the answers to which would be incriminating toward Datz. They never went there. During breaks, they consistently avoided me.

Strangely, I was called to the stand by Jack Nagley, on behalf of the defense. That's when the big mystery was solved. He lifted a file folder from his table, and started asking me about the names of several other prior suspects, information he wasn't supposed to know. Over the objections of prosecutors, he displayed letters and reports that I had written over a year before. He asked one question after another, certain to instill doubts in the minds of the jury. Somehow, Jack Nagley had managed to infiltrate the Homicide Office and obtain copies of the case file.

Russ Golden testified, as did Honey North. Nagley did his best to portray them as witnesses hostile to Datz.

The jury was out four hours.

Not Guilty.

Lest we not forget, the element that was on trial here.

* * *

Captain Roy Longbottom was a sore spot with E. Wilson Purdy. He had embarrassed the department during the 1968 riots when he spent down time marching police officers around Liberty City like a Parris Island Marine platoon. He was also one of the holdovers from the Buchanan regime who was suspected of taking payoffs from organized crime figures for protection. One of those, Dolores Costello (who was one of the targets during my days in Special Enforcement) was killed in January of 1968, along with her boy friend, Brian Perez, execution style, hands bound, blindfolded, and shot in the head while she lay on her own bed. The case was never solved. Longbottom was known to be friendly with her.

A large and overbearing man, Roy Longbottom was eventually pulled from his road assignment into the Shift Commander's Office, midnight shift. He spent many hours alone in Detective Bureau every night with access to the homicide files, during the period when those files were missing.

Under a cloud, Longbottom left the department and went to work as a maintenance man in a local church. From there, he was deemed clinically paranoid and committed to a mental institution. He later died of natural causes leaving a legacy that no one in the department really cared about.

CHAPTER THIRTY-FOUR
Detective Clouseau

Kermit Russell was dispatched to a routine DOA call where a man had been stricken at his home with an apparent heart attack, then taken to a local hospital and pronounced dead. When Kermit lifted the sheet covering the body, he saw that it was none other than his boss, Captain Lou Spaeth, commander of Homicide.

I never did get that steak dinner.

* * *

Someone once asked me who was the most famous dead person I ever handled. Certainly a sick question, but it didn't take long to answer.

The lieutenant sent me on a routine DOA call to a high rise apartment building in Bal Harbor, just north of Miami Beach on the same island. When I arrived at the penthouse overlooking the Atlantic Ocean, I was greeted by a well-dressed gentleman who had been attending to his boss, the deceased. He had stepped out of the bedroom for a few minutes, and when he returned, the old man was on the floor. He had heart problems in the past. Fire-Rescue came, but it was too late. After obtaining the gentleman's name and personal data, I entered the room and saw the dead man lying face up on the plush carpet, eyes partly open and a serene glow to his sculptured features. I recognized his face immediately, the distinctive part in his hair, though a little more gray now, that pencil-thin mustache, very distinguished.

I stood there alone for a moment and thought. Wow! Here I am, with the man who almost became the president of the United States. Matter of fact, according to the *Chicago Tribune*, he actually beat Harry S Truman.

Thomas E. Dewey.

* * *

I hate to dispel the long standing myth perpetuated by television and movies that all solved homicides are the result of clever sleuthing. Not so. Homicide detectives rarely solve murders. Of all the cases that are cleared, ninety-five percent can be attributed to information provided by witnesses and/or the weight of clear evidence, regardless of who worked the case. Homicide/suicides are an automatic closure every time. Domestic murders—which comprise a large number—usually yield an array of background information, motives, and other evidence. Suspects are often known to the witnesses who simply tell who did it. Fingerprints, blood, etc. identified on a crime scene are sometimes handed to detectives by the crime lab as a virtual gift in solving a murder. Stupidity of the killer, like getting caught on a surveillance camera, leaving a blood trail, or telling about his deed to a third party, results in many closed cases. In fact, detectives often act as facilitators and reporting agents, assembling evidence and compiling files into a neat package full of documents to support a conclusion and/or to bring a defendant to trial.

In all the years I was associated with Homicide, I saw but a handful of cases where I could honestly say the murder would never have been solved if it hadn't been for the unique handling by a particular detective. C.T. Clark's solving of the Patricia Rooks murder was one. I know of another handled by Kermit Russell, and a few others. Skillful interrogation, at times, causes a suspect to confess where another detective may not have had the same results.

The Jerry Springer murder is an example of one case that might never have been solved had it not been for the tenacity of the detective assigned. For that, the Homicide supervisory staff recommended me for the Officer of the Month Award, the most prestigious department recognition at the time. Presented by E. Wilson Purdy, marked only the second time in the department's history that a homicide detective was so honored.

The first was Ray Beck.

* * *

Lieutenant Chuck Harbolt stood in the squad room shouting names for roll call, when he called a new name:

"Pearson?"

"Here, sir," responded a female voice from the back of the room.

We all looked back. We had seen this young, slim, brown-haired woman milling around headquarters that morning and thought she was a new secretary. Not so. Madeline Pearson was the first female to be assigned to Homicide as regular duty. Previously, women were given temporary assignments for decoy operations, searching women prisoners, stakeouts, and such. Her sudden presence was an anomaly.

Until then, stereotypical homicide detectives had been white Anglo males between 25 and 45 years of age, who smoked at least a pack a day, drank moderate to heavy and wore the most stylish of suits. Females were clerical support or juvenile detectives. No way could a woman handle murder investigations, dead bodies, crime scenes, interrogations, and complicated prosecutions.

She must have known there would be animosity and resistance. Yet, this lady rookie stood tall and resilient.

Mike Coon was livid. "No way am I working with that pock-faced broad," he muttered, loud enough for her to hear. Pearson steeled herself. A divorced mother of a four-year-old boy, she'd been working as an insurance secretary for six years and saw police work as an opportunity for a better future. And so it was.

Because she was an unknown, E. Wilson Purdy ordered Madeline into Homicide direct from the academy t work with Ray Wertis investigating illegal abortions. But Wertis, a die-hard gambler, would have none of it. Each day, he would station Madeline at a select location with instructions to watch a house or a business and to take down all the tag numbers. Then he'd disappear for four hours, usually to Hialeah Race Track or his favorite bookie.

There were time when Wertis didn't show up for work at all. Some of us—including Kermit Russell and myself—felt sorry for the way she was treated and offered to take her with us on investigations. I made a particular point of bringing her to watch autopsies at the Medical Examiner's Office, a distasteful task which she handled like a trooper.

Her days in Homicide were limited, especially after Ray Wertis left the department and ended up in federal prison. Not only that, abortions became legalized, pulling the rug out from the black market.

After her transfer to General Investigations, (burglaries, thefts, assaults, etc.) Madeline's career accelerated rapidly. She became part of the movement that won equal rights for police women, leveling them in the same rank structure with their male counterparts. From there, she went on to become the first female Captain and Major on the Metro-Dade Police Department, before retiring in 1998.

Irony has its twists. Madeline was the last boss I worked under before I retired in 1990.

* * *

Speaking of illegal abortions, there were two murder cases in my career as a field investigator in which I failed to perform effectively resulting in them remaining open (unsolved). In other words, I bungled them completely.

One of those was the murder of [12]Bruce Milligan in May of 1968. A bruiser of a man, about thirty-five years of age, Milligan was found by a maid in a second floor room of a North Miami motel, lying fully clothed, face down on the floor, with several bullets in his body. Because this is an open case and officially remains under investigation, I must omit much of the crime scene detail. Suffice it to say, it appeared that Milligan was in the room to meet someone, he thought, friendly.

We learned that he worked as a veterinarian by day and an abortionist by night, using his office facility for performing the illegal deeds. He also had several friends and acquaintances within the netherworld of organized crime. Just as in the Springer murder, I compiled a list of unsavory people he knew, many of whom were capable of such an act.

Milligan's wife was a shapely young woman who seemed to be distraught over the death of her husband. She cooperated fully, providing details about the night before when she last saw her husband. The phone had rung. Milligan answered and agreed to meet someone at an undisclosed location away from the house. Clandestine little meetings with shady figures outside the house were not uncommon. At the same, time, [13]Harry Weissburg, a personal friend from out of town, had been visiting at the Milligan house. He verified the same basic story. She was candid about Milligan's illegal activities and even pointed out a number of handguns in his dresser drawer which he had collected over the years.

---

[12] Bruce Milligan – fictitious name
[13] Harry Weissburg – fictitious name

Several days after the investigation ensued, firearms experts in the Crime Lab unveiled an interesting discovery. Bullet markings indicated that the same gun used to kill Bruce Milligan had also been used to kill Dolores Costello and Brian Perez four months before. From that point, I worked on the assumption that a local organized crime (O.C.) figure, probably one of the suspects in the unsolved Costello execution, had also killed Milligan. I dogged the case in that direction, checking names, alibis, showing mug photos to Mrs. Milligan, comparing fingerprints from the motel room, interviewing known thieves, and spending hundreds of hours trying to solve this whodunit.

My best link to obtaining information, Mrs. Milligan seemed genuinely concerned. When I told her that the same gun had been used in another O.C. killing, she seemed startled.

Little did it occur to me that Bruce Milligan may have been a source for illicit weaponry to his criminal friends, and that the murder weapon had actually been sitting in that dresser drawer inside his own house. I should never have said anything to Mrs. Milligan. Weeks later, after that thought occurred to me, I asked her if I could see those guns again. Of course, the murder weapon was not there. And neither was Harry Weissburg.

What was it that Ralph Kramden used to say on *The Honeymooners?* "I've got a biiiiig mouth!"

* * *

The other case I botched occurred several years later.

Beautiful, young [14]Cathy Anderson was found on a September Monday morning by her ex-husband lying supine on the bedroom floor of her own house, partially clothed. She'd been strangled.

Cathy hadn't been seen since Saturday afternoon. When she arrived home from shopping, Mr. Anderson was there waiting to talk to her. He didn't want the divorce. She did. They argued. He left.

Thirty six hours later on Monday morning, after Cathy failed to show up for work, her boss called the house several times with no response. He then called Mr. Anderson, whom he knew, and asked him to go to her house and check on her. When he did, Mr.

---

[14] Cathy Anderson – fictitious name

Anderson found her dead. Distraught, he ran next door to an old friend and neighbor who called police.

The crime scene was like something out of a textbook, all the trimmings with which to reconstruct the murder. We took half the day sketching, photographing, collecting evidence and talking to everyone who knew Cathy. Everyone, that is, except, Anthony, who was in such distress, he checked himself into a hospital.

Later that evening, I tracked Mr. Anderson down and conducted an interview while he lay grieving in his bed. Cooperative and helpful, he related his movements, step by step, from the time he last saw Cathy on Saturday, to finding her on the floor that Monday morning.

Later that night, I mulled over the interview in my mind. Anthony said that he went into the bedroom, gasped, knelt down, lifted and cradled her head, gently kissed her, her eyes bulging, face blue.

Wait a minute. I examined Cathy's body in detail. Her face was not blue, her eyes were not bulging. Matter of fact, she was in complete rigor mortis, stiff as a board. How could he have cradled her head? Then it occurred to me. Anthony had been describing Cathy at the time of her death, not her discovery.

Why didn't I think of that when I had the chance to nail him in the interview?

Just when I thought it was not too late, and I was heading back to the hospital for a second interview, I received a call from a prominent local attorney who said he was now representing Mr. Anderson. I was not to talk to his client any further without him being present, at which time, of course, he would not agree to answer any more questions.

Well, you know how it is with innocent folks.

The murder of Cathy Anderson remains technically unsolved to this day.

My marriage to Joan had its ups and downs, a steady repeat of sex, drinking and arguing about attention and money, with a little fun thrown in from time to time, taking the kids to the beaches and making huge celebrations for birthdays and holidays. Each Christmas Eve, we spent the entire night quietly putting together bicycles, swing sets, racing tracks, dolls, and so many toys that they virtually covered the entire living room. With no sleep, we woke the kids at 6 A.M. to watch the glee. Definitely a rewarding experience.

Joan and I agreed that it would bind the relationship to have our own child together. She stopped taking the pill. Sure enough, she became pregnant in January of 1969.

She made no secret of it. Joan wanted a baby girl, and she wanted her to have black hair, just like her mommy.

CHAPTER THIRTY-FIVE
Rape

The most difficult aspect of investigating a rape is discerning truth from fiction. At the same time, the investigator must be aware that the victim has probably suffered a horrible and traumatic event. Showing sensitivity and compassion is as important as catching the perpetrator.

Before there was such a thing as specialized Sexual Battery Units, Metro-Dade homicide detectives also handled reports of rape. In the 1960s and early '70s, rape carried the maximum punishment: Death. Thus, investigations were pursued with the same vigor of a homicide. (Large police agencies today dedicate specially trained investigators to sexual battery cases, handling nothing else.)

During my tenure, approximately one-half of all rape investigations were deemed "unfounded." Translated, that means—after a thorough review of the facts—the elements of a crime were simply not present, and/or the rape didn't happen at all. Police were often used as a tool by angry women who swore retribution to a man over a domestic squabble. Also, crying "rape" was often a cover for being caught in compromising situations. Some "victims" were only concerned about explaining an unwanted pregnancy.

In a typical unfounded case, a woman called the Detective Bureau and complained that she was victimized with nonconsensual sex while out on a date. He drove to a lovers lane where he made advances. She didn't want to have sex, he did. He told her she'd have to walk home unless she gave in. She submitted. She defined that as rape. In reality, she was pissed off and wanted to stick it to the fellow.

Unfortunately, as the police were inundated with so many of unfounded reports, the onus was on bonafide victims to assure investigators they were, in fact, victims of a bonafide rape. These investigations consumed a tremendous amount of a detective's time and, yes, each call was screened with a touch of cynicism until the detective was satisfied that the report was a genuine crime. Just as in handling a homicide, I felt the same spirit of responsibility when investigating a true rape. At the same time, I resented so-called victims who distorted truth, wasted our time and energy, and disregarded the seriousness of the charge they were making.

Many reports were clearly valid where the victim had obviously been beaten or threatened with great bodily harm, or there were supporting witnesses. Others submitted to sheer power and threats of death. In cases of one-on-one, where there were no other witnesses, no physical evidence to support, and the parties knew each other, it was a matter of sorting out facts and praying that we did not arrest an innocent person.

One of the more horrifying cases occurred in the tiny blue-collar town of Opa Locka, Florida, just northwest of Miami. The assault will have left an indelible mark in the minds of two decent people, not only from the acts of the assailants, but the criminal justice system as well. Dennis and Maggie Strickland* were a young married couple heading for a Sunday night church service in their pick-up truck. They sought the shortest route, not thinking about the risks of neighborhoods they traveled through. Sure enough, at a traffic signal, they were accosted by three black males, one of whom boarded the cab of the truck holding a pistol to the head of Maggie, while the other two hopped into the back. Dennis was ordered to drive to a remote wooded location. In the semi-darkness amid thorns and cabbage palms, each assailant took turns with Maggie while forcing Dennis to watch at gunpoint.

Headlights appeared at a distance. The rapists then ordered Dennis and Maggie back into the truck, only this time, Dennis was in the back—held at gunpoint by one subject—while one of the assailants drove. As they traveled to a new destination, the third assailant continued to have sex with Maggie in the front seat.

After arriving at a more remote wooded area, they each took turns one more time before tying them with nylon cord and running away on foot.

Dennis managed to free himself and call for help.

Needless to say, when I first arrived at the hospital, Maggie was a physical and psychological wreck, as was Dennis. My heart poured out. Intellectually, I knew it was my job to investigate and bring the rapists to justice, but I felt a personal charge as well. This was a horrible crime.

After interviewing street people throughout Opa Locka and tying up physical evidence from the truck, I managed to find the first suspect. Maggie Strickland came to headquarters where she viewed a line-up and pointed him out. Arrest number one.

The next day, we found suspect number two. Maggie came down again for a second line-up, and made an I.D. Arrest number two.

That led to a third suspect who was brought in for his line-up. Maggie returned one more time and pointed him out. Arrest number three.

Nightmare over? Afraid not.

Dennis and Maggie Stickland came to know police headquarters and the courthouse as though it were their own back yard. They were summoned to the State Attorney's Office for statements. It was torture enough to suffer the lifelong trauma, they each had to relive the horror for officials of the court. It didn't stop there.

Somehow, each suspect acquired separate attorneys. That meant Maggie and Dennis were subpoenaed to give statements to each attorney on three separate dates, where she was subjected to accusations of lying and racism.

The attorney's wanted separate trials for each defendant. The judge consented. They would be grilled on the witness stand over and over.

The Stricklands responded to every demand made of them. But they shared their inner feelings with me while waiting outside the courtroom during the first trial. "If we knew what we'd have to go through in this so-called justice system, we'd never have reported it to begin with."

The subjects were convicted. The first got the death penalty. The second agreed to testify against the third, and got a life sentence. The third pled guilty after his buddy turned state's evidence.

Another horrific rape occurred in the upscale neighborhood called Sky Lake, north of Miami. A couple and their fourteen year-old daughter lived in a modest home. Four thugs broke into the house and proceeded to terrorize the entire family, threatening to kill, beating, robbing, desecrating. The parents were held at gunpoint and made to watch as each took their turns with the young virgin.

The subjects? One was caught, tried and convicted. The others were never identified. No consolation for the victims.

A similar case happened one Christmas night in Cutler Ridge. A teenage couple had attended a school dance, then parked in a remote area not far from the mall. They were accosted by three subjects, each of whom raped the girl before they shot and killed the boy.

They also shot the girl in the head, but the bullet did not penetrate the brain. She lived to tell the story, but could never identify the rapists. The case remains unsolved to this day.

As I did in researching suicides, I conducted my own unofficial studies about rape, particularly victim ages, suspect ages, and racial equations. Though most victims were under thirty, we handled some where victims were over fifty and even sixty. These were usually an afterthought during a burglary, where the subjects decided to take more than jewels and money. Nearly ninety percent of all rapists were under the age of thirty.

Interestingly enough, the most common equations among races were consistent with the same equations attributed to murder. The most common reports of rape were black victims, black suspects. The second most common, white victims, black suspects. The third most common were white victims, white suspects. And with the exception of one strange case, I never knew of a report where a white rapist attacked a black female. Hispanic subjects were a rarity in those days, though we did prosecute one or two involving Mexicans. But, as the Cuban population grew over the years, so did their inclusion in sexual battery crimes.

* * *

Dade County was in the grips of a serial rapist using the same ploy from case to case and conducting himself so blatantly, it was almost as if he wanted to get caught.

Greg Stead was a local hero, a young teen who had been paralyzed playing the game of football. Charities were formed as the news media went to bat for the stricken kid.

One day, a north Dade woman responded to a knock at the door and saw a small bespectacled man standing with a pad in hand, asking if she would sign a petition for the Greg Stead Foundation. Familiar with the news stories, she agreed. Before her name was signed, she was staring into the muzzle of a .38 caliber revolver. The suspect ordered her inside the bedroom, tied her up, removed her clothes, and proceeded to rape her. All the while, he never tried to conceal his face, nor any of his scars and tattoos which she described in detail.

A week later, another woman opened her door to a knock and suffered the same fate. A third victim a week later. The man was gentle and never imposed bodily harm to his victims other than the act of intercourse.

A fourth victim was a black nurse who lived in a hospital dormitory on Miami Beach. Along with having sex and showing off his markings, he took the liberty to give this woman a complete hot oil massage.

The fifth was an odd case. The woman was quite large, ruddy complexion, a large bulbous nose, and simply unattractive. Yet, she responded to a knock at the door, was ordered into the bedroom at gunpoint, tied up and stripped of her clothes. However, according to the victim, the moment he penetrated, he suddenly stopped, stood up, got dressed and ran from the house.

News media followed the case from day to day, publishing composite sketches of the suspect, each showing a fellow with dark rimmed glasses and shaggy hair covering his neck. We were going nowhere, until I received a clandestine call from a doctor who worked in the mental ward at a local hospital. "Don't tell anyone I called," he said. "But I've got a guy in here who says he's raped five women. Thought you ought to know."

Super sleuth. That's me.

Richard "Ricky" Leichtman, 31, had checked himself in claiming "depression", that he wanted to kill himself, and that he'd been on heavy drugs. In truth, there were no drugs in his system, and he was about as depressed as I was. Ricky was very cooperative, and after waiving his Miranda rights, started confessing to each rape, the easiest cop-out of my career.

A product of foster homes and no family, Ricky had been in and out of jails since the age of twelve, for every crime imaginable short of murder, including armed robbery, burglary, rape, theft, drugs and more. No bigger than a bantamweight, and most likely bi-sexual, he found *love* and acceptance within prison walls.

He had been released from prison two months earlier after serving eight years of a ten year term for robbery. He didn't know how to manage money from a job, he didn't know when to eat or take a shower, unless someone in authority was there. If ever there was a classic case of someone being institutionalized, he was it. Releasing Ricky Leichtman from prison was like releasing a lion or tiger back into the wild from a life of captivity. It can't survive.

Ricky wanted to be back in prison. And so he returned. That's where he died twenty-five years later.

I asked him about each crime, which he openly described in a video taped confession. The hot oil rub over the black nurse, he said, was fulfilling a fantasy. He never would have hurt anyone, he said. An admitted homosexual in prison life, he really didn't even want to have sex, but he felt it was necessary to play out the modus operandi. Such was the case with victim number five, the large unattractive woman. He said he had to carry it through, tie her up and have sex. But once he looked directly at her, the erection fizzled like a deflated balloon.

* * *

Then, there was the "Big Dick Rapist" from Opa Locka. No one could describe this assailant, other than the dimensions of his giant appendage.

Over a period of two months, at least six elderly black women who lived alone had been burglarized during the night by an intruder who threatened harm, and then had his way with them before dashing out the window. None of the victims got a good look at his face, but they were all consistent in describing his significant body part. "Big. Really big!"

If we ever caught this guy, we wondered how we'd hold a line-up.

[15]Willie Sams was finally caught by uniformed police after a foiled burglary when the intended victim blasted him in the eyes with her "Big Mama's" fist. Cops formed a perimeter around the neighborhood, and in thirty minutes, Sams was cuffed sitting in the back seat of a police car.

I interrogated Willie Sams for over an hour at headquarters, after advising him of his rights. Though cooperative and talkative, Willie would not own up to all the rapes. We knew this was our man.

Bob Lamont was now a detective in homicide, the same cop who partnered with me the day I was shot in 1965. Bob had a caustic, arrogant way, and I thought this would be the best time to try out the fabled "good guy/bad guy" interrogation ploy. I was already the "good guy," patting Willie on the back, feeling sorry for his life, feeding him cigarettes and Twinkies. I took Bob aside and suggested

---

[15] Willie Sams - fictitious name

he talk to him a few minutes. Perhaps his style would be more effective.

From outside the interrogation room, the entire floor could hear Lamont ranting in a loud voice, "You miserable son of a bitch, low life bastard, piece of shit, do you realize what you did to those poor ladies? We're going to put you under the Goddam jail and feed you to all the queers, you understand that? Damn, I hate people like you...you..."

With that, Lamont stormed out of the door, his face beet red, and muttered to me, "He's all yours."

Giving him a little time to think, I waited five, maybe ten minutes, then re-entered the room. Willie was sitting, hands in his face, weeping. "I'm sorry," he said. After another Twinkie and a cigarette, Willie gave me a full confession.

No. We didn't hold that line-up.

CHAPTER THIRTY-SIX
New Faces

On October 15, 1969, Joan went into labor at North Miami General Hospital. Along with the kids, Russell, 6, and Annette, 9, we all sat and paced and chewed nails in the waiting room. Later that afternoon, planet earth was graced with the birth of Jennifer Marie, who—to Joan's delight—had a full head of black hair.

Once little Russell learned of this, he scamper around all excited and began telling everyone on the floor,

"My mommy just had a little black baby girl. My mommy just had a little black baby girl."

* * *

Lieutenant Chuck Harbolt was one of those people nobody could dislike. His even-tempered manner, his fairness, smarts and common sense made him a prince whom anyone would be lucky to work under. He lived with his devoted wife, Jean, in a modest North Miami apartment. Soon after he learned they were expecting a child, Chuck found he had cancer of the brain.

We, in Homicide, worked around death and misery every day, shirking any sense of emotional attachment. But when it came to one of our own, especially someone as revered as this man, it was a shock, indeed.

Nevertheless, Chuck maintained a positive spirit while continuing on as the field lieutenant in homicide, undergoing radiation therapy at Jackson Memorial Hospital every other day. Liability issues dictated that he could no longer drive a county car, so I drove him to work and back every day, and—whenever possible—brought him to crime scenes and to his therapy sessions. We talked often, about marriage, about his baby to come, about my family, about the guys and about working murders. "Don't complicate things more than you have to," he said. "Look for the simple answer. You'll never go wrong."

I never heard him complain. I never saw him depressed. It was as though he had a cold and would be over it in a few days.

His little girl, Laura Jean was born on the April 14, 1968. After only two and a half years of adoring his child, Chuck died quietly. Jean never remarried.

The wake was held at the same funeral parlor where we had honored his Captain, Lou Spaeth, two years earlier. Honor guards were present, reminding me of the same honor guard Chuck once stood among earlier in his career.

We all wept. He wouldn't have wanted it that way, but we did anyway.

* * *

Over the next few years, Homicide experienced a wave of new blood, including lieutenants and a captain named Dick Smith who had no homicide experience. He was known more for his administrative acuity. Small, athletic, Frank Wesolowski, looked like a blond teenager with a flat top just out of high school. At twenty-five, a former Marine, Ski had already been on the police department for four years in uniform. Someone must have thought he was sharp, or he wouldn't have been transferred into Homicide. It was my job to break him in, as I already had done with a number of other detectives. At this point, I was also teaching death investigation and interrogation techniques in the police academy.

Frank was easy to train, because he cared and he wanted to do things the right way. Whatever was taught to him stayed etched in concrete. With Frank Wesolowski, the job was done right, Ray Beck style.

But Frank had two other problems to worry about. His first love, baseball, consumed much of his off duty time (and—as we learned later—some of his on-duty time as well). Apparently, his wife felt much the same as mine, that she played second fiddle to job and hobby. (Or would that be *third fiddle?*) Often, I'd pick him up at his house in the mornings only to hear her scream at him from the window, followed by a baseball glove flying through the air out the door.

Riding with Frank was always an event. One day, we were heading for work when a dump truck turned over directly in front of us.

As we pulled out from his driveway the next day, a high speed police chase whizzed by. Of course, we had to join in.

Frank and I drove through upstate Florida for an investigation. As we traveled at 70 mph, for no apparent reason, this shy kid pulled out his snub nose revolver, pointed it out the window, and began shooting at birds and signs. Crazy guy. He scared the shit out of me.

His first whodunit was memorable, indeed, because it demonstrated how important it is to be completely certain before taking anyone's freedom away.

Early one August morning, Sherivon Wooten's body was found fully dressed under a tree in the middle of Liberty City. Young and shapely, she had been manually strangled. Information was sketchy about her whereabouts the night before, but we did learn she had performed as a prostitute in past times. Among other items, a tiny plastic-like item was found atop her thigh, like a small round chip from a fingernail, translucent, irregular edges, only a quarter-inch in diameter.

Three nights later, we picked up, [16]Walter Jones, a bus driver who was one of the last to see Sherivon alive, brought him to headquarters and asked a number of questions. The man was cooperative and friendly. As we talked, we noticed the top of his thumbnail had been gouged, about a quarter-inch in diameter. My heart started to race. It must have felt the same as C.T. Clark when that suspect double-snuffed a Benson & Hedges cigarette. Jones said he'd hurt his thumb working on a car.

Yeah. Sure.

This was too important to wait. I phoned Criminalist, Bill Hartner, the top forensic man in the Crime Laboratory. He said he'd come in from home and take a look.

When Hartner arrived at 1:00 A.M., we brought Walter Jones upstairs to the lab and had him sign every waiver form we could think of, to make it solid for court. Hartner examined the little piece of evidence under a microscope, then lifted it with tweezers and carefully laid it into the man's gouge spot. It fit like a jigsaw puzzle piece. This was our man. Hartner took us aside in the hallway and said, "Book him."

---

[16] Walter Jones – fictitious name

But wait. The most important thing was for the lab expert to testify that the item was, in fact, human fingernail material. We held off booking Mr. Jones, keeping him with us until the next morning, and into the afternoon, while Hartner brought the evidence item to a number of university labs in the county.

Final disposition: The item was actually a fish scale, from a bream or a bass. Walter Jones was released. Hartner sucked back his now infamous decree: "Book him."

And we learned once more, that most folks who are truly innocent are more than happy to cooperate.

The murder of Sherivon Wooten remains unsolved to this day.

* * *

Another newcomer showed up in Homicide on day, Gary Minium, the North Miami High School bully who shocked me when he showed up at the North District substation in uniform. Now it was my job to train Minium to become a homicide detective. Minium was a natural bloodhound, so I assigned him to Wesolowski, and I took another rookie who didn't work out so well.

At first, Wesolowski was intimidated by Minium's powerful personality, but he prevailed and became a fine trainer, imparting the same rules of procedure I had taught him and as Ray Beck had taught me. Minium became one of the best homicide investigators in Dade County history (in my opinion).

* * *

Transitions continued in Homicide into the 1970s as several of the sharpest men took high ranking jobs in other departments outside of Dade County. C.T. Clark, Marvin Pittman, Bob Laws and Mike Coon all moved on to become bigger fish in smaller ponds leaving Homicide open to new blood.

Meanwhile, E. Wilson Purdy issued a decree saying that anyone who wanted to be promoted must either have a college degree or be working toward one. I knew that other detectives would be studying for lieutenant, and I had no wish to work under many of them, so it behooved me to start thinking about a future promotion.

But, the word was clear. No college, no promotion. I had to sign up. That meant more time away from home and more pressures. Joan wanted attention. I wanted advancement. The two didn't mix.

CHAPTER THIRTY-SEVEN
A Litany of Murder

In moments of violent circumstance, when someone is seriously injured and facing possible death, it's natural to try and comfort the victim and assure him/her that everything's going to be all right. "Don't worry, fella.

You're not going to die. Hang in there."

Well, it doesn't always work that way. The hearsay rule in Florida dictates that any conversation outside the presence of the defendant is not admissible in court. Therefore, if a murder victim had once told a third party that Joe Blow had threatened to kill him, that third party cannot be called as a witness. One exception to that is when the dying person tells Joe Blow the name of his assailant while *knowing* he is going to die. These are rare instances.

Frank Wesolowski and I were coming back from another DOA, passing through Liberty City when we heard a call go out on the air. Shooting. It was neighborhood pandemonium when we pulled into the ghetto street five minutes later, hundreds of people milling around, some running to and fro, while a pair of ambulance attendants loaded a victim into the vehicle on a gurney. Sheets were stained in blood. We had to think fast.

I asked an onlooker what happened. "That's Sammy Bender*, he been shot."

"Do you know who shot him?"

"No."

I checked with the ambulance people. They said Sammy was still conscious and lucid, but that his wound might be fatal. That's all I needed to know.

Frank and I agreed to separate; he would take the streets and start rounding up witnesses, while I hopped in the back of the ambulance, badge in hand, to ride with the victim en route to Jackson Memorial, pondering the prospect of a dying declaration.

The ambulance interior was tight, with one attendant applying an IV, me kneeling next to the gurney, and the victim gasping for breath, looking to the ceiling, a small caliber bullet wound dead center in his lower chest. I hated to (it's a tough job, someone's gotta do it), but it was time to think of the court proceedings if Sammy didn't make it. If Sammy could tell me the name of his killer, I wanted that admitted into the record. Two legal; elements were necessary. First, that he knew he was dying and, two, that he actually died.

While the ambulance sped through city streets, siren wailing, I formed the courage and blurted what would otherwise be against the grain of decency. "Sammy, I'm Sergeant Frank, Homicide. Can you hear me, do you understand?"

He gasped. "Yeah. Yeah."

"Sammy, (gulp) I gotta tell ya. You are going to die." No response. The attendant gave me the evil eye.

Again, I asked," Are you aware you are going to die?"

Sammy's acknowledgment was essential.

"Yeah. Yeah. Oh Lord, I'm agonna die."

"Okay, Sammy, who shot you?"

He strained, barely audible. "Bait Man. The Bait Man done shot me."

"Who's the Bait Man, Sammy? What's his real name?"

"I dunno. Oh, Lord. I'm agonna die."

"Tell me where I can find Bait Man, Sammy."

"Bait Man do numbers. Hang out at Eddie's. Oh Lord."

Well, the statement was trial perfect, and in the presence of a witness, no less. For the first time in my homicide career, the victim actually told me who killed him, and the process was admissible, everything performed according to rules of court. There was only one problem.

Sammy didn't die.

The case was turned over as an Aggravated Assault to detectives in the General Investigations Unit. Sammy's statement was not admissible.

* * *

Like the graying grandfather he was, barrel chested Larry Foreman had been a homicide detective in the early '60s and was now brought back as a field lieutenant after a series of promotions and transfers of two or three short-tenured supervisors. Larry had a cynical and humorous side to his otherwise serious veneer, often telling straight-faced jokes that left everyone in stitches. They say, timing is everything.

I had been investigating the murder of a fifty-year-old woman whose head was bashed by her son-in-law with a hammer. The subject was Louis Carpenter, an oversized, affable fellow no older than twenty-four, who was madly in love with his wife, [17]Karen. Apparently, Karen's mother never approved of Louis, thinking he was too dumpy for her lovely daughter, and made no secret of her feelings.

Karen must have been the first pretty girl ever to accept poor Louis. She was his trophy.

An argument broke out in which the mother insisted that Karen leave her husband and come home with her. Louis sensed he was about to lose the great love of his life. Tempers flared. As Louis screamed and ranted, he spotted a claw hammer lying on a table. In the heat of anger, he lifted it, and swung down upon the woman's head in one smashing blow.

Emotionally wrecked and soaked in sweat, Louis Carpenter was easy to cop out. (police jargon for gaining an admission) What I needed was a full confession, signed and packaged for the prosecution. The tiny interview room had one desk, two chairs and a telephone. The mood was intense. He was on a roll, telling me everything that occurred, blow by blow (excuse the pun) when I was distracted by the local buzzer on the phone. I wondered who was calling.

I raised my hand to signal Louis to stop talking for a second. I answered, turned my head and cupped the receiver. "Hello?"

On the other end of the line, Larry Foreman's deep voice was unmistakable, singing to me, "If I had a hammer, I'd hammer in the morning... Uh, by the way, that's by the Carpenters." He hung up.

I know that moments like this are supposed to be solemn, when one person has lost a life, a daughter has lost her mother, and another otherwise law-abiding man is about to go to prison, but I had to turn my back away and begin coughing violently; otherwise, I'd have burst out laughing. Louis never knew.

---

[17] Karen – fictitious name

Ironically, Louis liked me. He pled guilty to manslaughter and did hard time for about four years. When he was released, he went out of his way to visit me at headquarters, like a child who was proud that he did well, and told me about his time and his future.

His wife? She divorced Louis and moved on.

* * *

Then, there's Judge Ralph Ferguson, the pudgy ex-football tackle who performed the wedding with two of my wives, each for a bottle of scotch.

The law required that anytime we arrested a suspect on a warrant for a major crime such as rape or murder, he/she had to be brought before a magistrate within twenty-four hours for a reading of rights. This was to ensure that the person arrested was fully aware of the charges and had not been abused or denied access to representation by authorities.

During weekdays, this was easy. We could always find a sitting judge to take a few minutes to conduct the brief formality. On weekends, we had to hunt for an available off-duty judge. Judge Ferguson was a true law enforcement advocate, ready and willing to help out anytime we asked. And, he lived near headquarters. That' why we usually called him first, before shopping for any other judge.

It was a Sunday morning, when my partner and I busted a young black man for rape. The suspect offered no resistance and was willing to talk about his crime. After a formal confession was taken, I called Judge Ferguson's house and spoke to his wife who had answered the phone.

"Yes, the judge is in. Come on by."

Twenty minutes later, we arrived at the old frame house near Miami's Orange Bowl where Mrs. Ferguson let us in, two cops in suits and one solemn black man wearing a ratty tee-shirt, shorts and handcuffs. "The judge is just getting up," she said. "He'll be down in a moment. Please have a seat."

It seemed unusually long before we finally heard footsteps coming down the wooden stairs. Judge Ferguson must have had a rough night, as he forgot to put on his pants. Clad only in his skivvy shorts and an undershirt, the judge waddled barefoot—or should I say, staggered— over to the couch, plopped into a sitting position and picked up the arrest warrants which lay upon the table. He looked like I used to feel after an all night binge.

Trying to maintain a sense of decorum, my partner and I stood up before the hungover judge and held the suspect by the arms waiting for the formality to begin. The judge sat at the edge of the couch reading the charges, and reciting rights by rote. "Do you understand these rights as I have just related them?" he asked.

"Yes suh," replied the arrested man.

With his gut hanging over, teetering from a sitting position, Judge Ferguson's boney knees swung open. That provided a visual treat rarely experienced by criminal defendants anywhere, a pair of legal testicles dangling from his shorts.

We always said that Judge Ferguson had a lot of balls. Now we knew it.

*   *   *

People used to say I had an uncanny knack for memory. After having a few beers with friends at a local pub, a car mechanic named [18]Ed Gunther returned to his trailer on Christmas eve only to find that his wife had been joined for a surprise tête-à-tête by his girl friend. This was a very awkward situation, because he loved his wife and loved his girl, but never wanted either to know about the other.

The two women sat together on the couch, angrily telling Ed to get lost, they never wanted to see him again. Drunk and in a near stupor, he thought about his little baby lying in a crib in the back room, and his role as a father, his future, and of losing his wife, and his girl at the same time. He paced the floors as the two women relentlessly screamed at him. Then he went outside, removed a .38 caliber revolver from his car, and stepped back inside the trailer. He knelt before his girlfriend and pointed the gun to her heart. "Did you mean what you said," he asked, weeping. "That you never want to see me again?"

That's when the girl friend made a fatal error.

"Yes," she said, probably thinking it was an empty threat.

Bang!

When the shot fired, Ed's wife went hysterical. Ed then shifted the muzzle toward her head and fired another shot.

---

[18] Ed Gunther – fictitious name

Bang!

The two women lay dead, listing to their sides. His crying baby could be heard from the back room. Ed walked over, stood over the crib and pointed the gun at his child, but did not fire. When he fled from the trailer and headed to his car, a group of neighbors had assembled in the darkness outside, having heard the commotion. He fired one shot into the crowd and wounded an elderly man in the liver. From there, he drove away.

Several minutes later, Officer [19]Blaine McGowan, a young cop over six-foot five, arrived on the scene, entered the trailer and checked the victims for signs of life. When he stepped back onto the porch, Ed Gunther was standing on the street below, drunk, teetering, pointing his revolver at the uniformed cop. Officer McGowan had to think fast. Like a scene from a Clint Eastwood movie, he spun around, drew his weapon and exchanged gunfire with Ed Gunther. The officer was unharmed. Gunther took a bullet in the arm.

When Frank Wesolowski and I arrived on the scene, we could see that Officer McGowan was clearly shaken. Gunther had been taken into custody and then transferred down to Jackson Memorial Hospital for treatment. My brain thought in terms of obtaining an admission, if at all possible, because it is ultra powerful as prosecutorial evidence. With the subject injured and in a hospital setting, time was of the essence if there was any chance of a confession. Subjects usually cop out within a short time after the crime, when they are emotionally charged, not after they have too much time to think about defense strategy, or worse, are contacted by a lawyer.

Wesolowski remained behind at the trailer park to handle the scene, collect evidence and interview witnesses while I rushed to the hospital to talk to Ed Gunther.

On the way to Jackson Memorial, I radioed ahead to the hospital police office to check on the condition of the subject. They said he was awake and lucid. I then contacted headquarters and asked that a court reporter be transported over to meet me—just in case.

Already treated for a minor wound to the arm, Ed Gunther lay shackled in bed when I arrived. I informed him of his rights.

---

[19] Blaine McGowan – fictitious name

Weeping and quite remorseful, he said he didn't want an attorney. With the steno present, I took his statement in which he detailed the events, step by step, starting with his drinking at the bar and ending with the shootout with Officer McGowan.

Two hours later, the steno had the statement all typed up, ready for review and signing. I brought the document back to Jackson Memorial and presented it to Gunther. "Please read and, if everything is correct, sign on the dotted line."

"No."

Geez. In the two hour wait for transcribing the statement, Gunther had been talking to other hospital jailbirds who told him not to sign anything. Now, I worried that the confession might be useless.

This mattered most when the trial began six months later. Gunther acquired a flamboyant local lawyer named Mitchell Goldman, a well-known Miami figure who was often seen strutting around downtown wearing a suit and a white ten-gallon cowboy hat. His private investigator was none other than Max Berman, Bernie's friend who helped me get on the department. Goldman tried to have the entire confession thrown out, but only succeeded half way. The judge ruled that the document was inadmissible, because it was unviewed and unsigned by the defendant, but that I could testify to anything Gunther told me, from memory only.

The prosecutor ordered me to brush up on the confession during a break and do my best.

The courtroom was packed. I took the stand. Twelve jurors listened intensely as Mitch Goldman sat at the defendant's table with a copy of the twelve-page unsigned confession before him, checking word by word. The prosecutor asked me the same question, one after another.

"What did you ask the defendant, and what did the defendant reply?"

With my hands on my lap, I responded to each point in chronological order, eyeballing the jury as I spoke. The questions and answers came easily as I recalled those moments at the hospital. About halfway through the testimony, Mitch Goldman abruptly stood up. "Objection, your honor! I demand to see what the witness is reading from."

I raised my empty hands with a quizzical look toward the jury. The prosecutor smiled.

"Objection overruled. The defendant is not reading from anything."

According to the lawyers, who were able to follow the written statement, I recited the confession nearly verbatim.

The next morning came the verdict. Guilty.

Today, I can't remember what I just wrote in this chapter.

As for veteran Officer McGowan, he quit his job after that eventful evening. Six months later, I spoke to him outside the courtroom during a break and asked, "So, what are you doing these days, Blaine."

"I just hang out on my sailboat, smoke my dope, and don't worry about nothin'."

* * *

It was a Friday night when [20]Mark Fida*, 24, tried calling his apartment several times from his workplace with no answer from beautiful young wife, Linda. Worried, he left early and arrived home, only to find her nude body lying on her side in a bath tub full of blood-soaked water. He pulled the plug and tried lifting her out, but it was no use. She was dead.

Three homicide detectives and I responded to the four-story, U-shaped apartment building and worked as a team, canvassing neighbors, interviewing the husband, coordinating with crime lab personnel and examining the death scene in apartment 216, at a corner of the building on the second floor. As a bonus, one of the most meticulous prosecutors from the State Attorney's Office happened to live in the same building. Never without his Abe Lincoln beard, James Woodard offered to help.

Linda Fida, a former high school beauty queen, had been stabbed numerous times, then submerged in the tub of water. Stuck to her leg, was a small mangled Band-Aid style bandage.

In the adjacent bedroom, a toppled basket and miscellaneous clothing were strewn about the floor indicated that the victim had been attacked while carrying a newly dried wash from the laundry room downstairs. Also on the floor, was another crumpled bandage

---

[20] Mark Fida – fictitious name

which appeared to have fingerprint ridge patterns imbedded on the adhesive side.

A closer examination of the victim's body revealed petechial hemorrhages—little blood spots—in the whites of the eyes, usually attributed to some form of asphyxiation. Nail marks on the neck confirmed our preliminary thoughts, that she had first been strangled. The autopsy
would later show this.

News media assembled outside. Our first press release would say that the victim was found submerged in water with multiple stab wounds. We withheld the information about strangulation, hoping that a killer would one day tell us about that.

When opening the Band-Aid, it appeared it was pulled off an extremely large finger, so large that it might have been from a big toe. I.D. Technicians confirmed that the sticky-side print was identifiable.

A canvass of the building by detectives interviewing residents unveiled no useful witnesses. We regrouped and came to the conclusion that the killer was probably barefoot, and therefore, someone who lived or was an invited visitor in the complex, not some delivery or repairman wearing shoes. We decided another full canvass was in order, but to pay special attention to people's feet.

The next evening, Frank Wesolowski and James
Woodard, the prosecutor, teamed up knocking on doors. Paul Rowles, 23, a tall, blond tennis player, answered the door to apartment 218, adjacent to the victim's. As they began talking, they looked down and saw he was wearing sandals, and a Band-Aid around each big toe.

Bingo.

Rowles' wife, an airline stewardess, stood next to her husband as they both decried the horrible crime in their building. They had not seen or heard anything.

Paul Rowles' bandages were not enough to make an arrest, and it would be stupid to start questioning him at that point and reveal what evidence we had. The question was, how to get his standard toe prints to compare to the evidence. Woodard helped us to obtain a creative search warrant for the physical body of Paul Rowles. Before that, in the event that the legal issue did not hold up, it was important to try and get him to volunteer his inked toe prints. If so, we'd never have to use the warrant.

We secretly assigned a fingerprint I.D. technician in Woodard's apartment with copies of the evidence print, while Frank and I proceeded to the Rowles apartment. "We have some footprint evidence," we told him, and his wife. (Carefully worded, not to say *toe print*) "And we're going to every apartment in this complex asking all residents to cooperate and voluntarily submit their standards." I watched closely when I asked. "You won't mind, would you?"

What could he say, especially with his wife standing right there? After a short hesitation, "Yes, of course."

We inked his bare feet and then pressed them onto glossy paper. We didn't bother with any other apartments and took the fresh standards directly to the technician waiting in Woodard's apartment. It was a positive identification. We knew the killer.

Now armed with strong probable cause, we returned to the apartment and, to the chagrin of Mrs. Rowles, took Paul into custody. He strongly denied having anything to do with the crime. We perfunctorily advised him of his rights and placed him in the car.

Always in need of that valuable confession, I didn't start questioning him right away. Rather, we wanted a perfect interrogation setting. I called ahead and asked that a room be made available at headquarters.

Wesolowski and I had conducted interrogations together in the past, and with rare exception, the main questioning was left to one detective, while the other stood by as a witness. This was better than barraging the suspect from two sides.

Wesolowski remained in the room as I reminded Paul Rowles of his rights. Again, he denied the crime. After an hour of recounting his family background, his psychological problems, and personal issues, and while we showed him sympathy, he began to break down. "When was the first time you had these kinds of urges?" I finally asked, getting more to the point.

"I almost did it before, a couple times," he said.

That broke the ice. As long as the momentum was not interrupted, we knew a confession would be forthcoming.

"I followed a woman on an elevator once. Just when I was going to attack her, she acted unafraid, and started talking to me. It stopped me."

We had ourselves an almost serial killer.

Gradually leading into the murder of Linda Fida, Paul said he had been watching her through his peep hole carrying clothes to and from the laundry room, and could not control himself. He wanted sex. The last time she walked out of her apartment, he snuck in and waited for her behind the bedroom door. When she returned, he grabbed her. She screamed. He held her down by squeezing his hands around her throat. "It was the only way to stop her from screaming," he said. "But, she opened her eyes, and then saw my face. I knew I had to kill her."

Paul Rowles had just shared information that was never in the news. Only the killer would have known she was strangled. Apparently unaware that the girl was dead, he took a table knife from her kitchen drawer and began stabbing her. After three or four stabs, the blade was so dull it failed to penetrate, so he returned to the kitchen for another knife. He then dragged her into the tub, opened the faucet full blast and held her head under water. I asked, "Why?"

He said, "I wanted to make sure she was dead."

The confession was reiterated before a stenographer, then signed.

Months later, his attorney, Bob Josefsberg, tried to have the confession thrown out in court on the basis that I had coerced him by being too nice.

Who knows? Perhaps another Ted Bundy was brewing in the form of Paul Rowles. One can only imagine how many lives were saved by a crumpled bandage.

CHAPTER THIRTY-EIGHT
Moving Up

These memoirs would not be complete if I failed to mention the names of two important cops whom I helped usher into Homicide.

Some say Douglas Hughes marched to the tune of a different drummer, and that may be true. I met Douglas when he was a young uniformed officer reputed to possess an extra bag of smarts. Once a New York City cop in the Serpico era, Douglas left the big apple in favor of Miami-Dade in 1970 because he was too honest to survive the corruption around him. After only two years in Miami-Dade, his talents were recognized and then transferred into Homicide.

Considered a flaming liberal among a sea of conservatives, Douglas unabashedly set himself apart from mainstream cops, most of whom were somewhere to the right of Barry Goldwater, including myself. Like all of us, Douglas possessed his share of weaknesses, but always as a true gentleman. I never heard him utter a racial slur or a derogatory word about another human being or any ethnic group. He was the only cop I ever knew who didn't curse. While his liberal nature made him unpopular in police circles, Douglas maintained the highest standards of honesty and respect for everyone. In some ways, his benevolent nature was part of his downfall as a detective, for he was so busy helping others, he often forgot about his own cases.

Tall, robust and very Italian, Frank Mussoline and I were friends before we were cops. He lived in the same neighborhood, around the corner from where I practiced violin daily, enjoyed Mom's mobster dinners and talked with Bernie about his old cronies. Frank was riding motorcycle duty when I called one day asking if he wanted to work Homicide. He jumped at the chance. Like a charge of electricity, Frank's personality lit a room with humor and ebullience, forever finding the light side of a tough issue.

Frank worked on the afternoon shift, a journeyman detective who could handle more cases in a week than anyone I knew. And a better friend, no one could have.

I'm happy to boast that I kissed his wife-to-be before he did. He brought beautiful AnnMarie to the Kimberly Bar on a New Years Eve, proud to show off his new date, an airline stewardess. Already inebriated, I shocked Frank by planting a wet one directly on her lips Hmmm. Not bad. As of this writing, they have been married nearly 50 years.

* * *

In 1971, a new phenomenon altered the nature of investigating homicides forever. Once, unthought-of, overtime pay now titillated the working detective. And, supervisors were presented a new challenge in holding down unnecessary hours and expenditures, something that hadn't concerned them in the past. The question was, what could specifically be deemed "necessary" and "unnecessary?"

The police union (PBA) won a class action law suit which awarded retroactive overtime to existing detectives, and provided future overtime to the ranks of police officers and sergeants. We were all ecstatic. Back pay for me amounted to $8,000, based on records gleaned from time sheets maintained in the office for the past six years. (It helped to bail us out from a mound of department store charge accounts) In one 1970 case, I had worked 110 hours of overtime in two weeks, which seems physically impossible, but the case—a double homicide—was nonstop hustle for ten straight days. Finally, some form of reward for all the extra work was forthcoming. But, not without a down side.

No longer could a pro-active detective arbitrarily go out into the field to follow up hunches, check leads, chase potential witnesses and hunt clues without prior approval from a supervisor. If the off-duty activity was not justified, it wasn't done. Had overtime pay existed years before, cases like Jerry Springer's murder—and many others—may never have been solved.

Worse yet, was the potential for abuse. And abuse there was. As the years passed, some enlightened (though few) detectives found ingenious ways to pad their overtime, inflating paychecks beyond comprehension by justifying "necessary" interviews and informant contacts after hours. Most of these were the newer, post-overtime detectives who hadn't dogged cases without the padded paychecks on their minds, as we had in the 1960s. Consequently, cops began to adjust their lifestyles based on fifty percent extra income, buying expensive cars and houses. If and when they were involuntarily transferred back to uniform, financial setbacks left them in bankruptcy, while families suffered and divorces mushroomed.

Few of us remain who remember how it was when nothing but pure initiative and conscience dictated how we would pursue and investigation, and not the almighty dollar.

* * *

By the early '70s, I was a regular teacher at the academy, plus an instructor in a number of state certified criminal investigation seminars. We had also set up a squad system of handling cases, with five men to a squad supervised by one sergeant, three squads all on the day shift. The night shifts worked in a different premise, without squads, just detective rotation.

I headed one squad, Kermit Russell another, and Rick Fowler, the third squad. Each had its own reputation for competency and hard work, though Fowler's group was known more as the party boys, carousing bars after hours, and sometimes during. I had trained Fowler, who was one of the brightest and charismatic cops I'd ever encountered, a man who could have reached the top. With youth and good looks as his downfall, Rick was an incorrigible womanizer and a borderline alcoholic.

My squad, which included Frank Wesolowski and fellow academy classmate, Jim Duckworth, was known for their athletics. More than once, I had to summon my good friends to a crime scene while they were sliding into home plate somewhere across the county. Also on my squad was one of the slickest cops I ever knew, Wade O'Keefe. Matter of fact, that was his nickname: Slick. More about O'Keefe later.

The Major of Detective Bureau, Charlie Black, had experienced staffing and budgetary restrictions, which led to my assignment as the Acting Field Lieutenant in Homicide for six months. That nailed me to a desk, working night and day assigning and reviewing cases, supervising twenty-five detectives though they held the same rank as I, plus responding to call-outs on virtually all murders and other questionable cases that required Homicide's attention. Attending community college two nights a week in pursuit of that fabled

Marshall Frank

degree, studying and writing papers, added to the family stress situation.

The new captain was a bald-headed neatnik named Harvey Singer whose reputation had been earned as a tough rules monger. Singer, who had worked in Homicide in the early '60s, expended his energy in enforcing odd little idiosyncrasies, like prohibiting detectives from carrying an umbrella, or a hair brush exposed from their pocket, while never seeming to give a crap about murder cases. I often wondered if he knew the difference between important and unimportant. It also amazed me how his desk remained in showroom condition at all times, not a piece of paper anywhere, other than a small note pad sitting next to a telephone. Administrative lieutenant, Bob Norris, served as his assistant, which basically meant that Singer had nothing much to do other than attend meetings, sign papers and delegate.

He and I were the proverbial odd couple. Singer would walk into my office, which was constantly in turmoil—files and papers stacked and strewn everywhere, and an ash tray piled high with cigarette butts—see the condition of things, and turn an abrupt about face without saying a word. I didn't think he really cared about anything other than doing his time with his eyeballs on retirement. I cannot recall a time where we sat and informally discussed personnel or murder cases or problem issues, unless they were required formalities, like staff meetings or submitting a statistical report. Unless, of course, he came under fire during a high profile murder investigation.

Singer and his administrative lieutenant often left for lunch together, not to be seen the rest of the day, while I stayed behind, buried with work and no assistance. To say the least, they took advantage of me. Time to move up. I had taken lieutenant's exams before, but flunked them all, happy to remain a homicide sergeant. The 200- question tests were difficult, covering the gamut from police procedure, law, psychology, weaponry, reading comprehension, administrative organization, and more. Reaching the rank was highly competitive, with over three hundred sergeants vying for a handful of open positions.

Ready as ever, I bought all the books.

Besides his foibles, Rick Fowler was an ambitious young man who had eyes for the department ceiling. Rick was smart. He and I formed a study union, consuming two weeks of vacation time to cram for the test. We met for twelve hours a day at a neutral location, peppering each other with questions, reading from stacks of books, memorizing tables, and principles, and thousands of rules and laws. At home, I kept the books in the bathroom. I became a virtual stranger to my family as I secluded myself even further.

Rick came out number one on the list. Beat me by one question. I was number two.

* * *

When the promotional list was published, most people assumed that I would be elevated in rank while retaining the same position as the field supervisor of Homicide. At the same time, the director announced several changes among the higher ranks, promoting Charlie Black to Division Chief in charge of all central services, including Communications, Records and the Crime Laboratory.

The assumption that I'd remain in homicide turned out dead wrong.

Shortly after Black's promotion was announced, he called me to his office. I never thought he noticed me, until he showed me a copy of a memo he'd prepared for E. Wilson Purdy. I was his first choice to be his aide in Central Services, assigned as supervisor over forensic Crime Scene personnel. In reality, I'd be his trouble shooter. He left the final decision up to me.

It was not an easy choice. Homicide was my passion. In Crime Scene, I would still be involved in overseeing the physical evidence aspect of murders and other crimes, but no longer in the loop of investigations. Black was considered the number two power in the department, and future heir apparent to the director's job. It would be career suicide to turn him down. April 9, 1973. My friend, Frank Wesolowski, was promoted to sergeant and remained as a squad leader in Homicide. That same day, I received the lieutenant's badge and reported to a new station under Charlie Black. Later, it would be known as CSI Miami.

CHAPTER THIRTY-NINE
Crisis

In the fall of 1971, when Bennett was eleven, his stepfather, Bill Gertz left the house one night and never came home. Gertz had been a chef at the very pricey Forge Restaurant on Miami Beach's Arthur Godfrey Road. When the owner opened up the next morning, he found the safe wide open and $16,000 missing from inside.

At first, police figured this was just employee theft. But as their investigation unfolded, it appeared that Gertz had a gambling problem and was in significant debt to a number of mobsters. As of this date, he's never been found. Some suspect he went shopping for cement shoes.

The sudden change in family arrangement had a negative emotional impact upon young Bennett. During the ensuing year, Betty Jo turned about-face from her attitude of ten years and started teaching Bennett to accept me as his father. A little late, perhaps, but now she summoned me to his school whenever he was in trouble, which was nearly every day.

I noticed a change in Bennett's behavior during the infrequent times he visited with us, constant fidgeting, forced smiles, incessant lying. His grades plummeted. He skipped school often.

At the age of twelve, Bennett ran away from home with another boy and was missing for three days. He was finally located on Miami Beach where they had been sleeping in parks and beaches. I picked him up and returned him to Betty Jo. The relationship between him and me was not comfortable. He did not accept me as a father figure, and understandably so. He'd been coached for ten years that I was the bad guy and Gertz was the good guy. Bennett seemed genuinely disturbed over the disappearance of his stepfather. His sadness triggered a spark of jealousy deep within me.

Bennett now visited at our house more often and spent overnights and weekends, previously not allowed. I had hoped to forge a new union with my boy, to integrate him as part of our family, even if it was part time. But it was an uphill struggle.

Meanwhile, pressures mounted on the home front to upgrade our living standards. Now flooded with higher incomes, homicide detectives were buying larger pool homes in upscale neighborhoods. We felt the need to keep up. Besides, our family now consisted of four full-time kids and a part-timer in Bennett.

The modern new house in Miramar had four bedrooms, two baths and a screened in pool, matching those of my peers. The house cost more than we could afford, but Joan worked (waitress), and I tried to manage.

Debts soared. Joan had expensive taste in clothes. We needed furnishings. All I needed was a couple of polyester suits from J.C. Penney's, four packs of cigarettes a day and a well-stocked liquor cabinet. As a lieutenant, overtime pay came to an abrupt halt. Sergeants and patrolmen detectives, even Crime Scene technicians made more money than me. But, I figured the promotion was a step toward making captain in two years.

The day came that I had wished for, for twelve years. It might have been too late. Betty Jo called and said she could no longer handle Bennett. He was incorrigible, stealing from relatives, getting involved in drugs. He needed a father. I felt the calling, I had to take in my son and do what I could to repair his soul, and become a father to him after so many years of estrangement. But how much time could I devote, with a full time job, a college schedule, and a new boss with his own set of demands.

Joan was gracious. We brought him home and into the family but it was a colossal disaster. Bennett had psychological disturbances which I could not nail down. He lied constantly. He used drugs away from the house, mostly marijuana. He stole liquor from the cabinet. And he wouldn't integrate as a brother to the kids, remaining aloof, not wanting to participate in family outings.

In a few rare moments of sincerity, Bennett told me that his mother had taken on a new identity when Bill Gertz disappeared. New relationships with men blossomed. She openly used marijuana around the house, once offering him a toke saying, "Go ahead and take one. I'd rather you not do it behind my back." A pattern of dysfunctional behavior ensued. Bennett discovered his mother's *stash* in the closet and took handfuls to school to sell. He began using marijuana, in great quantities. He felt that his mother must not have loved him very much. After all, she had encouraged him to engage in an activity that the rest of the world taught him was wrong.

While I made efforts to spend quality interaction with Bennett, Joan became the fairness referee, monitoring my actions closely, making sure that I did not devote any more time with him than I did the other kids. I sensed eyes watching me at all times. Household undercurrents mounted, day by day. After Bennett had committed several more acts of dishonesty, and sensing the pressure from Joan, I lost my sanity, whipping him with a belt on the butt before turning into another room where I broke out crying. Later, I realized it was not so much a punishment as it was to satisfy others, to prove he was not "favored." Perhaps I blew that concept larger in my mind than was necessary, but it was real to me.

Charlie Black turned out to be a loyal boss, placing his confidence in my abilities. But responsibilities mounted there as well, to perform in the work place, writing staff studies, evaluations, statistical analysis, personnel issues, grants, meetings, budgets, training, and more. Just like before, I responded to major crime scenes at all hours of day and night, unpaid overtime. Crime Scene Technicians and other forensic personnel were a challenge to supervise. Most were bright and independent minded, yet sensitive to the perception that they weren't full-fledged police officers. Personnel conflicts arose. The job became more demanding as time went on.

Sometimes, Black would call me at the end of a day and suggest we stop for a drink on the way home, perhaps meet friends and other county officials. Sure, why not. Happy Hour began as social time with the boss once in a while, and eventually progressed to two or three times a week. Commiserating with police chiefs and high ranking officials fueled my ego. Joan wasn't happy. Sometimes Black and I stayed out for hours, drinking and talking.

College classes, school papers, Bennett's problems, Joan's demands, the kids, the booze, Charlie Black, the Crime Scene Unit, call-outs, bills, debts, it all spiraled. Joan wanted more. I pushed away, wanting only a drink and a bed when I came home. I tried to spend a few minutes with the family now and then, reading little Jennifer a bedtime story, making breakfast for the kids on Sunday mornings, but my time with them was sparse.

I managed to bring my friends Frank Mussoline and Doug Hughes into CSI to assist me in running the office. They were competent and loyal supervisors who I could count on. But no matter, my life was out of control, like a runaway roller coaster.

Once I stopped and looked closely in the mirror and wondered who I really was, all this performing, matching up to expectations, standing up to pressures, doing it all the right way. I should have won an Oscar, playing the role daily, presenting a facade of a high-spirited police administrator, but a churning pile of garbage on the inside. From the outside, nobody could tell the difference. It made me realize how serial killers and other criminals could intermingle with society undetected, seemingly normal, while they were internally fractured. A virtual Dr. Jekyll and Mr. Hyde.

Love-making became a chore, a responsibility, just like my job, satisfying personnel. I enjoyed it less and less until I dreaded every moment I had to "perform." I began to shut down. Joan presented an ultimatum. "If I don't get it from you," she said. "I'll get it from someone else." And she did.

After an injury at the restaurant job, Joan found work selling drapery. That's where she met her lover.

She began staying out late one or two nights a week. She didn't lie. When confronted, she admitted having an affair. In the beginning, I felt a warped sense of relief, that the onus was now off of me, and she could get all the sex she wanted and leave me alone. But that was short lived. I still cared for Joan. I became all-consumed, obsessed. Every night that she stayed out, I knew she was probably in a motel room somewhere with him. I paced floors, poured powerful Manhattans, scurried out to bars, blurring the entire world from my consciousness.

I started an affair of my own with a department employee, but it was sporadic and meaningless. I felt no guilt. I figured if Joan could, I could. It served a good purpose, validating virility to myself, that I was okay. It was sex for pleasure, not for obligation. I would have done anything to return to a life of normalcy, but didn't know how. Our relationship had plunged down a slippery slope, and there was no turning back.

Joan's affair became more bold and intense. At first, I had selfishly consented to this sickery, but I couldn't stand it any longer. I pleaded with her to stop. She refused. Bills mounted which I couldn't pay. Charlie Black wanted my attention. So did Frank Mussoline, and Doug Hughes, and Bennett, and Annette, and Russell, and Randy, and Jennifer, and forty personnel in my office, my debtors and my professors.

I had seen it many times before. Easy. Fast. Painless. I came home one night, after drinking, and her car was gone—again. I sat in the driveway. I pulled my three-inch revolver from the holster, and checked the ammo, contemplating under a starlit night. Inside, four children were asleep in their beds. Annette, the eldest at 15, had done well to manage things when her parents were out carousing in separate directions.

I didn't want the taste of blue steel to be the last sensation of my life. I thought about those kids and the shame I would bring upon them. I thought about Jennifer, my baby girl, and how I'd leave her just like my father had left me, without ever knowing me. Squidgie had reached pinnacles he never dreamed of; from a Harpo Marx lookalike, a middle school fairy, a ballet dancer, violinist, the butt of bullies, he'd evolved into a hot-shot homicide detective, now a rising police administrator with connections to the top. I would finally have made my mother proud. But not in doing this. When I put the gun back in the holster, I felt like a coward. But a live coward.

* * *

February 15, 1975 was a date that reversed the spiral.

The evening before, I'd come home at 7:00 P.M. from work. Joan was out. The kids informed me that "Mommy called. She won't be home. Said for you to make dinner." The utter embarrassment in front of my kids was all I could handle. They knew. They knew I knew. I must have looked so small to them.

I bottled up the emotions and made the dinner.

After work the next night, I stayed out with Charlie Black and Ray Beck, calling home occasionally. Joan was not there. I figured she was in a motel room somewhere. I pretended it didn't bother me, but it bothered me big time. I could not stop dwelling on her.

I arrived home after midnight, half inebriated. Joan was asleep in the bed. In that darkened room, something snapped within me. As though another force took charge of my hands and arms, I suddenly started slapping at her head, cursing her, waking her, crying aloud. I grabbed her hair, screaming, "How could you do this to me? How could you do this to me?" I pulled her hair until she fell to the floor.

...he screamed at my mother until he was hoarse, squealing, angry, loud, throwing things, breaking lamps, out of breath like he had run a marathon. I cracked

open the door again and spotted my father dragging her across the floor by her flaming red hair while she grasped at his hands and holding her head, grimacing, crying, that transformed face.

The entire house awakened; kids standing in the living room watched in horror as I pounded on their mother. Annette called the Miramar police. I was out of control, hysterical, causing little physical damage to Joan, but scaring the living hell out of everyone.

Two cops handcuffed my wrists behind me and hauled me into a police car, down to the station. The scene was familiar, I'd been there many times, but from the other side.

I had always prided myself in maintaining control, no matter how stressful the situation. But this time, I not only shocked everyone around me, I shocked myself. Violence was not my nature. I abhorred violence. I avoided violence throughout my police career, with great success. Yet, I had become a wife beater. I had become mentally unbalanced.

Still barefoot and wearing nothing but underwear, I paced the concrete floor behind bars in the tiny station house cell in Miramar, scared like I was never scared before. For my allotted phone privilege, I called Charlie Black. Someone from home had called Doug Hughes. I could see my entire career, my life, family, future, everything, vanish before my eyes. Once E. Wilson Purdy learned that any lieutenant had beat his wife and gone to jail, he'd be fired. Pension, gone. Job security, gone.

Prestige, gone. Back to selling women's shoes to tangle toes, hunting for a job, maybe two jobs, perhaps a security guard.

Silver-tongued Doug Hughes came to the police station and talked with the local police officers. Then, Charlie Black made a phone call behind the scenes. I was released. No booking. No media. No record. No E. Wilson Purdy. Black risked his job to save mine.

I had to get away from this life and start anew. But how?

CHAPTER FORTY
Recovery

I dreaded this moment. After losing custody of my baby boy to a mother who ultimately shut him from my life, I swore I'd never let my Jennifer grow up without her dad.

At a tiny wrought iron table at a local ice cream parlor, I watched as she scooped and ate, and savored the flavor of sweet vanilla, knowing my little six year-old was unaware of the impact this decision would have on her life.

When it came time to drop the bomb, I started to choke. I didn't want to do this. Never wanted to do this.

"Darlin', listen. I have something to tell you."

"What's that?"

"Uh. Daddy's leaving. I have to go away."

"What do you mean?"

"I mean, I have to go away. Live somewhere else."

"Why?"

"Because it's best for you, and your brothers and sister, and for Mommy."

"Where are you going?"

"To an apartment. I'll be real close. I'll always be real close."

"Okay."

"I'm sorry, Jenni. I'm so sorry."

"I love you, Daddy."

"I love you too."

* * *

For one year following February 15, 1975, I focused on paying off debts and securing financial help from a friend in order to move out of the house. Other than my wardrobe and a few personal items, I left everything behind to Joan and the kids and borrowed from a friend to buy a clunker for transportation. Thank goodness, I still had my job.

As an institution, our family was dead. Our kids would grow up in a broken home, which we had dreaded. The children all saw me as the bad guy, so I thought. The image of beating on their mother would remain imprinted in their minds forever. All those years of loving, caring and supporting, now gone to the winds. Joan was sad. I was sad. But it had to be. We could have ranted on with the blame game, but in truth, we both let our separate agendas get in the way of what was important. We lost sight of the true priorities. Now, it was too late.

I'll not forget the sensation the first time I inserted the key in the door of my apartment and walked inside, like a cool breeze washing over me after years of pressure and stagnation. I sucked a long wonderful breath, reveling in freedom. I sat at the piano, laid my fingers onto the keys and struggled through a version of Beethoven's Moonlight Sonata. Then I opened my violin case, and resurrected the neglected instrument and played like I never played before.

This was as close to being reborn, as reborn could be.

As another bonus, my wayward son had my complete attention for the first time since he was a year old.

Now I could devote time to this fractured soul and try to mend those cracks in his foundation. At first, it seemed to be working. We played tennis, shared meals, talked and went over his school work. But the gap remained. he still pushed away. Three months later, fifteen-year-old Bennett ran away with a friend. When he called from Iowa, hungry and needing help, I bussed him back home. He ran away again. The cycle never ended. Bennett had become a drug addict.

Months later, Joan and I listened to a distinguished gentleman in a black robe tell us we were no longer man and wife. Then we walked across the street to a local pub and lifted a toast to our new lives.

* * *

Focus, focus. I had to think about the future. For a time, I dropped from college classes in order to study for captain. After all, I didn't want to stay a lieutenant when the upper ranks offered opportunity for higher appointments, more pay, and—what else— prestige.

Because of our great success three years earlier, Rick Fowler and I formed a study team again and crammed for two weeks of our vacation time. It paid off. We both came out in the top five. Six months later, I was handed a captain's badge.

Not a bad recovery, considering what could have been.

* * *

My mother once said, "If you can do something well by yourself, anything, you'll never really be lonely."

She was right. I was no longer a virtuoso. The term "well" is subjective, depending on who is doing the listening. But I don't know what I would have done without my music. Often, in my solitude, I resorted to my long dormant violin for solace and comfort, playing for no one but myself, enjoying the creations of Beethoven, Sarasate, and Brahms, and many pieces which I could barely struggle through.

I joined a small local orchestra in North Miami Beach, played a few concerts and met new and creative friends outside the police arena. From there, we formed a chamber quartet and met for jam sessions once a week, case load permitting.

That spun off into a newer circle of social friends, including many professionals such as lawyers, psychologists and college professors. I enjoyed the acceptance, because they accepted me as I was, not as I had to portray myself. The only drawback was money. They all had money. I didn't. But so long as they didn't care, neither did I.

CHAPTER FORTY-ONE
Skin Prints

The 1971 murder of Cathy Anderson was mentioned in Chapter Thirty-Four, describing my interrogation failure of her ex-husband, whom I considered the prime suspect.

The classic crime scene took place in the master bedroom of the victim's house, which was an ideal setting for reconstructing the events that led up to the killing and what followed after. It appeared that she was with someone in a friendly environment, then attacked from behind and strangled to death. The layout of items in the room indicated she was treated with love tenderness after death arrived. Because it's still officially unsolved, we'll not go into any further detail.

Mr. Anderson's fingerprints were in the bedroom and throughout the house. But that solved nothing, because they belonged there. Mr. Anderson had recently shared ownership of the house and still visited often when he'd come to pick up his child. He had chatted with his ex-wife in the bedroom as well. Any defense lawyer would make mince meat of his prints as evidence.

If only we'd had the means to develop latent fingerprints directly from her flesh, that would have nailed the killer. We didn't.

After my appointment as lieutenant in charge of the Crime Scene Section, and later as captain, with the Anderson case in mind, I assembled several talented members of the unit to ask what they knew regarding the development of latent prints from skin. No one in Dade County had worked with such a process. That's when we formed the research team. If another murder took place where the subject manhandled a victim, perhaps we could identify the killer by this new process. What a coup that would be.

At the time, the only known system for developing latent prints from human skin had taken place in laboratories within other states, where lead powder was used in a sterile, morgue environment to dust a cadaver, then followed by X-ray. While this yielded some results, the process becomes invalid the moment the body is handled by investigators on the scene and those who transported.

Inspired by the thought of innovative fingerprint technology, the small cadre of Crime Scene Technicians, led by Eddie Stone (who later committed suicide) eagerly went about testing new methods for recovering latents from skin; they visited the morgue in their spare time, and gained the consent of the chief Medical Examiner, Dr. Joseph Davis, a great friend of law enforcement, a renowned progressive in his field. Working with him were Dolly Wiemer, Jim Carr and Dave Gilbert.

It was important that any new method, if successful, be applied while at the crime scene before a body was moved around. Eddie Stone and his partners excitedly came into my office one day to demonstrate a discovery on his Eddie's own skin. It was a simple technique using metal filings on the body, sweeping a pen-like magnet over the filings until only the particles which adhered to a latent print remained on the body.

All we needed now was a real victim. Dade County had always been bountiful in that regard.

* * *

Shortly after midnight in July of 1978, three bodies were discovered in cavernous health spa in North Dade County, each shot. I was summoned to the scene along with Homicide personnel, Crime Lab and other department brass.

The male victim, half owner of the spa, lay slumped in the business office. The office had been ransacked. A cleaning woman was dead on the tile floor of the Jacuzzi room. The third victim, young Patricia Beck, the cleaning woman's assistant, lay nude on the floor in an adjacent room, surrounded by mirrors. Only eighteen years of age, Patricia had obviously been raped, then shot in the head. Air conditioning kept the interior cool. Patricia Beck had definitely been manhandled. Her skin was young and taut. Conditions were ideal.

It took nearly an hour for Eddie Stone's response from home, but we held the scene unmolested until he could arrive. Eddie was the expert. We'd settle for nothing less.

Meanwhile, a small crowd formed outside behind the tape along with news media who were interested in the story. The other half-owner, Steve Beattie, had been a well known and popular figure in Dade County, touted by several newspaper stories about his fitness regimen. Beattie arrived at the scene wailing in hysterics behind the tape, outraged over the horrible crime in his fitness center.

Slowly, deliberately, sweat forming on his brow, Eddie Stone took his time with the pen-magnet, sweeping the body up and down with metal filings. His assistant, Officer Dolly Wiemer, took photographs of every step. We watched with anticipation. When Eddie reached the victim's ankles, two prints developed like an apparition.

They seemed to have identifiable ridges. It was, indeed, an incredible moment. We were ecstatic.

The prints were treated like fragile treasure. First, Dolly took photographs from various angles, Polaroid and 35mm. Then came the lifting process, using tape to white backing paper.

Later the next day, an I.D. Technician looked at the prints and identified the killer.

Steve Beattie.

Three years after his conviction for First Degree Murder, Beattie hung himself in prison.

It has been said, that for all that is bad, comes good. Whoever killed Cathy Anderson seven years earlier may have escaped justice. But he left a legacy that ultimately resulted in the solution of a triple murder—and uncounted other killings—that might never have been solved otherwise.

That made us all feel good. All, of course, except Mr. Beattie.

CHAPTER FORTY-TWO
Back In The Saddle

On the March 26, 1979, the day that President Jimmy Carter presided over the historic signing of a peace treaty between Israel and Egypt, Rick Fowler called asking if we could have lunch. Through his own bouts of personal turmoil, Rick had been the Homicide captain for two years.

Rick said he'd had enough of running Homicide. He'd just recovered from aneurism surgery in his brain and was mostly concerned about his health. He asked if I'd agree to a trade: He'd go to Crime Scene and I'd take over Homicide.

Darn right.

What made it better, Charlie Black had recently been transferred as Chief of Police Division, meaning the liaison between me and the boss who saved my job would be sustained.

I chomped at the bit to take over the position held by so many homicide captains before me, Pat Gallagher Lou Spaeth, Dick Smith and, yes, Harvey Singer. But, all's not always as it seems.

Homicide had gone through a huge personnel transition in the years I was in Crime Scene, and I barely knew many of the detectives. Inherited were two salty lieutenants who'd been around for years, Bobby Willis and Fred Smith. Thin and wiry, Willis had no background as a homicide investigator, a well-known good ol' boy whose father had been a legendary career officer. We'd never worked together before, though I knew him by reputation as a hard-nosed, no nonsense cop who didn't mind a physical brawl now and then, the perennial winner, of course.

I immediately felt like an outsider. The men avoided me. Hallway chats clammed up when I walked by. There seemed an absence of camaraderie, and no one with whom I could confide. It wasn't the same as when I left in 1973. I had a total understanding of how homicides should be investigated from front to end, the reporting and the administrative process. When it came to murder investigation, I couldn't be snowed. The old standards, in my opinion, had collapsed. Supervision was lax, to say the least. The good detectives were on their own to follow their conscience. Case reports, supposed to be prepared immediately after conducting a field activity or an interview, were days and weeks behind. In some cases, detectives failed to write any reports at all, on whodunits, no less.

Ray Beck would have been appalled.

Overtime had become a major issue for detectives and sergeants. I suspected that hundreds of hours were trumped up. If they were or not, the lieutenants had to approve them. One detective had been awarded paid compensation for 191 hours of overtime—over and above the standard 80—in a two-week period. Humanly impossible. That's 81 above my own record of 110 overtime hours in 1970. Yet, it went unquestioned. One trusted detective told me that he suspected one or more of the lieutenants were involved in an overtime conspiracy, taking a piece of the action for every approval form they signed. This was never verified, but there was no doubt in my mind that many investigations were guided by the opportunity to conduct interviews and searches after regular hours.

I hadn't realized the nest of skullduggery I would inherit. Dade County had become a haven for drug murders, particularly within the Hispanic community. Every Latino body found in some dumpster, creek, or alley was attributed to The Cocaine Cowboys. They became brazen one noon day, using Uzi's and Mac 10s to shoot up a liquor store in Kendall, leaving four dead, then speeding off in a van.

Established policy was to have Spanish detectives conduct these investigations, often riding four to a car, unsupervised. As it turned out, those four Spanish detectives would become well known outside of their investigative accomplishments.

While the majority of detectives were hard working and honest, a small percentage were bringing shame to their profession. For added support, I brought Frank Wesolowski, who I trusted, back into Homicide from the Sexual Battery Unit.

Then I learned Rick Fowler's real motive in offering to swap. He knew something few others knew. Miami's Channel 10 News, under the title: "I-Team Reports," unleashed a media expose' that caught the department, and me, completely off guard. For several weeks, the FBI had been conducting a covert investigation into mass corruption with the county's Homicide Bureau, focusing on at least twelve detectives and supervisors. Newspapers and other television stations went wild with rabid stories about detectives in cahoots with Mario Escandar, a known drug criminal, selling, buying, ripping off, and using drugs. Huge amounts of drug money recovered from murder scenes—in the thousands and millions—had been released to bogus relatives, then found its way into the hands of corrupt cops. Detectives would pull over trucks known to be hauling a shipment of cocaine, then hijack the drugs, stranding the driver who certainly couldn't call the police. Detectives stupidly flaunted their new found wealth, driving expensive sports cars, wearing heavy gold jewelry, buying mansions and keeping girl friends on the side.

While I dealt with the surge of murder cases and day-to-day personnel issues, the FBI's investigation added more pressure to the job. Often, the public focus turned to me. I thought it was necessary to be completely open to the media. I never wanted it to appear like we had anything to hide, and that we—the department's administration—were cooperative in every way. As the Homicide Bureau representative, my job was to buffer the director from any embarrassment.

Phones rang incessantly. I consented to newspaper and television interviews every time they asked. The questions were tough. Sometimes, I couldn't answer a question because I simply did not know the answer.

Most of the news groups did their jobs fairly and honestly. Not so with the I-Team, Clarence Jones and Joe Bergantino. These two men, led mostly by Bergantino, seemed on a mission to win a Pulitzer by nailing every cop in their path, whether guilty or not. It came to a head when they started pounding me with accusatory questions on camera, wording and slanting in such a manner to clearly leave an impression I was corrupt as well. When I watched the evening news later that day, I was astonished to see how they had manipulated and edited my answers out of context, cutting off at key words and phrases, or actually attaching some answers to a different question that was asked.

Even I thought I looked guilty.

These guys wanted someone higher in the chain than low-level detectives, a bigger fish for their Pulitzer Prize. And, they were apparently fueled by FBI agent Andre Fortier, who headed up the massive case trying to tie me to all the thievery and drug money.

They failed to consider that I was not working in Homicide when the FBI launched the corruption investigation. All of that activity had gone on long before my arrival. Two captains had been there before me when the scurrilous activities were running rampant, but no one asked them a single question.

I halted all television interviews. There was a unit of fifty personnel to run and 350 murders a year to investigate.

But the fallout caused damage that nearly put my career in jeopardy. In one instance, an inmate in the county jail, charged with a serious felony, contacted the State Attorney's Office claiming he had been watching television from his cell when he spotted me in an interview. "That's the cop who I saw taking a payoff from a drug dealer," he told the prosecutor. "I'm positive, that's him. Captain Frank, from Homicide."

They sent the jailbird to the county's best polygraph examiner, George Slattery. Known for his sharp interrogative skills, Slattery copped him out. The inmate was looking for a deal. He saw me on television all right, but the payoff story was all a lie.

Dodged another bullet.

* * *

Somewhere in the interim, a new County Manager named Merrett Stierheim summarily fired Director E. Wilson Purdy because the stubborn old man would not bend with the times. He refused to promote and appoint minorities into higher positions unless they met the same criteria he had set for the department. One African-American lieutenant, Willie Morrison, had passed the captain's test, and was within reach of a legitimate promotion. But Purdy didn't like Morrison, so he stonewalled and promoted all whites instead. Purdy's dark ages mentality earned him an unanticipated stint of unemployment.

At the same time, a clandestine unit within the Organized Crime Bureau (OCB), emboldened by the corruption scandal in Homicide, went about their own witch hunt. They targeted Charlie Black for an alleged involvement in a drug deal and for his close association with a lawyer named Paul Pollack. I'm certain that internal politics played a role in this. Nevertheless, OCB had tagged Pollack as corrupt and Black guilty by association. I'd been with Charlie Black several times during visits with Paul Pollack at his office, usually during lunch. When I was there, there was never any talk about illegal activity or any other business union between the two men.

They were, simply, friends. Knowing Black as well as I did, I would never have believed him corrupt, unless he told me to my face.

Paul Pollack was a colorful character, indeed. In a stand-alone building near downtown Miami, his dimly lit office reminded me of The Godfather's, with a large curved desk at one end of the huge room. Behind his desk, a black curtain camouflaged a wrought-iron spiral staircase leading up to a secret parlor on the second floor, complete with liquor bar, fireplace and comfy furnishings. Hmmm. Wonder what that was for?

Because of the on-going investigation, Stierheim could not name Black as the interim director. That appointment went to Bobby Jones, the same man I worked with during my first days in Homicide in 1966. Jones took the appointment reluctantly, claiming he would serve as a stand-in until a full-time Director was appointed. He didn't want the job.

Several months after Jones took over, with the corruption probe at full steam and negative publicity saturating newspapers, the department felt compelled to act in some manner, even though there was no clear evidence or indictments against anyone. I was ordered to transfer twelve detectives and supervisors out of Homicide and back to uniform. The number of sudden vacancies at one time was unprecedented. With the murder rate spiraling, that was like removing a full one-third of the infantry from Europe in the height of WW II. We went into a frenzy searching and interviewing for new officers, sergeants and lieutenants. Many who might have applied for the job, did not for fear of negative perceptions associated with Homicide.

It was not uncommon to lose one or two detectives for replacement. Twelve was an untenable burden. The transfers left several active murder investigations suspended. The remaining detectives were under tremendous pressure to work their cases while training new people, all the while fending off horrid perceptions from the public and fellow cops.

New supervisors—sergeants and lieutenants—brought in from uniform were at a disadvantage with no background in Homicide. The onus was on me and the few remaining supervisors to get them trained.

I saw the transfers as a knee jerk decision to appease media. The powers saw it as politically necessary. Our job was to keep the Bureau running. Meanwhile the lives and reputations of twelve cops, whose names appeared in the newspapers, were stained forever, guilty or not.

Homicide was in total chaos.

The next year, eight of those officers were charged with corruption-related crimes. Four were acquitted. Another four went to federal prison.

CHAPTER FORTY-THREE
Hill Street Blues

The divorce from Joan was followed by more years of personal struggles, facing Bennett's drug problem, earning a bachelor's degree, keeping Jennifer with me as much as possible and, of course, dealing with the job and all its demands. Bouts of depression led to more drinking and frequent solitude. I dated intermittently, but it became nothing more than a sporadic attempt at overcoming impotency until I dared not fail one more time. Nothing is more humiliating to a man who flirts with a woman, wines, dines, and then begins the love making process, then finds himself incapable.

Worse than anything, I thought I had failed Bennett.

Loneliness and financial straits plunged me further downward. I began drinking heavily again. Again, I contemplated suicide. After all, it was easy. I'd seen hundreds of painless journeys out from a sea of misery.

Doug Hughes knew I was in bad shape and suggested I see a shrink. "I'm not crazy," I said.

"It has nothing to do with being crazy," he said.

"It's about getting yourself on track, to be happy with who you are."

With reluctance, I began therapy with a woman psychologist once a week. At first, she only listened, rarely making a comment, just a question now and then. Weeks later, I was amazed how she had memorized every detail about my past and present life. I began to look forward to our appointments. While the sessions were kept to a strict clock, I had her undivided attention during every hour. We delved into the many deep corners of my life and of those around me, and the revelations that unfurled remain with me to this day. She was nothing less than marvelous.

During one session, I was lamenting about Bennett and all the craziness with his past and present life, what more I could do to help him become a whole person again. Then she shocked me with a comment. "He's got you, Marshall. Just where he wants you."

I stopped and pondered what she had just said. I realized how right she was. Bennett knew my weaknesses and was playing on my emotions to get from me anything he wanted. I had become his enabler. He fed off of my shroud of guilt.

I realized, also, that much of my behavior in other ways, was triggered by a deep sense of guilt and the need for acceptance.

Naturally, I did not tell anyone that I—a Metro- Police Captain—was in therapy for mental problems. Yet it was one of the best decisions I ever made. The sessions went on for over a year. I had little money to spend, but this was well spent.

* * *

I had not forged any great friendship with public defenders. Their job was to humiliate me, undo my work, and set the guilty man free. Justice didn't matter. Winning did.

Maxine Cohen was a 29 year-old liberal brown-haired lawyer with her sights on becoming a judge one day. We met through a mutual friend. She heard I loved classical music.

I received a phone call. She had tickets to an afternoon concert by Vladimir Horowitz, the great pianist of that era. Her date couldn't make it. She didn't want to waste a ticket. "Sure," I said. "I'd love to go."

Horowitz performed concerts only at four o'clock in the afternoons because the evening hours, he thought, found patrons too sleepy and inattentive.

We had a marvelous time. After the concert, we enjoyed dinner at the Sonesta Beach Hotel on Key Biscayne, dancing , drinking, and then making love at her waterfront apartment along Biscayne Bay. My virility had been resurrected.

The affair lasted six months. During that time, a popular new television program hit the airways. We figured the producers used us as a model for the main characters. Hill Street Blues was about a right wing Homicide captain and his liberal girl friend lawyer who worked for the Public Defender's Office.

As casual dates, we were ideal. As live-in lovers, we were a disaster, both hard-headed when it came to domestic duties. Nor could I afford her Nieman-Marcus taste with my Wal-Mart wallet. But the relationship formed a confidence in myself I'd never experienced before. We remained friends.

Judge Maxine Cohen Lando sat on the Circuit Court Bench starting in 1993. She passed away in 2012. She was an amazing woman.

* * *

Bennett didn't make life easy. I never knew what strange things he would do next. Now nineteen years of age, he stayed with Maxine and me for a period of time in 1979, while we tried to help him recover from drug addiction and other behavioral problems. One night,

Bennett went on a rampage, stealing my gun from home, then driving to the Haulover Beach inlet where he stood on rock pilings shooting off rounds, scaring the hell out of everyone. Fortunately, he only aimed at the stars above.

I received a call from police headquarters. Bennett had been arrested. I managed to retrieve my weapon and Bennett ended up on probation for Reckless Display of Firearm.

I brought my son to a local psychiatrist named Arnold Lieber, M.D., touted as being an expert in cases such as Bennett's. Reflecting on my own father's plight with mental illness, I wept the day I entered him into three months of lock-up treatment at Highland Park Hospital. He engaged in therapy daily, was given medication, and allowed visitors once a week. Lieber would see Bennett for fifteen minutes, twice a month. Based on that, Lieber diagnosed Bennett as manic-depressive. After his hospital release, Bennett was to take powerful drugs, Lithium and Haldahl, to keep him balanced.

Bennett started sleeping sixteen hours a day. When conscious, he walked around like a zombie, short little steps, drooling, jaw shaking, monosyllabic, unable to converse. In one instance, he defecated in his pants. After a week, I called Doctor Lieber, who said this behavior was normal, that he would have to be on this medicine for the rest of his life.

After a month, I lost confidence in the psychiatrist and stopped the medicine. Bennett recovered as if he awakened from a long sleep. In reality, Bennett's primary problem was drug addiction, along with some psychological issues stemming from family dysfunction. Doctor Arnold Lieber, in my opinion, was incompetent.

Not long after Bennett's reawakening, he was caught—once again—stealing from me in my house. An old habit. He ran away. Again.

* * *

Out Bennett. In Jennifer.

After two years in the apartment, I managed to save enough money to put down on a small house in a lower-middle class neighborhood. I had already been keeping Jennifer during my days off and vacation periods. Joan was having her own personal problems, and allowed my nine-year old daughter to come and live with me full time.

So, in addition to my duties as the captain of Metro- Dade Homicide, I happily became a Mr. Mom.

CHAPTER FORTY-FOUR
The McDuffie Case

I'd known Edna Buchanan since the early 1970s as a tenacious crime reporter for The Miami Herald with an insatiable nose for stories. Dealing with Edna was like being plugged into an electric outlet. She could be a colossal nuisance to detectives in Homicide who occasionally caught her shuffling through papers in the office while casually asking questions, wanting to know more and more about some case. Away from the office, she was on the phone constantly, probing for more information than the Public Information Office was willing to give her. I'd seen her dozens of times at crime scenes standing behind the tape, pad in hand, dressed handsomely, her hair coiffed perfectly while I admired her sultry curves. I never knew anyone who could ask more questions in less time. In spite of a somewhat adversarial relationship, I respected the woman for her incredible skills as a reporter. (In 1986, she won a Pulitzer Prize for outstanding reporting with *The Miami Herald*)

It was sometime around the 23rd of December, 1979, when I received a call at home from my friend and Division Chief, Charlie Black. "What do you know about an Arthur McDuffie?" he asked in a gruff tone.

"Never heard the name, sir."

Black sounded angry. "Edna Buchanan just called asking questions. This McDuffie guy is at the morgue.

Something about a police chase, and suspicious wounds to the head, that he might have been beaten by cops several days ago. Why don't I know about this? Get on it, right away."

I spoke to Edna. She had been at the Medical Examiner's Office talking with Doctor Ron Wright, who had just completed an autopsy on a motorcyclist who had been chased by Metro-Dade Police six days before, the night of December 17. According to reports, Arthur McDuffie, 32, a black man, drove head-on into a light pole, causing his deadly injuries. However, Doctor Wright found suspicious wounds to the skull consistent with being beaten by night sticks. Edna peppered me with questions I couldn't answer, but I vowed to find out.

Police reports stated that McDuffie had been speeding through Liberty City after 1:00 A.M., when he refused to stop for a police unit. The inner city chase accelerated in and out of private yards, parking lots, as police units smashed into poles, parked cars and trash cans. Eventually, ten to twelve police cars entered the fray. According to those reports, McDuffie crashed head-on into a light pole on North Miami Avenue and 38th Street, just at the ramp to the interstate. From there, he was taken to the hospital where he remained on life support systems for six days.

Once Edna sunk her teeth into the story, the incident became the most publicized police brutality case in Dade County's history. Scrutiny was intense from all sides: Politicians, citizenry, media, courts and law enforcement. Sensational reports saturated the news every day. Following her first article, the black community was up in arms, demanding a full investigation, and that due justice be administered to those officers who may have killed an innocent black man. The cops were white.

For me, a major roadblock was the manner in which the upper echelon had already dealt with the case. Written orders had long been established stating that any incident in which a citizen is killed by police, or where death was imminent after injuries were sustained at the hands of police, was to be investigated by Homicide. Not Internal Affairs. Not the District Commander. Not the news media.

For the six days that McDuffie lay comatose on life support, that didn't happen.

Homicide was structured under the Police Division, headed by Charlie Black. With Purdy gone and the bogus corruption investigation hanging over his head, Black was struggling with internal political forces.

Once McDuffie's life support plugs were pulled, and it got out into the media, Acting Director, Bobby Jones, turned the case over to me, asking that I personally head up the probe. But because the upper echelon had already violated orders regarding investigative protocol, I started off at a major disadvantage, picking up the pieces six days late.

I learned that Internal Affairs had, indeed, been investigating this matter since the morning after it happened. Charlie Black and I, captain of Homicide, had been kept in the dark. The reasons why Homicide was categorically excluded was never explained.

The Internal Affairs investigation had been triggered by the Central District (Liberty City Police Station) Captain, Dale Bowlin. He was the first top official to be made aware that some blows were struck after McDuffie allegedly rammed into the pole, and that the man's condition was critical. Bowlin had discussed it with

Bobby Jones, who turned it over to Captain Jack Rafftery of Internal Affairs. Better known as "Smilin' Jack", Rafferty then delegated the case to Sergeant Linda Saunders, an amicable young woman with little experience or knowledge in the field of criminal investigation. No one called Homicide.

It's important to point out here that Bobby Jones' prior announcement that he didn't want the permanent director's position spurred at least a dozen applications for the top job, many from within the department, including Dale Bowlin and Charlie Black.

From the onset, Bowlin accused Black of transferring too many problem officers cops into Central District, thereby casting blame up the chain. Black accused Bowlin of mismanaging his district.

On the morning of the incident, Linda Saunders had taken statements from four of the involved officers who basically told her what they wanted her to know. McDuffie, they said, had rammed into the pole, but was conscious and combatant, requiring the police to use force in subduing him. I took note of Saunders' inexperience just by reading the statements. The subject officers had taken charge, narrating their lies unchallenged. She avoided confrontation. I was struck by the total inept handling of the entire case from the beginning, not necessarily by Saunders, but by the upper echelon who had taken control.

While Saunders lacked experience, she may have followed the lead of experienced supervisors, had any bothered to lead her. Such was not the case. During those first six days, Saunders—and her boss—had not even inspected the most crucial item of physical evidence available: The motorcycle. When I inquired of its location, she didn't know. She thought McDuffie's next-of-kin might have it. The motorcycle, in fact, had been impounded.

The burden should never have rested on Saunders' shoulders.

I proceeded to the pound and viewed the motorcycle, bringing with me an expert in traffic homicide investigation. An expert wasn't needed. The obvious stared us in the face. There had been no accident. There had been no ramming. The damage was obviously fake. Smashed speedometer, dented gas tank, dented fenders, all had been the work of sticks and rocks, made to look like an accident. Conspicuous by their absence, striations should have been present in any accident in which the motorcycle laid down at a high speed. Nor was there any major damage to the front, which would indicate that a "ramming" caused McDuffie's injuries.

Meanwhile, Doctor Wright—a friend of law enforcement—had signed off the death as "accidental", accepting the chase officer's statements at face value. But he also pointed out that several suspicious, unexplained trauma wounds were visible to the scalp, indicating possible blows by a blunt instrument.

It was not enough that our murder rate was soaring beyond all records; that we had recently been at the core of a major corruption scandal, resulting in the transfer of twelve detectives, and the indictment of eight; that we were training new detectives by the dozens, trying to keep up. Metro-Dade Homicide, once again, was in the center of another firestorm, raging with internal misconduct, fending off accusations of racial bias and cover up. Television and the print media intensely followed every step of our investigation, calling press conferences daily at the Director's Office and the State Attorney's, headed by Janet Reno.

Twelve and fifteen hour work days kept us all jumping out of our pants. (Well, Reno jumped out of her skirt) I assigned two outstanding detectives to assist, men I trusted implicitly, Al Singleton and Frank Wesolowski. I took statements from several of the officers, knowing I was not going to get the truth. In the interim, two City of Miami officers who had arrived at the scene as bystanders after McDuffie went down, came forward and gave statements. They described the assault as a shark frenzy, cops bending over an unarmed man lying on the street, uniformed officers wailing away at him with night sticks and long steel flashlights. The scenario sounded so familiar. I could envision the final images of Arthur McDuffie as he lay face up on the street.

They formed a circle around me. chanting to the tune of ring around the rosie, only the lyrics had changed; 'Marshall is a fairy, Marshall is a fairy', over and over, and over again. They punched me in the shoulders, stomach and face, then tossed me to the ground, kicking, spitting. I wrapped my hands over my face to protect myself from the onslaught of hands, arms and shoes. It was like a shark frenzy. I thought they were going to kill me.

Of all the statements, I was struck most by Sergeant Skip Evans, one of two supervisors that had arrived on the scene. (The other supervisor was Sergeant Ira Diggs, who was part of the on-scene frenzy) Evans told me that he had phoned Captain Dale Bowlin at 6:00 A.M. that morning and informed him that McDuffie had been beaten with night sticks and flashlights, after the accident.

If true, and considering McDuffie's near death condition, that information should have placed the investigation square in the Homicide Bureau. Bowlin, Rafferty or Acting Director Bobby Jones deliberately kept it from Charlie Black and me.

Janet Reno's top assistants, George Yoss and Hank Adorno, had become deeply entrenched in the investigation from a prosecutorial standpoint. We met and spoke four to five times a day with updates on progress, while pinpointing legal issues that could result in charges. Besides nailing the obviously guilty cops, they asked if I thought Lieutenant Don Arney, the on-duty shift supervisor who did not respond to the scene, had been involved in the cover up. I found no evidence of that. They had Arney take a series of polygraphs, which he passed.

They also wanted to know if Captain Dale Bowlin was guilty of any part of the cover-up. In fact, Bowlin did not cover up the crime because he hadn't known, yet, that a crime had been committed. In truth, he had covered his ass by turning it over to the Acting Director, who gave it to Internal Affairs. The main violation here was administrative: Not informing Homicide or the Police Division Chief. I struggled with the question, feeling a sense of duty to Reno's office as well as the department, knowing—in light of the frenetic pace of things—that Bowlin would probably be subjected to prosecutorial scrutiny if I mentioned the revelation by Sergeant Skip Evans. Feeling the matter was more an issue of internal politics, I elected not to mention Bowlin's situation to the State Attorney's Office.

In the midst of another harrowing day, I received a surprise visit by one of the on-scene officers, Charles Veverka Jr., who presented me with the blue copy of a police report. He was accompanied by another on-scene cop, Mark Meier. With the media blitz, Veverka had seen the writing on the wall and was prepared to preempt everyone else with his own mea culpa. The report, he said, was his original copy written on the scene which he was told (by his sergeant) to throw away, alter and rewrite before turning it in. In it, he described what he called an accurate account of what happened on the scene.

Veverka stated that he and Meier were the first to catch McDuffie at 38th Street. McDuffie, he claimed, did not have an accident. Rather, he parked the motorcycle. As he is telling me this, I imagined the scene as it was described by the City of Miami officer, who told me he saw the motorcycle leaning upright on its kick stand.

According to Veverka's statement, he and Meier screeched to a halt in separate cars after McDuffie finally stopped. When he ran over to make the arrest, McDuffie threw a punch, thereby resisting arrest and precipitating the fight that followed. Meier did nothing but stand and watch. Other officers began screeching onto the scene and entered the fray, several taking their shots at the man lying on the ground, until a Latino officer straddled the unconscious McDuffie and whacked him three more time in the head with his night stick. (One of the officers involved, Bill Hanlon, aka, "Mad Dog," had since taken vacation time and was out of town, unavailable and non-locatable, a lucky break for him).

When it was all over and McDuffie lay there, Sergeant Skip Evans arrived and huddled with his cops. (Sergeant Ira Diggs had been there all along) That's when they organized a charade by smashing the motorcycle with night sticks and flashlights, to make it look like damage from an accident. Sometime later that morning, Evans must have felt a pang of guilt, for he phoned his commander, telling him that McDuffie had, in fact, been beaten.

I believed most of Veverka's story, but not all. If McDuffie had parked his motorcycle on its kick stand, that indicated intent to surrender. It made no sense that McDuffie would give up, then throw a punch at a uniformed officer. More likely, Veverka's adrenalin had pumped to overload after eight long minutes of a harrowing chase and he simply charged after McDuffie like a bull, causing the man to pull away or resist. When other cops arrived on the scene, they saw Veverka in a scramble with McDuffie in what appeared to be a resisting mode. That's when they all piled in with night sticks and flashlights. Veverka—I thought—had to come up with McDuffie's "first punch" scenario, to cover his own ass. In my opinion, Veverka was the cop who sparked the chaos that followed. Had he and Meier simply taken the man into custody, the name, *McDuffie*, would never have been a household word in Dade County.

As he spoke on, I reflected on a scene back in 1963, when I was part of a phalanx of police cars who caught up to a possible murder suspect, and a detective name Jack Kahn lost his cool.

"You son-of-a-bitch!" Kahn continued hollering, his face red, until a more even-tempered, Joe Kogan, physically pulled Kahn away. Kogan was a true leader who stepped in to quell the fray instead of joining in. His actions made a lasting impression. If all sergeants were like Joe Kogan, terms such as police brutality and corruption would almost be rendered obsolete.

Veverka and Meier essentially broke the case, giving us the first witnesses we needed. Janet Reno's office was under pressure to come up with an arrest as soon as possible to placate the community. Yoss and Adorno, great lawyers each, seemed under the gun to charge as many cops as possible. In fact, only about four or five of the responding officers actually struck the man, while others stood back or arrived after the fact. One of those, a Spanish cop named Ubaldo Del Toro may have kicked McDuffie one time, but that couldn't be verified. And, he may have participated in some of the motorcycle cover up, but the reports were iffy. I thought the case against him was weak, at best, but they wanted him charged as well.

After he finally returned from vacation, prosecutors gave Bill "Mad Dog" Hanlon immunity for his testimony against the others. This was done to add insurance to a case that would be difficult to prosecute for the lack of independent witnesses. As it turned out, and by his admission, Hanlon was one of the principals on the scene.

Also immunized from prosecution in exchange for testimony, were Mark Meier and Charles Veverka Jr. Coming in to volunteer information was a smart move for those two men.

In January of 1980, after warrants were issued by the State Attorney, I had the distasteful responsibility of summoning five police officers to the Homicide Office where I placed them under arrest and booked each in the County Jail for conspiracy to obstruct justice and the manslaughter death of Arthur McDuffie. They were the last physical arrests I would ever make as a sworn cop.

* * *

The McDuffie aftermath plunged the department into several administrative and operational quagmires. External scrutiny by media, politicians and citizen's groups, still brimming over Purdy's narrow-minded legacy, demanded sweeping changes to the promotional and hiring processes so that minorities would be better represented within the rank structure. Willie Morrison, the only black on the captain's list, was promoted to captain and then major. Bobby Jones eventually changed his mind and decide to accept the director's job on a permanent basis.

Meanwhile, Jones turned over final review of the McDuffie cops (as they were now known) to Robert Dempsey. Dempsey was a New York lawyer originally hired as a legal advisor to Purdy, who later promoted him to Assistant Director. I was no fan of Bob Dempsey. Neither were many cops who felt he was a carpetbagger with no roots in the department. I viewed him as a weasel who rested on his law degree, and ever condescending toward the rank and file. Dempsey's job was to determine and recommend the disposition for the remaining seven police officers who, in one manner or another, had arrived on that fateful scene. I had contended that each cop should be looked at individually. One officer arrived long after the fact and only tended to Sergeant Ira Diggs who appeared to be injured. Another two or three late arrivals clearly had nothing to do with the beating, and had no idea what actually happened. They had no particular history of being abusive. It was unclear which peripheral officers were present when the primary officers engaged in the on-scene cover up.

Nevertheless, Robert Dempsey, another Director wannabe who had thrown his hat in the ring for the big job, had made a decision. "Fire them all," he said. I couldn't believe my ears. Some of these guys were good men with careers at stake and supporting families. Dempsey made an arbitrary decision that would affect the rest of their lives, though they were found guilty of nothing. "Let the union try and win their jobs back." Dempsey's only concern was department image, or his image, and to hell with police officers who had served and risked their lives faithfully for many years. My esteem for Dempsey plunged to rock bottom.

Some of the McDuffie cops (Michael Watts, Alex Marrero, Bill Hanlon and [21]Charles Veverka Jr.) had assembled track records who the department should have red-flagged as potentially brutal

---

[21] Charles Veverka Jr. was the officer accused of brutality in the elevator which led to the suicide of Crime Scene Technician, Eddie Stone. Stone's death left no witness and the allegations were not sustained.

officers. For sure, they never should have been assigned to patrol the streets on a midnight shift within a volatile district such as Liberty City, supervised by the likes of Ira Diggs and Herbert "Skip" Evans. (Where or where have the Kogans and Becks gone?)

While hindsight is always 20/20, it boggles the mind how and why these kinds of men were assembled in one squad unharnessed, harassing citizens night after night with their personal brand of street justice.

CHAPTER FORTY-FIVE
Shake-up

There was no love lost between Bobby Jones and Charlie Black. When Jones was named the permanent Director, he wanted to form his team of loyal upper level managers. He demoted Charlie Black to Captain and promoted Dale Bowlin into Black's job as Police Division Chief.

Black had been a department powerhouse for twelve years, promoted to Major of Detectives Burea when he was but 32 years of age and later, a Divisio Chief. During that time, he was often considered the heir apparent to the department throne if and when Purdy left.

Now, he was reduced in rank and farmed out from headquarters to take charge of the department air and sea support units at the airport station in Opa Locka.

I remained as the Homicide captain. But it was an adjustment, for I'd lost my rabbi. Black and I would remain friends, always, though it may have bode poorly for my future.

When Bowlin took over as Police Division Chief, he inherited an old-timer name Dick Shelton as the Detective Bureau Major. Shelton was never known as a slick cop or dynamic administrator. Rather, he was a steady, by-the-book gentleman who Purdy liked because he was uncompromisingly honest and had survived the old Buchanan regime unscathed. Previously, except for official protocol, I usually by-passed Shelton and reported directly to Black. Now, I had to go through Shelton for everything.

I never sensed acceptance by Dale Bowlin. That became clear one day during a private talk in Dick Shelton's office. The major must have felt morally compelled to impart an ominous fact. Either that or he was speaking on behalf of his boss. I'll never know. But it went like this. "Marshall, there's been talk about your friendships."

I sat back, amazed at what I was hearing. "You mean Charlie Black?" I asked.

"Yes. If you want to go anywhere in the department, you might think about who your friends are."

I knew Dale Bowlin held animosity toward Charlie Black. But I never figured that would spill over to me. I thought about my—then—twenty years of service in the police department, and then taking charge of Homicide during its most trying of times, staying in the proverbial kitchen while it was hot, dealing with a unit that was under the gun from the day I took over, handling the McDuffie matter and representing the department with honor and dignity. And, it all boiled down to my friendship with a man who was out of favor with the new regime. Well, that's politics.

"Charlie Black is my friend, Major. I wouldn't be much of a friend if I turned my back on him just because he's not Division Chief any more."

"Well," he said. "Just thought I ought to tell you."

* * *

For a while, the violin had become personal therapy for maintaining sanity. Besides playing with a quartet, I managed a first chair position in the Broward Symphony in Ft. Lauderdale, where we held concerts once a month and rehearsed at a college campus music hall two nights a week. Being a symphony musician wasn't always easy, wearing that beeper and praying it didn't go off during a rehearsal. I reveled in the experience, not just for the music, but for the environment, being surrounded by such wonderful and creative talent. For so many years, the rigid structure of a traditional police agency had somehow thwarted independent thought and feeling. Being immersed in music was like opening the heavens and finding my true identity.

The most important concert of the year featured a renowned young virtuoso, Eugene Fodor, as the soloist who was to play *Paganini's Concerto in D Major*. One evening, during rehearsal, as I played four chairs behind the concertmaster, the musicians, the conductor and Fodor were working hard at refining some passages. Suddenly, the double doors flew open and the room lit up like a stage setting. A small well-dressed man holding a microphone and a television cameraman boldly entered with the hot lamp glaring. Seeing he was now on camera, the conductor stiffened up and began flailing his arms like he was in Carnegie Hall. Fodor stood taller and began playing his heart out for the camera. But the two newsmen walked past them and directly to my chair, pointing the camera down toward me. I could see a look of confusion, or perhaps, disgust on the conductor's face.

Someone had tipped off the media that the captain of Homicide was a symphony violinist, and thought it would make an interesting story. An interview followed.

The story was aired two nights later as a short feature. Neither the conductor or Eugene Fodor received any press.

After a number of call-outs, and too many beeper signals during practice, I realized that schedules and work demands were too conflicting. I dropped out of the symphony after playing there for two years.

CHAPTER FORTY-SIX
Charade in Washington

In the early part of 1980, a representative of Senator Lawton Chiles' office invited me and a City of Miami Homicide Captain to testify in Washington D.C. before the United States Congress concerning the problems of violence in America and what was needed to combat crime in general.

I was floored. Imagine that. The school fairy from Nautilus Junior High had finally arrived. My mother would have been proud. Bernie would probably have laughed his guts out wondering which politicians were on the take. It never occurred to me that our highest officials had paid any attention to our local dilemma. And, of all people, that they thought I was worthy of being heard.

I decided to take Jennifer with me. At ten years of age, she would have a golden opportunity to learn something about her government, and as a bonus, do a little sightseeing. That's why I added two extra days onto the trip, one on the front end, one on the back.

I was to arrive at the capitol building one day early to go over my testimony with aides. Enthralled by the sheer atmosphere of the seat of our government, the rotunda and circle of presidents, the chambers of the house and the senate, I tried showing it all to my daughter. Actually, it was I who was intrigued. She just enjoyed being out of school.

Jennifer was edgy and restless. I had to keep her occupied while I talked with the aides. Once we found books and papers and pencils, she was fine. Meanwhile, I imagined all those hearings I'd previously watched on television, and now here I was, a dot in the annals of U.S. government history. Small, perhaps, but a dot nonetheless. My congressional testimony would be recorded for all time.

Now I learned how the system really worked. The aides went over my prepared speech with a fine-toothed comb, suggesting a minor edit job here and there, but basically accepting what I had written about the scourge of crime, why it had risen, spewing statistics, and getting to the core of what I felt was needed to combat it all. Then they informed me of what questions would be asked, and by whom. "Senator Nunn will ask you this. Senator Cohen will ask you that. Senator Chiles will make commentary, and ask you this." They wanted to know, in advance and specifically, what my responses were going to be. Nothing extemporaneous, like rehearsing for a school play.

The next day, my colleague from the City of Miami Police Department and I sat before the panel of distinguished senators and recited our prepared speeches. Then, sure enough, those exact questions spewed forth from the panel as though they were from the top of their heads. I was tempted to wing a couple of surprise comments, but gave it a second thought. No guts.

In all, it was a wonderful experience, taking my daughter to see the White House, the Lincoln Memorial and the Tomb of The Unknown Soldier.

When we got home, a friend had clipped an article from a newspaper with a large photograph of me sitting and waiting to speak in the senate chamber with Jennifer next to me, mouth agape, yawning.

I always told her that she had a big mouth. Now she believed me.

CHAPTER FORTY-SEVEN
The Verdict Aftermath

Between the onslaught of daily news coverage, the outcries of the black community and the pandering politicians, tension piqued throughout Dade County like a huge bomb ready to explode. As long as we (police officials) were white, no one escaped accusations of racism, either in letters to the editor, television street interviews, by demonstrators or community leaders themselves. We simply had to shrug it off and do the best job possible.

Janet Reno was gracious enough to personally congratulate me on a job well done.

Because of the enormous publicity for nearly six months, a change of venue was awarded. The McDuffie trial was held in Tampa, Florida. I flew there four times during the trial to assist and to give testimony.

Hank Adorno and George Yoss did a credible job as prosecutors, working with problem witnesses and no other evidence. The defendant cops each secured the finest of lawyers, all of whom put one-hundred percent of their effort into the defense. The charges against Ubaldo Del Toro, the cop I thought should not have been charged, were thrown out by the judge after his lawyer, Gerald Kogan won a motion for dismissal. (Kogan later became Chief Justice of the Florida Supreme Court.) That left four primary defendants.

The defense was based on infusing reasonable doubt into the minds of the jury, that the officers who gave testimony in exchange for immunity—Charles Veverka Jr., Mark Meier, and Bill "Mad Dog" Hanlon—may have been equally as guilty, or more so, than those on trial, and that they flipped on fellow officers and even lied to save their own hides. It was one's word against the other. No independent witness could say that any one cop committed a specific act that murdered Arthur McDuffie. Had I been on that jury, I might have had those same doubts.

The earth's moon must have been full on Saturday, the 17th of May, for it was a day never to be forgotten. Not because it was the same day that the Mount St. Helens volcano erupted in the State of Washington. Not because it was the first day of the infamous Mariel Boat Lift from Cuba that eventually brought 120,000 new immigrants into the South Florida community. But because the long-awaited McDuffie verdict was announced. All defendants: Not Guilty.

It was as though the insurgents had been holding the county hostage for six months, waiting for justice as they wished it to be, and if it didn't go their way, we all—the white establishment—would pay. Never before had the county been so divided along racial lines. The department was on the ready with twelve hour shifts, but it didn't matter. Being on the ready stopped nothing.

On or around 7:00 P.M., while visiting at a friend's house, I received a call from a frantic Lieutenant Bob Elliott at the shift commander's desk letting me know that the headquarters building might be under siege. Our worst nightmare had started. Rioters were storming the streets of Miami, setting fires, turning cars over, and terrorizing unsuspecting motorists. I'd seen civil disorder three times before in my career, but they paled in comparison to what would become the worst race riot in the history of the Southeast United States.

It was just getting dark as I rushed down I-95 toward headquarters—about 20 minutes away—to assemble my people at the Homicide Bureau and see the status of things. But I had inadvertently left my hand held radio at the office and could not communicate with anyone while driving the car. I didn't know the extent of what was happening.

It was now dark as I neared the Civic Center and pulled off the ramp at Northwest 12th Avenue. A black man was standing at the corner frantically waving drivers back.

"Get out of here!" he said. "Get back. Get away." When he walked over to my window, I showed him my I.D., assuring him I was an official. "You don't want to go in there," he said.

As the light turned green, I disregarded the heroic citizen at the corner who probably saved a few lives and pulled across 12th Avenue toward the Justice Building.

Hundreds of people were scurrying about in the darkness ahead, like insects from a nest. One car was upside down, burning. Another was on fire, further on. I stopped the car as a frisson of fear suddenly came over me. A man's voice hollered at me from the overpass above. "Get out of there.

Get back NOW!" I heard a shot. My heart raced. I was trying to get into my headquarters building two blocks away but the rioters had the area under attack. Trapped, I backed up and headed down 12th Avenue, wishing I had my radio. I took the advice of the powerful voice from above and fled.

I was the Homicide Commander, running from the scene to save my own life, no communications, and no knowledge about the status of our employees back at headquarters. This was not good.

I learned later that the rioters had been on the verge of storming the five-story police headquarters building on 14th Street. A rookie black female named Betty Johnson and Clarence Balanky, an old-salt drunkometer technician, were manning the lobby desk when a band of angry sweat-soaked blacks threw rocks and bottles smashing the front window and glass doors, then stood in the doorway, menacing, threatening to come in, sticks in hand. No one else was on the first floor, but they didn't know that. Frightened beyond words, Betty Johnson and Clarence Balanky pulled their revolvers and pointed straight ahead. The rioters stood as a pack and stared. The officers stared back. Not a word was spoken. The elevators leading up four floors were a few steps away. Communication systems for the entire Metro-Dade Police occupied the fifth floor as well as the Crime Laboratory and all its forensic evidence and million dollar equipment. The fourth floor housed Central Records; every police report, every local criminal record, was filed there in hard copy. No computers then. Civilian employees were on duty. The third floor housed the upper administrative offices, including the Organized Crime Bureau and all its records. The second floor: Homicide, and all the other detective offices.

Why the rioters backed away and did not enter will forever be a mystery. The building was theirs. So was the chance to cripple all police communications and destroy thousands of criminal records, not to mention terrorizing the employees.

Those two desk cops should have been awarded medals. Their calm, steel resolve probably saved the department from total disaster and tremendous embarrassment. If they had pulled off a macho Clint Eastwood routine and started shooting, the rioters may have responded with violence.

I still needed to connect with my people. With nowhere else to go, I thought of Edna Buchanan at The *Miami Herald*, knowing they had access to all police communications. She met me in the parking garage of the bay front landmark and led me into the building and onto the elevator leading to the fourth floor. Alone now, we looked at each other with a dire expression, knowing local people were out there being killed, that this was going to be a sad and momentous day in the annals of Dade County. I don't know what really came over me when I ignored the crisis of the moment and pressed closer to Edna, wrapping her in my arms and kissing her. We were both stunned. For a few moments, we stared at each other, thoughts raging, until the door slid open. Then I felt a pang of guilt. After all, my guys were out there in harms way, and here I was making out with the queen of media.

What can I say. Some things never change.

By the time I connected to the police radios, I learned that a City of Miami Captain, Mike Cosgrove of Special Operations, had sent in his squadron of troops and secured the Civic Center complex. The lieutenant at the Homicide office and other supervisors assured me they were all right. It was safe for me to penetrate the streets and get back to headquarters.

When I checked my car, sure enough, a bullet had grazed the right fender. That shot near the Justice building was meant for me.

The department went into an emergency mode, with twelve hour shifts, and squads of uniform officers battling the insurgents in the streets, trying desperately to save lives. Our job in Homicide was to investigate every murder within the county's jurisdiction. Teams of detectives responded to every call en masse, with special support as back-up protection. Along with Crime Scene technicians, they handled scenes as fast as possible, shipped bodies, collected evidence and got the hell out.

Meanwhile, the rest of the county wasn't standing still. Crimes and death cases everywhere else still had to be investigated. Fortunately, little activity was going on outside the riot zone.

White citizens who normally drove home from work through parts of Liberty City were in great peril.

Some were trapped and surrounded by rioters at stop signs and red lights, rocking their cars until they turned over. One citizen was pummeled to death as the rioters stood on the side of the car, poking the driver with sticks and clubs.

Another had his tongue cut out. Businesses were set afire throughout the five square-mile area, gas stations, retail stores, schools, grocery markets. From there, wide-spread looting stripped business owners of their livelihood. It was a night of pure terror, not only for whites, and for police officers, but for the decent citizens of Liberty City as well. For it was their own community that had been destroyed, pillaged and burned, not the white's. A billion dollars in damage would later be assessed.

In the end, the body count attributed to the riot stood at eighteen with over 250 serious injuries.

With twelve-hour shifts, detectives worked around the clock. I remained in the office until 7:30 A.M. the next morning and left when my relief showed up. Oh yeah. In the office. After all, I hadn't really seen the carnage, other than radio and television news, and briefings by other cops.

I was one of the lucky ones, safe and sound within an air-conditioned building while the rest of the department was out in combat, risking their lives.

An overcast sky now cloaked Miami at dawn as I drove north on I-95 from downtown, emotionally weary and physically exhausted. I glanced west over the city landscape, then looked a second time, and shuddered. I could hardly come to grips with what I witnessed. The city, my city, was burning. For miles and miles, great pillars of black smoke rose to the heavens, like so many pictures I'd seen from WWII, where cities were bombed and building were turned to rubble. The tension bomb inside Dade

County had indeed exploded. Hair rose on my arms. I pulled the car over to the side and watched in macabre fascination; Miami had been a death trap for many innocent people who had nothing to do with Arthur McDuffie or the justice system.

On the way home, I tried to imagine the impact upon thousands of citizens, black and white, rebuilding lives and suffering with tragedy, and for what. Because a handful of opportunist thugs used an excuse to commit mass murder and plunder their own community in the name of racist revenge. I have always maintained that McDuffie was not a victim of racism at all. Because those officers were out every night, whomping on citizens for the sheer joy of it, exercising their anointed power in the name of law enforcement regardless of race. They had been abusing whites, Hispanics and, yes, blacks. And considering the nature of that chase, had Mr. McDuffie been a white man, the same would have occurred. A white Arthur McDuffie would have been beat to death.

So, what was gained?

Nothing. Other than sating the appetite of street thugs.

Driving north, my mind wandered in a myriad of channels, good cops, bad cops, my first day at the county jail watching Wes Harmon beat a defenseless inmate, detectives asking me to break into houses and snatch purses, Bernie's cronies inside the department hierarchy, the corrupt homicide cops and now, the McDuffie gang. All the while, the 99 percent that are good and honest police officers manage to survive the onslaught of public stain, and go on serving their communities with dignity and honor.

It was a night never to be forgotten. I was lucky to be alive. I wondered who was that man atop the bridge hollering down at me? *"Get out of there. Get back NOW!"*

I learned later on: Gary Minium.

Thirty years had passed since I answered to sobriquets like "Squidgie," and "Bubbala," and "Harpo Marx," that seventh grade "Fairy" who danced the ballet and succumbed to brutal young peers who set out to leave a mark because I didn't fit in, letting me know I must change.

In the long run, they succeeded.

After arriving home, the image of Miami burning etched into my brain. So exhausted, I could not sleep, I did the next best thing. I took out my violin and played *Fiddler On The Roof* and thought of Nero.

CHAPTER FORTY-SEVEN
In The Long Run

President Jimmy Carter opened his arms to the, "tired, poor huddled masses yearning to be free," and welcomed the incursion of 120,000 unanticipated foreigners into the already dense *urbania* of South Florida. In reality, Fidel Castro pulled off a clever coup by emptying his jails, prisons and mental institutions, dispatching them permanently from his country onto rickety boats that sailed from the Port of Mariel to the promised land. Many thousands of good and decent Cubans also arrived on the shores of paradise.

Dade County was not ready for the onslaught. Thousands of make-shift quarters were erected under the overpasses of downtown Miami which became known as "Tent City." Virtual unknowns roamed the streets, terrorizing citizens and wrecking cars without any record of who they were. The rate of violent crime—rapes, robberies and murders—virtually doubled overnight and stretched the resources of police, courts and jails beyond capacity.

Investigating Mafia murders was a piece of cake compared to the blitz of bodies that were turning up all over Dade County. We knew who the Mafia were. They had birth certificates, driver's licenses and police records. Mariel criminals had no roots in the United States, and we had no access to their backgrounds in Cuba. Unless they were caught in the act, we might as well have been searching for ghosts.

Up until the mid 1970s, the clearance rate for murders had stood around ninety percent. In 1980, it plunged to fifty percent.

Homicide could barely keep up with the demand, particularly with so many new and inexperienced investigators. But we managed. They became ace detectives in no time and some of the best cops I'd ever known. I was proud to be their captain.

* * *

A year later, the relationship between me and Division Chief Dale Bowlin had not gelled. He summarily transferred me from

Homicide to the Civil Process Bureau, while retaining the rank of captain. I had hoped Director Bobby Jones might have reflected on my hard work and loyal service when the kitchen was hot, and intervene. It was not to be. My knowledge and skills in homicide investigation were put to waste. I didn't know a writ from a subpoena. No one asked. No one cared.

That was the day my career morphed back to a job. It became a matter of marking time, like many do, until pension time collecting that check at the beginning of every month.

Thirty years later, long after retiring, I visited Dale Bowlin at his home in North Carolina where we reminisced as though old friends. I was taken aback by his unsolicited and tearful apology for wrongfully altering my career. He admitted that his motives had been unfounded.

Nevertheless, damage was done. But that was then, and I was glad that he had the will to man-up. He has since deceased.

Of the next nine years, I served one year in Civil Process, two years in Staff Inspections, another four as captain of a 255-man district station and two in charge of Transit Police, manning the new Metrorail system in Dade County. I performed well in these positions, but not outstanding. My heart wasn't there.

In those same nine years, I managed two more marriages. Debbie was a pert Jewish school teacher who I'd hoped would be the last of my wives. By marrying me, she willingly took on the role of being a stepmother to my little Jennifer, especially during some tough times. But, while we may have sung the same song, we were always in a different key. The chemistry just didn't work out and we lasted but six years

Enter, sweet Suzanne, a French Canadian hairdresser who had just moved to Florida. We met at a small party of friends. She'd been married twice. Losers both, neither of us wanted a relationship. We did everything we could to just be friends and not fall in love. I suppose, when you're not searching so hard, you find what you're looking for. Without question she is the woman of my dreams, my soul mate for life, the woman who, in truth, I had married four times before, only they all turned out to be somebody different. As of 2015, we have been together twenty-eight years, a record. We finally got it right.

I am blessed with solid friends I've made over the years, and still maintain close contact. Among them; Frank Wesolowski, Kermit

Russell, Dick Ward, Frank Mussoline, Charlie Black, and my best friend, Harvey Glaser, (the little Napoleon). I wish I could name them all, but they know who they are. My friend and mentor, Ray Beck, died of cancer in October of 2003. My old buddy, George Reincke, (*walks like a giraffe*) died in 2009.

My kids?

Randy, the deaf boy, is now fifty-six years old.

When he reached adulthood, he resumed a relationship with his natural father and took back his birth name.

Annette is a thirty-five year executive secretary for the Metro-Dade Police Department and married to, what else? A homicide detective. She's the mother of two wonderful adult kids.

Russell, now fifty-two, is—of all things—a fire department captain full time and a small business entrepreneur the rest of the time. He's married and stepfather to two boys.

Jennifer, forty-five, is remarried to Mr. Right and owns a Ph.D. in Neuropsychology. She is also a major in the U.S. Air Force reserves while she works full time for the Veterans Administration.

My first born, Bennett, has led a life of ups and downs, mostly downs, struggling with a drug addiction problem and a diseased liver. His is a tragic life worth another book one day. He was married twice and had two beautiful kids. Because his lifestyle, and the children's mother's lifestyle, was not conducive to parenting, Suzanne and I assumed custody of his children from the time they were ten and eleven. They are our kids, not just grandkids.

Jason, now 30, spent four years in the U.S. Air Force and now manages a Miami Beach hotel. Lacey, 29, lives in North Carolina and has a ten year-old daughter named Brookley. (See this book's dedication)

It's not over yet.

Remember in Chapter Four of these memoirs: *One day, a young twenty-year-old bespectacled redhead named Yvonne emerged from obscurity, along with her lush mother, claiming to be a long lost illegitimate daughter of Willie Strauss.*

In January of 1986, I received a call at the station office from a 21 year-old woman who was demanding answers from her elusive mother. Her mom had finally told her the identity of her biological father: That was me. In the early 1960's, her mother had been among my too-many dates when I worked in uniform. At the time, I was reckless, not in love, unwilling to marry and already supporting another child from a broken marriage. So she quickly married someone else.

It was true. My blood runs through this young woman's veins. She and I have since formed a loving father-daughter relationship, bonded further by her drawing me into the lives of three beautiful grandchildren I might never have known had she not garnered the courage to seek me out. Her name: Lysa.

When I fully retired from a security firm in 1994, Suzanne and I gave up a lucrative income and moved to the Smoky Mountains of Western North Carolina, where I began chasing my dream of being a writer while Suzanne pursued her dreams in sculpture art. We go to work every day, doing what we love to do, not what we have to do, exploding in creative juices and reveling in knowing that people of this planet have appreciated the fruits of our labor. My only regret is that we both had not discovered this incredible freedom of expression earlier in our lives.

Today, my musical side is further explored as I enjoy frequent interaction with audiences at residential communities, private clubs, civic organizations and libraries where I talk about the world of policedom and the writing experience, and then entertain folks with violin renditions of Fiddle on the Roof or The Ashokan Farewell, or whatever. Ironically, my piano partner is a retired Medical Examiner who is doing the same with his music, Doctor Jay Barnhart.

Whether through ignorance, selfishness, or instability, there are those I've hurt, people I've loved and who have loved me. I cannot turn back the clock and change history. But I can atone, I can acknowledge and I can apologize. You know who you are. I'm sorry. Truly, I am, very sorry.

Meanwhile, I could write a full chapter of acknowledgments to those who formed the mosaic of my life, and guided me one way or another into the final stages of true happiness. Of all, I will forever be grateful to a mobster who steered me straight with a crooked rudder, and to a struggling mom who loved me so, and kept me focused on my natural talents. She was right when she said, "Someday, music will be an important part of your life."

I may have disappointed her by my journey from violins to violence. But she'd be happy today to know that Squidgie has come full circle, from violence back to violins.

About the Author

Author, Marshall Frank, is a retired police captain from Miami-Dade, Florida where he served sixteen of his thirty years, in law enforcement investigating murders or commanding those who did.

In 1980, he was called to the U.S. Congress to present testimony regarding violent crime in America. Since retiring, Frank has authored six novels, a book of short stories, and five books of non-fiction, plus over 1,000 editorial articles published in various newspapers and magazines. He is frequently invited as a guest speaker at libraries, civic organizations, schools and conferences.

Visit his web site: www.marshallfrank.com
E-mail: MLF283@aol.com

Other books by Marshall Frank

The Way Things Oughta Be

Beyond The Call

Dire Straits

On My Father's Grave

Call Me Mommy

The Latent: A Miami Novel

Frankly Speaking

Militant Islam In America

Criminal Injustice in America

The Upside to Murder

Messages: Short Stories for the Thoughtful

So You Want To Write a Book?